CROSSING THE RUBICON

CROSSING THE RUBICON

The Shaping of India's New Foreign Policy

C. Raja Mohan

First published 2004 by PALGRAVE MACMILLAN™
175 Fifth Avenue, New York, N.Y. 10010 and
Houndmills, Basingstoke, Hampshire, England RG21 6XS.
Companies and representatives throughout the world.

PALGRAVE MACMILLAN is the global academic imprint of the
Palgrave Macmillan division of St. Martin's Press, LLC and of
Palgrave Macmillan Ltd. Macmillan® is a registered trademark in the
United States, United Kingdom and other countries. Palgrave is a
registered trademark in the European Union and other countries.

ISBN 1-4039-6462-9

Library of Congress Cataloguing-in-Publication Data available from
the Library of Congress.

First published in 2003 in Viking by Penguin Books India.

First PALGRAVE MACMILLAN edition: February 2004.

10 9 8 7 6 5 4 3 2 1

Printed in the United States of America.

To
K. Subrahmanyam
who taught me the virtues of staying ahead of the curve and standing up against conventional wisdom

Alea iacta est.
(The die has been cast.)
—Julius Caesar upon crossing the Rubicon

Contents

Acknowledgements

I owe a debt of gratitude to many who made the writing of this book possible. My employers, Kasturi and Sons, created for me in New Delhi a job that was unusual in the world of Indian media. The position of strategic affairs editor at the *Hindu* gave me the time and space to pursue my academic interest in world affairs and all the benefits that come from being a senior journalist in a major newspaper. Earlier they had hired me, a researcher with no experience in reporting, to be their Washington correspondent. Thanks are especially due to my editors, N. Ravi and Malini Parthasarathy, who gave me extraordinary support at the workplace, freedom to travel and the liberty to go against the grain in the pages of the *Hindu*. I am also grateful to N. Ram, who first drew me into one of India's great institutions as a columnist.

Without the ringside view of Indian diplomacy that the *Hindu* opened up for me, this volume could not have been conceived, and without the intensive interaction with the Indian Foreign Service (IFS), it could not have been written. Officers of the IFS, posted abroad as diplomats and minding the headquarters at the Ministry of External Affairs and the Prime Minister's Office in New Delhi, are the real heroes of the fascinating story of India's foreign policy transformation. They shared information with me on a daily basis about India's new engagement with the world. The warm friendship, generous hospitality and stimulating interaction offered by the Indian diplomatic corps went beyond the call of duty and the normal confines of a relationship between reporters and policymakers. Despite violent disagreements on the pace and direction of India's new foreign policy, they were ready to deal with me on the basis of trust and confidence.

Monika Kapil Mohta at the External Publicity Division of the Ministry of External Affairs was of great help in acquiring much of the primary source material on Indian foreign policy that is not easily accessible. Many senior diplomats from other countries posted in India over the years, too, spent long hours with me to give a sense of the story from the other side. I am especially grateful to key political decision makers of Indian foreign policy who always found time for me. I must acknowledge, in particular, the long discussions with Inder Kumar Gujral, Jaswant Singh, Brajesh Mishra, Yashwant Sinha, Naresh Chandra, N.N. Vohra and J.N. Dixit.

Many friends from the IFS who had served in key positions since the end of the cold war reviewed various parts or the whole of the book. They offered important factual corrections and valuable clarifications on key events in Indian diplomacy. I thank K. Subrahmanyam, Amitabh Mattoo and Kanti Bajpai for reading the manuscript and suggesting changes. Deepa Prakash and Soundarya Chidambaram provided valuable research assistance. But I alone am responsible for the inaccuracies that might remain in the volume.

Krishan Chopra, my editor at Penguin Books, kept faith with the project despite my erratic ways, which led to many delays and constant changes. It was a pleasure to work with Heidi Vierow, who copy-edited the book with an unremitting thoroughness and got it moving through the production cycle with precision.

Many journalist friends on the diplomatic beat in New Delhi encouraged me to take up the project and stay with it. Indrani Bagchi, Rashmi Saksena, Pranay Sharma, Seema Guha, Aunohita Mojumdar, Shobori Ganguly and many others made reporting on Indian diplomacy a happy vocation. Jyoti Malhotra, who has been covering the rapid flow of Indian foreign policy since the mid-1990s, was a constant source of argument and enthusiasm for the book. Nandan Unnikrishnan kept egging me on whenever I slowed down.

Above all it was my wife, Nirmala George, who would not let me give up. Her vigorous support of the project and a cheerful readiness to suffer its consequences are not easily compensated. Always shielding me from the routine, Nirmala took on an even a greater share of our common burden and yet found time to polish the manuscript. Special thanks to my daughter, Vasudha, and son, Prashant, for being indulgent with a father who spent far too much time at the computer than with them over many weekends.

Introduction

Shortly after the devastating aerial attacks on the World Trade Centre on 11 September 2001, Prime Minister Atal Bihari Vajpayee shot off a letter to President George W. Bush expressing India's outrage at the heinous terrorist acts. India offered even more than sympathy. The government communicated to the American mission in New Delhi that it would extend whatever support the United States wanted, including military bases, in its global war against terrorism. India soon went public with its offer of full operational military support to the United States.[1] The Indian offer seemed entirely out of character with its foreign policy. It was in sharp contrast to an India that built its international profile in the name of non-alignment, whose central principle was the refusal to get drawn into military entanglement with the major powers. Nor did it fit in with its long campaign against American military presence in its neighbourhood. Why was India, so proud of its anti-imperialist and anti-hegemonic orientation, throwing itself into a full-fledged military alliance with the United States?

India's response to the events of 11 September drew much political flak, not just from the Leftist editorialists of the English-language newspapers in the country, but also from the foreign policy community in the capital—the proliferating band of analysts at think tanks, columnists, former diplomats and countless retired generals. They were deeply dismayed that

India was losing all sense of perspective in its rush to embrace the United States. Equally surprised was the US embassy in New Delhi. There was nothing in the record of Indo-US relations, even in the improved atmosphere at the turn of the millennium, to suggest that New Delhi would offer unstinting military support to the United States. The American mission sought written clarification to figure out if India meant what it seemed to say—expansive and unconditional military support. And pat came the reply from the government: Yes.[2]

The Indian offer of military bases and facilities to the United States on 11 September seemed of a piece with its earlier decision to support the Bush administration's controversial initiative on national missile defence (NMD) announced on 1 May 2001. When the rest of the world, including American allies, was attacking the US plan as a dangerous recipe for a nuclear arms race, India was among the first to welcome it as a positive move towards the reduction of nuclear arms. Were the Indian moves on missile defence and on 11 September decisions by an absent-minded government, or did they reflect a fundamental transition in Indian foreign policy? Both within India and abroad it had been long assumed that anti-Americanism was ingrained in the world view of the Indian political elite. What might happen, it was argued, if India would oppose the United States rather than support it? Even reputable South Asian scholars concluded that, despite considerable political evolution in the last decade of the previous century, New Delhi would find it hard to say yes to the United States. Yet India was embarrassingly positive. By September 2001, it seemed, the anti-Americanism passed on from generation to generation of the Indian political elite after Independence had finally been exorcized.

The decision to support missile defence and the American war on terrorism was neither impulsive nor individually rooted; it was the product of incremental changes in Indian foreign policy through the last decade and a half of the twentieth century. By the turn of the millennium the quantitative adjustments in

Indian diplomacy after the cold war ended up in a qualitative transformation. The changes in India's foreign policy certainly accelerated during the late 1990s under the Bharatiya Janata Party (BJP)-led government, which conducted the nuclear tests in May 1998. Yet much as the nuclear tests were emblematic of the new Indian foreign policy, since the mid-1980s the foundations had been laid by different governments that included all political stripes of the Indian establishment. As the Left, Right and centre of the Indian political class had a shot at preserving and enhancing India's standing in the world, they prepared the ground for a radically different approach to world affairs in New Delhi.

This book is about the journey from the uncertainties of the early 1990s to a more self-assured diplomatic posture by India at the turn of the century. The change was in relation to not just the United States but other great powers, India's neighbourhood and beyond, and global issues. *Crossing the Rubicon* is also about the changing philosophical premises of India's engagement with the external world. Most nations, especially large ones, do not easily alter their international orientation. States tend to be conservative about foreign policy. Fundamental changes in foreign policy take place only when there is a revolutionary change either at home or in the world.[3] In 1991 India confronted just such a situation. The old political and economic order at home had collapsed, and the end of the cold war removed all the old benchmarks that guided India's foreign policy. Many of the core beliefs of the old system had to be discarded and consensus generated on new ones—state socialism yielding place to liberal capitalism, one-party rule to coalition governments at the centre, upper-caste dominance to accommodate those at the bottom, and attempts to redefine the notion of secularism—to name just a few. Externally the collapse of the Soviet Union and the new wave of economic globalization left India scrambling to find new anchors for its conduct of foreign relations. *Crossing the Rubicon* is by no means a record of India's diplomatic history at a critical moment in its national life. That laborious but rewarding job is for historians, who will have to dig into the copious records of Indian foreign policy in the 1990s. My objective is to capture the essence of India's foreign policy transformation after the cold war.

Unlike Jawaharlal Nehru, his successors in the 1990s had little time or inclination to articulate the ideas behind the new foreign policy in the making. If Nehru both enthused and educated the political elite with his frequent speeches and writings on foreign policy, the Indian leaders of the 1990s neither had the conceptual flourish nor a burning desire to communicate their foreign policy objectives with their constituents. Although Inder Kumar (I.K.) Gujral, who shepherded India's foreign policy from 1996 to 1998, tried to keep up with the Nehruvian tradition of vocalizing ideas, both P.V. Narasimha Rao and Atal Bihari Vajpayee chose to be reticent about the foreign policy transition. Nevertheless, all the Prime Ministers were under the constant pressure of circumstances to tinker and innovate on the diplomatic front. Despite the substantive changes in Indian foreign policy beginning in 1991, few major speeches signalled a change of direction or a break from the past.[4] This narrative of the transformation of Indian foreign policy, then, has been constructed from the decisions themselves and insights gathered from ringside observations of the events and conversations with key decision makers.

Despite the absence of a verbal articulation of the new directions in foreign policy, the period since the mid-1980s has been one of unending excitement in this arena. India dragged itself into an extended debate on its nuclear policy as it saw Pakistan acquire nuclear weapons. India decided to acquire nuclear weapons in the late 1980s even as it stepped up its disarmament activism, engaged in diplomatic flip-flops on the Comprehensive Test Ban Treaty (CTBT) from 1993 to 1996, performed the nuclear tests in 1998 and the post-Pokhran diplomacy to limit the damage from the nuclear tests, and supported the controversial American proposals on missile defence in 2001. India's nuclear debate ended up as the fulcrum of change in its foreign policy. The nuclear tests at Pokhran in the summer of 1998 were about redefining India's approach to the question of power. They were part of the effort to temper the idealism in its foreign policy with a strong dose of realism.

The end of the cold war put India's attachment to the idea of non-alignment into an unforgiving political spotlight. Non-alignment, for reasons right or wrong, has been widely seen as the singular feature of India's foreign policy since Independence. The altered world forced India to examine the relevance of non-alignment in the conduct of external relations during the 1990s. As it rethought its commitment to it, India had also to reconsider its earlier rejection of formal alliances with great powers. The decade also brought up the deeper question of where India stood vis-à-vis the West, when the East and its economic model stood shattered. Returning to the West became of vital importance for India after the cold war. For India was the only liberal democracy in the world that stood apart from and often against the West throughout the cold war; this position defined India's first four decades of engagement with the world as an independent nation. Its attempts to reconcile with the West had run against entrenched sources of antagonism to the West in the past—the anti-imperialist tradition, the nativist ideologies and the security imperatives of the cold war dynamics in the subcontinent, which put India and the West at opposite poles. This story of Indian foreign policy in the 1990s is about the struggle to overcome the sources of opposition to the West.

Through the decade of the 1990s India had to restructure quickly its relations with the major powers. Injecting political and economic substance into its long emaciated relationship with the United States, now the lone superpower, became the principal national strategic objective. At the same time India was unwilling to let its old ties to the former Soviet Union, now a weakened Russia, wither away. Moreover, China now had become the second most important power in the world. Reconfiguring relations with the major powers, riding the roller coaster relations with the United States and China and salvaging the formerly dense ties with Russia were the key markers of Indian diplomacy during the 1990s. But that was not all.

Throughout the decade India was severely tested in dealing with a newly aggressive Pakistan. It sought to cope with Pakistan in the radically changed context that brought nuclear weapons into the bilateral equation and increased Pakistan's ability to intervene in the disputed state of Jammu and Kashmir through what has now come to be called cross-border terrorism. The diplomatic history of Indo-Pakistani relations in the 1990s is a rich, if frustrating, tapestry that included every possible development—from a limited conventional war to a total military confrontation, to many summits that struggled to define a new framework for peace between the two neighbours. While Pakistan consumed India's energies, the rest of the neighbourhood would not leave New Delhi alone. India's policy towards the smaller neighbours reached a dead end in the 1990s and had to be recast. Economic globalization opened up the prospect of regional economic integration, and deep-seated suspicions in both New Delhi and the neighbouring capitals kept the political tone of the subcontinent uncertain.

Even as India struggled with defining a new approach towards its smaller neighbours, the regions abutting the subcontinent beckoned India to reassert its claim for a say in the affairs of the Indian Ocean and its littoral. The 1990s saw India making a determined effort to reconnect with its extended neighbourhood in South-East Asia, Afghanistan and Central Asia, and the Middle East. India's renewed engagement with the surrounding regions had to be within a new framework that emphasized economic relations and energy diplomacy rather than the traditional notion of Third World solidarity. The cold war and India's insular economic policies in the first four decades had undermined India's standing to the east and west of its neighbourhood and prevented New Delhi from ensuring its much vaunted primacy in the Indian Ocean littoral. But India's new economic and foreign policies have given it an opportunity to realize the vision of Lord Curzon, the British viceroy at the turn of the twentieth century, of Indian leadership in the region stretching from Aden to Singapore.

At a moment when Islam and its troubles with the West have come to centre stage, India's approach to citizens of Islamic faith at home and its dealings with Islamic nations abroad will be crucial for the emergence of India as a great power. Its attempts to develop a more substantive relationship with the Islamic world was complicated by the rise of the regressive forces of Hindutva at home, the creation of a new strategic relationship with Israel and Pakistan's support to Islamic militancy in India. Despite the growth of the communal cancer in India that began to colour the discourse on foreign policy, India could not shake off the reality that it is an Islamic nation—both because it hosts the second largest Islamic population in the world and its national culture has been deeply influenced by Islam. A pragmatic engagement of the Islamic world, then, inevitably became a cornerstone of India's foreign policy in the 1990s.

While every one of these subjects merits a separate and full-length study, this book takes a brief but sharp look at all of them and weaves together a single narrative on the changing orientation of Indian diplomacy. Beyond the specific moves India has made in different regions and on major global issues, the key feature of the 1990s was the changing conceptual bases on which Indian diplomacy had been founded. If Nehru defined a unique foreign policy for independent India in search of its manifest destiny, the Indian leaders of the 1990s had to break out of the straitjacket to which Nehru's foreign policy ideas had been reduced. Finding new ways of doing things and putting aside old ideas—for rejecting them formally would have invited serious political trouble—while embarking on new approaches was central to the handling of the extremely challenging international environment in which India found itself in 1991.

This has not been easy. The tension between the imperative of the new and the resistance of the old ideas on how to conduct foreign policy is real and unlikely to end in the near future.

The fear of the new and fondness for the old continue to be reflected in all aspects of Indian diplomacy, from engaging the United States to an optimal strategy towards the smallest of the neighbours. For the new foreign policy of India is a work in progress. Equally important is the flux in world affairs after 11 September, which has left largely uncertain the direction of the international system in the coming decades. By focusing on change and advocating more, this book does not detain itself with the arguments of those who denounce the reorientation of Indian foreign policy since the mid-1980s. Instead it contends that the direction of Indian diplomacy has changed radically amidst internal and external impulses. Such a contention does not negate the value of a continuing argument about Indian foreign policy; rather it should sharpen the great Indian debate on its external relations. The country has begun to move towards a new set of assumptions about the nature of its interaction with the world. Not all of these were articulated self-consciously or clearly by the Indian political leadership, but its actions since the mid-1980s have slowly but surely transformed the ideas that have guided India's world view. Many of those changes are unlikely to be reversed.

First was the transition from the collective national consensus on building a socialist society to a consensus on building a modern capitalist one. The socialist ideal had so dominated the Indian political discourse by the early 1970s that a constitutional amendment was passed in 1976 to make the nation a socialist republic. Yet 1991 saw the collapse of the Soviet Union, the veritable symbol of socialism, and the crumbling of the edifice of India's state-led socialist economy. Whatever the remaining pretensions of the political class, there was no question that building modern capitalism, in tune with the trends of globalization, was now the principal national objective. India's internal socialist orientation had its foreign policy complement in India's closeness to the Soviet Union and the socialist bloc. From now on, however, the success of Indian foreign policy depended on the pace of India's globalization, its ability to strengthen links with the West and its ability to bring its economy up to speed with China's.

Implicit in this was the second transition, from the past emphasis on politics to a new stress on economics in the making of foreign policy. India began to realize in the 1990s how far it had fallen behind the rest of Asia, including China, in economic development. Having got into the groove of socialist rhetoric, Indian diplomats had little time for commercial diplomacy in the past. Now they were marketing India as a big emerging market and the biggest new information technology power. With the socialist hubris gone and the pressures to compete with other emerging markets, Indian diplomacy now entered new uncharted waters. In the past, the begging bowl for aid was symbolic of Indian diplomacy that sought to meet the nation's external financing requirements. India was now seeking foreign direct investment, and access to markets in the developed world. Trade, not aid, would be the national priority. India also recognized the basic truth that its claim to great power status could no longer be sustained without rapid advances on the economic front.

A third transition in Indian foreign policy was the shift from Third Worldism to the promotion of its own self-interest. By the 1980s, for most Indians, striving for the collective good of the Third World and standing up against the Western world became the natural responsibility of India. Many of the international and regional security issues were viewed through the prism of the Third World and anti-imperialism. Any other approach was seen as a betrayal of the long-standing Indian consensus on foreign policy. The 1990s, however, brought home some painful truths. There was no real Third World trade union, in the form of the Non-Aligned Movement, that India believed it was leading. After a radical phase in the 1970s, most developing nations had begun to adopt pragmatic economic policies and sought to integrate with the international market. Much of the developing world had made considerable economic advances, leaving South Asia way behind. If there was a Third

World, it was largely within India and the subcontinent. This meant that if India helped itself and developed faster, it would be uplifting much of the remaining Third World. While rhetoric on the Third World remained popular, the policy orientation in India's external relations increasingly focussed on India's own self-interest. There was a growing perception, following from the Chinese example, that if India developed rapidly, it had a chance to gain a place at the international high table. The 1990s saw India step up its campaign for a permanent seat in the expected enlargement of the United Nations Security Council (UNSC). All this implied that India would now be more interested in becoming a part of the management of the international system and not remain just a protesting leader of the Third World trade union.

Rejecting the anti-Western mode of thinking was the fourth important transition of Indian foreign policy. As the world's largest democracy, India was the most committed to Western political values outside the Euro-Atlantic world. Yet the cold war saw India emerge as the most articulate opponent of the Western world view. India joined the losing side of the civil war within the West—between the US and western Europe on one side and Soviet Russia on the other—in both the economic and diplomatic choices that confronted it after Independence. By the late 1980s, India was voting more often against the United States and the West than even the Soviet Union was. And within the Indian political class, rejection of the Western economic model as well as its foreign policy goals became second nature. In short, the anti-imperialism that had been at the heart of the India's struggle for decolonization had degenetared into knee-jerk anti-Westernism. The cold war alignment of the Western powers with the military dictators in Pakistan and the Chinese communists reinforced the opposition to the West in the Indian security establishment. India's liberal intelligentsia was deeply influenced by the Labour Left in Great Britain until the 1970s and American university radicalism after that, and it gave itself the role of critical opposition to the West, albeit within the framework of Western thought. In the process it ended up supporting the counterproductive anti-Western foreign policy of India. Further, there were the traditional nativists, who dominate the BJP and are deeply suspicious of the supposedly corrupting Western influences on the traditional Hindu society. As a consequence, a strong anti-Western bias crept into Indian foreign policy, supported by the Left as well as the Right and underwritten by the security establishment. The end of the cold war also meant that the United States finally won the civil war within the Euro-Atlantic world. The Soviet Union became Russia and returned to the Western fold, which in turn forced India to break the decades-old anti-Western approach to foreign policy.

Finally, the fifth transition in Indian foreign policy in the 1990s was from idealism to pragmatism. Idealism came naturally to the Indian elite that had won independence from the British by arguing with them against colonialism on the basis of the first principles of Enlightenment. Newly independent India mistakenly believed that it could conduct foreign policy on the same rationale. It believed a new world order could be structured on the basis of the first principles of peaceful co-existence and international cooperation through multilateral endeavours. The new leaders of India had contempt for power politics. They believed it was a negative but lingering legacy from nineteenth-century Europe and had no relevance to the mid-twentieth century. India tended to see its role in world politics as the harbinger of a new set of principles, which, if applied, would transform the world. It had little time for dark analysis of the world in terms of a clash of interests and the pursuit of power by individual states. Although India's first Prime Minister and foreign minister, Jawaharlal Nehru, was quite a realist in his thinking about foreign policy and the importance of protecting national interest, the public articulation of India's foreign policy had the mark of idealism. As India rediscovered statehood and the challenges of independent engagement with the world, the creation of domestic political support for foreign policy hinged on popularizing a simplistic set of principles. The country's elite so internalized the moralism and idealism of India's foreign policy that it had to unlearn a lot as it confronted a transformed world order at the turn of the 1990s.

India has moved from its past emphasis on the power of the argument to a new stress on the argument of power. The conscious rediscovery of power as the crucial dynamic by Indian foreign policymakers does not mean India has become a cynical nation unconcerned with the normative dimension of global politics. Instead India has merely reconfigured the mix between power and principle in the pursuit of its national interest.

February 2003

ONE

The Nuclear Leap Forward

Buying Time and Space

As he came out of a special session of the United Nations Security Council (UNSC) at the summit level in January 1992, India's new Prime Minister P.V. Narasimha Rao did what he knew best—finesse the issue at hand and obfuscate India's position. The UNSC had just passed a historic measure declaring that the proliferation of nuclear and other weapons of mass destruction was 'a threat to international peace and security'. It is a phrase that Narasimha Rao understood well. It meant that the UNSC could take collective action either in the form of economic sanctions or military action, under the UN charter against any nation that violated the newly declared norms against proliferation of nuclear weapons. For a long time India topped the list of countries likely to acquire nuclear weapons. As far as India was concerned, it was under no legal obligation not to do so; only its own moral ambiguity on nuclear weapons held it back. But now the UNSC was warning countries like India that they could go nuclear at the expense of incurring the wrath of the entire international system, and it was saying so with the Indian Prime Minister present.

British Prime Minister John Major, who presided over the special session of the UNSC, declared that the resolution was passed unanimously, but Narasimha Rao briefed the accompanying media party that India had not agreed with the formulation that proliferation was a threat to international peace and security. Did India explicitly dissociate itself from a formulation that was going to tighten the nuclear noose around it? The answer was to be found in Narasimha Rao's speech at the UNSC:

> Mr. President, the statement you will be reading out on behalf of the members of the Council at the end of today's meeting has been subject of intensive, productive discussions. We were happy to be part of the exercise and to have made our contribution to it. We consider it an important statement. However, I find that the statement does not reflect one or two of India's crucial concerns. . . . This, of course, does not detract from the significance of the statement you are about to make or from India's cooperation.[1]

Narasimha Rao was walking the tight rope on one of India's most difficult diplomatic moments. The new international approach to nuclear proliferation was a stark reality staring at India. It was in no position to confront the international community, nor could it acquiesce in a self-defeating formulation on an issue of core national security concern to India—the preservation of the nuclear option.

Narasimha Rao's evasiveness was about the nuclear pickle that India found itself in 1992. Just three and a half years earlier in June 1988, Narasimha Rao's predecessor, Rajiv Gandhi, was making a thundering case before the United Nations Special Session on Disarmament for total abolition of nuclear weapons by 2010.[2] Narasimha Rao could no longer afford to lecture the rest of the world. He was representing an economy that was nearly broke and dealing with a United Nations that no longer had the comforting presence of the Soviet Union, which had split up just a month before. Moreover, the United States, fresh from its triumph in the Gulf war, was strutting on the world stage as the sole superpower. Previously, the world was either amused or irritated by India's grandiloquent moral posturing on nuclear weapons—India was a nuisance that would be tolerated. Now the world was restricting its nuclear option. If India could not make up its mind on what to do with nuclear weapons, the world would decide for it by demanding India give up its nuclear option. If the UNSC resolution had been just another routine one, India could perhaps have lived with it. But it had the imprimatur of the United States and the backing of the other permanent members of the UNSC. The real political challenge for New Delhi was to engage with Washington intensively on the nuclear question—as it turned out for the entire decade that followed.

Much to his distaste, Narasimha Rao had to handle it then and there in a meeting with President Bush on the margins of the UNSC meeting. It was undoubtedly the most challenging diplomatic encounter Narasimha Rao had had in his tenure as the foreign minister under Indira Gandhi and then as Prime Minister of India from 1991 to 1996. In normal circumstances, India would have taken the ususal moral high ground on nuclear weapons and worn the American side down. 'Dialogue of the deaf' was the traditional description of any nuclear discourse between the United States and India. It was also called the meeting between an irresistible force and an immovable object. Yet the equation had dramatically altered in 1991-92. The United States' irresistible force became unstoppable at the end of the cold war. Having had to confront potential dangers of nuclear weapons in the hands of Saddam Hussein in the Gulf war, the US was now determined to deal with the question of nuclear proliferation and elevated it to the top of its foreign policy agenda. Thus it had already unveiled a framework for arms control negotiations in the Middle East and sent a high-level envoy to New Delhi and Islamabad in November 1991. The envoy, Ronald Bartholomew, had given the Indian government written proposals on what the US expected India to do on nuclear arms control, and now Bush was going to demand that India act. India no longer appeared the immovable object. The economic and other crises at home and a weakened international position had made India shakier than ever before. Narasimha

Rao and his principal foreign policy aide, Foreign Secretary J.N. Dixit, understood that the moment of nuclear reckoning was at hand. They knew they had to summon all the intellectual guile to wriggle out of the situation. India could not have found diplomats more wily than these two.

President Bush had a simple proposition: India must join a conference of five nations—along with the US, Russia, China and Pakistan—to discuss nuclear non-proliferation in the subcontinent. On the face of it, there seemed no reason for India to object, but in effect the proposal went against everything that India stood for on the nuclear question. New Delhi had argued for years that the nuclear issue could only be discussed within a global framework and that the focus should be on the total abolition of nuclear weapons within a specific time frame. Bush's proposal instead called for a discussion focussed on Indian and Pakistani nuclear programmes within a multilateral format. Worse still, the negotiating framework proposed by Bush was deeply offensive to India's sense of standing. Not only would the conference concentrate on getting India and Pakistan to behave on the nuclear issue, but their conduct was going to be supervised by Washington, Moscow and Beijing sitting at a higher table. The ultimate insult was that China, which India saw as an equal, was to become a guarantor of peace and stability in the subcontinent. This was a China that India knew had helped Pakistan acquire nuclear weapons. In no way was India going to accept such a set of negotiations. It had already rejected a similar proposal by Pakistan six months earlier when Prime Minister Mian Mohammed Nawaz Sharif called for a three-plus-two conference on nuclear proliferation in the subcontinent. It was one thing to refuse Pakistan but entirely another to reject the same proposal from the United States.

In typical fashion, Narasimha Rao was non-committal. Pointing to the political difficulties at home, he said that he would prefer to discuss the problem in detail with the United States bilaterally before he could join multilateral nuclear negotiations. It was agreed that bilateral nuclear talks would begin within a few weeks.[3]

Having found an escape route at a critical moment, Narasimha Rao launched India on a two-track policy—engage the Americans in a nuclear dialogue and prepare for conducting nuclear tests. The first was a visible track and the second invisible. Narasimha Rao gave orders to the atomic energy establishment in Bombay to get ready for another round of nuclear tests, but the scientists wanted time—at least two years. Meanwhile, the pressure from the United States was relentless. Immediately after a bilateral dialogue was started with the Americans, key Western nations and Japan demanded and got similar bilateral nuclear negotiations with New Delhi. The Western powers began to consult each other on the nuclear situation in the subcontinent and occasionally delivered collective demarches on New Delhi's nuclear and missile programmes. 'Buy me time' was the constant refrain from Narasimha Rao to Dixit. The Foreign Office bobbed and weaved and found every trick in the diplomatic book to avoid getting into multilateral negotiations on the nuclear issue. Formerly immovable on nuclear policy, India had to transform itself from a rock to a thin reed that bent with every gust of wind but held firm with its roots. In the talks India invented arguments for expanding the multilateral negotiating framework to include every possible country from Israel to Japan. It modified its position at the disarmament negotiations in Geneva to support talks on drafting a Comprehensive Test Ban Treaty (CTBT) and a Fissile Materials Cut-off Treaty (FMCT).

By December 1995, India was ready for Pokhran-II. Narasimha Rao had achieved the impossible. He had managed to fob off the various international pressures on India to close its nuclear option. The economy, formerly the weakest element in the country's portfolio, had turned around and was now an attractive feature that created the basis for a different relationship with the world. In addition, he was ready to conduct nuclear tests and hence put India on a different strategic pedestal. But the United States began to notice the Indian preparations for nuclear tests in the Pokhran desert by the end of 1995. A story in the *New York Times* on 15 December 1995 put the word out. The Indian government did not immediately deny the report, and since very few in India knew that the country was getting ready to test, newspapers speculated about a new plot by the United States to defame India. Meanwhile, the US ambassador to India, Frank Wisner, was on a flight back to New Delhi with pictures of the satellite imagery showing the wiring for the underground at tests at L-shaped tunnels in the Pokhran Desert. Wisner handed them over to the Prime Minister's Office. He was not going to suggest to Narasimha Rao that India should not test; after all, India was a sovereign country and could choose to do what it wished. But he firmly reminded the Indian government of the consequences of India's tests—wide-ranging American economic sanctions. The implicit threat worked. Fully three days after the *New York Times* report, the government formally denied that it was going to conduct any tests. The diplomatic community in the capital heaved a sigh of relief. India had been coaxed into not going ahead with the tests—which were due in less than seventy-two hours.[4]

While the United States got what it wanted, India was back to square one. Once again all the traditional inhibitions that prevented it from taking the nuclear leap seemed to come back into play. Indira Gandhi had put her toe into the nuclear waters and pulled back in 1974. Narasimha Rao did all that was necessary to cross the nuclear Rubicon in the early 1990s. In the end he decided to keep India in limbo—neither exercising the nuclear option nor being able to give it up. Since he never suggested he was going to test nuclear weapons, Narasimha Rao did not feel compelled to give any reason for not doing so. But the reasons were quite clear. India had yet to resolve its moral concerns about nuclear weapons. It would wring its hands rather than come to a decisive view about national policy for nuclear weapons. Uppermost in Narasimha Rao's mind was the question of economic costs. Throughout 1995, the finance and external affairs ministries were engaged in studying the likely economic consequences of nuclear tests. The finance ministry insisted that sanctions would significantly undermine India's economic progress, then in a good curve. The Foreign Office was divided but eventually tended to back the finance ministry's view. A second factor that bothered Narasimha Rao was the prospect of Pakistan following the footsteps of India and testing its own nuclear weapons. Would it provide explicit nuclear parity to Pakistan, internationalize the Kashmir dispute and put India at a disadvantage? It was an important question that would trouble India later, but the proponents of nuclear tests believed that Pakistan had already acquired nuclear weapons and there was little to lose by both sides bringing them out of the closet.[5] That was the assessment of Atal Bihari Vajpayee, who chose to act.

Overcoming Inhibitions
In the sweltering heat of May 1998, India finally ended its long-standing nuclear ambiguity. By conducting two rounds of nuclear tests on 11 and 13 May, its first right-of-centre government led by the BJP, resolved nearly five decades of nuclear debate in India in favour of an overt nuclear posture. For good or bad, and whether the world liked it or not, India decided to cross the nuclear Rubicon. Fifty years after Independence, India now wanted to become a normal nation—placing considerations of realpolitik and national security above its until recently dominant focus on liberal internationalism, morality and normative approaches to international politics. The shock waves from this decision would certainly haunt the domestic politics of India, the regional equation in the subcontinent, the balance of power in Asia and the global nuclear order for a long time to come. There was no turning back now from India's decision to explore the uncharted waters of a nuclear future.

India's dalliance with the nuclear question goes way back to the early 1940s, well before India shook itself free from British colonialism, the American use of atom bombs against Japan and the full story of the efforts—unsuccessful in Germany and successful in the United States—to build nuclear weapons came to light. India's interest in the nuclear issues was spurred by the emergence of an impressive community of scientists in the early decades of the twentieth century in India who managed to produce world-quality work despite the country's utter backwardness. Scientists like C.V. Raman, Srinivasa Ramanujan, and S.N. Bose were substantively contributing to international scientific development. Indian scientists, with a long tradition of excellence in mathematics, took eagerly to modern physics that was about to transform the world fundamentally. They were part of the exciting developments taking place in Europe in atomic physics, and some of them were familiar with the economic and political implications of the prospect of harnessing nuclear energy. One of them, Dr Homi Jehangir Bhabha, was determined to ensure that when the Second World War ended and India became independent, it would be ready to enter the atomic age quickly. In 1944, fully three years before Independence, Bhabha wrote and got a grant from the Dorabji Tata Trust to set up the Tata Institute of Fundamental Research at Bombay for advanced work on nuclear and allied areas of physics. Prime Minister Jawaharlal Nehru took a strong interest in the development of India's scientific capabilities and gave unstinting support to Bhabha in building a wide-ranging national nuclear programme.[6]

Bhabha and Nehru focussed on peaceful uses of nuclear energy. Like all the physicists and politicians who backed them in the 1950s, they believed that nuclear research would lead to electric power too cheap to be metered and that energy was to be the cornerstone of India's rapid development. Nehru's high-profile international diplomacy and Bhabha's wide-ranging contacts in the community of Western physicists—many of whom were close to policy-making circles—ensured that India got substantive international cooperation in building an infrastructure for atomic research and development. Bhabha's standing was such that he was elected president of the world's first UN International Conference on Peaceful Uses of Atomic Energy in Geneva in 1955. Even as they laid the foundations of a broad-based nuclear programme, Bhabha and Nehru were not unaware of its military potential. Nehru, however, clearly ruled out the military application of nuclear energy, although he said he could not vouch for the policies of the future generations of Indian leaders. With Nehru's emphasis on peace and disarmament in India's foreign policy, it could not have been otherwise. He took the lead in calling the world to come to a standstill on nuclear weapons development and to adopt a ban on nuclear testing and a freeze on production of nuclear material.

Even as they campaigned for nuclear disarmament, Nehru and Bhabha were clear in their minds that India should not give up the option to make nuclear weapons in the future. For this reason, they refused to support any control mechanism— whether it was the Baruch Plan of the US in 1945 or the international safeguards system—that sought to limit India's nuclear potential and future decision making on the bomb.[7] Until the mid-1960s, the Indian nuclear policy focussed on building civilian nuclear technology, de-emphasizing the military spin-off and campaigning for nuclear restraint at the global level. This policy mix came under tremendous pressure in October 1964 when China conducted its first nuclear test and declared itself the fifth nuclear power. China's test, coming barely two years after Beijing humiliated New Delhi in a border conflict, forced India to debate openly for the first time its nuclear weapons option. There were strong demands within India for acquiring nuclear weapons, but there was also considerable hesitation arising from the deep revulsion against nuclear weapons and the notion of deterrence. Nehru's death five months before China's test had made it even more difficult for India to make up its mind on nuclear weapons.

India tried three approaches to resolve its nuclear dilemma. First, it sought security guarantees from the United States, the Soviet Union and Great Britain to cope with a hostile nuclear

China on its borders. India was rebuffed by all three. Second, it attempted to develop a multilateral solution by calling for a non-proliferation treaty (NPT), under which the nuclear powers would give up their nuclear weapons and others would not acquire them. The NPT that came out of the negotiations turned out to be entirely different. Third, Prime Minister Lal Bahadur Shastri decided in 1965 to go ahead with a subterranean nuclear explosion project (SNEP), but both Shastri and Bhabha died in January 1966, and given the large political and economic crisis that India went through in that period, the project was postponed. It was left to Indira Gandhi and Bhabha's successors to complete it in 1974 by conducting the first underground nuclear test. Nonetheless, the test—a delayed response to China's explosion a decade earlier—did not end India's nuclear problem. It demonstrated the country's atomic capability, but New Delhi remained unwilling to call itself a nuclear weapons power. Moreover, India confounded the whole world by calling the test a peaceful nuclear explosion and declaring that it had no intention of embarking on a nuclear weapons programme. The tension between India's moral rejection of nuclear weapons and the security imperative of acquiring them remained unresolved. Further, India's action in 1974 provoked the world into acting against it—through an expanding series of non-proliferation sanctions—without completing the task that challenged the global non-proliferation order.

From the late 1970s, India faced renewed pressures to reconsider its ambiguous nuclear position. This time they came from the western border, where Pakistan had embarked on a clandestine nuclear weapons programme. China had begun to assist Pakistan in its nuclear quest. The United States, which had renewed its strategic alliance with Pakistan in the early 1980s to drive the Russians out of Afghanistan, was unwilling to challenge it. Indira Gandhi considered conducting nuclear tests in the early 1980s, but word about the preparations got out, and they had to be cancelled. As the scale of Pakistani nuclear weapons programme began to be understood in New Delhi in the mid-1980s, Rajiv Gandhi tried to persuade the United States to stop the Pakistanis, but the gambit did not work. Gandhi, who had embarked on an international campaign against nuclear weapons at the height of the cold war, resisted pressures from the strategic establishment at home to go nuclear. When the Pakistani leaders began to flaunt their nuclear weapons capability in early 1987, India was left with few choices. Gandhi ordered nuclear weaponization in 1988, and the project was completed in 1990 under his successor, V.P. Singh. Nonetheless, the ambiguity in India's nuclear posture remained. India could not get itself to claim it was a nuclear weapons power.[8]

The Security Imperative
The end of the cold war did not bring the expected peace dividend for India; instead it accentuated the Indian security problems. India was confronting a radically transformed world order. With few reliable friends, the importance of self-help in managing its national security was coming to the fore with greater clarity. New questions about India's nuclear options were now being debated. Was India's untested nuclear deterrent—composed of a few air-deliverable weapons— credible against its two nuclear adversaries in the neighbourhood? The new pressures on India became irresistible, and it moved inexorably towards testing its nuclear weapons by the end of 1990s. All that the BJP government did was give the final political clearance for the tests, which were under active consideration for at least a few years before.

In addition, the end of the cold war removed one of the most important constraints against India's overt nuclearization: the strength of Soviet Union, India's de facto military and political ally since 1971, when the two sides signed a treaty. It provided enough of a security assurance for India to avoid going fully down the nuclear road. The collapse of the Soviet Union in 1991, however, left India without a reliable ally in the new world order dominated by one superpower. The end of the cold war raised expectations in India of a new relationship with the United States, but these hopes in the early 1990s were quickly dashed as the United States drifted towards a strategy that sought to pressure India rather than befriend it. As the world's largest democracy sought to cope with massive threats to its territorial integrity posed by intensive insurgencies—rooted in domestic political mismanagement but fuelled by Pakistan—in the sensitive border states of Punjab, Kashmir and north-eastern provinces, the administration of President William J. 'Bill' Clinton was determined to highlight India's human rights problems. The new US strategy towards India also highlighted the dangers of a nuclear war between New Delhi and Islamabad and emphasized the importance of rolling back India's nuclear and missile capabilities.

The decline of Russia's standing in the world after the cold war also saw the rise of China and the growing recognition in the United States that Beijing was now the second most important power in the international system. The huge gulf that emerged between the international statures of India and China—who were seen as peers offering different models of social and political development until the late 1970s—was now a major source of concern for New Delhi. Although India embarked on a process of normalization of relations with China at the end of 1990s, its self-esteem and pride were badly hurt by the way the world treated the two Asian giants—communist China as a global power and democratic India as a regional power locked into a conflict with a hostile smaller neighbour, Pakistan. China's policy of buttressing the strategic capabilities of Pakistan, with added cooperation on missiles in the 1990s, was seen in New Delhi as an attempt to balance India within the subcontinent. Regaining the psychological parity with Beijing, reasserting a role in the Asian balance of power and getting out of the subcontinental box became important national objectives that had a significant bearing on India's nuclear policy in the 1990s.

The Gulf war and the Western concerns about proliferation of weapons of mass destruction saw a dramatic expansion of the technology-denial regime against India, which was seen as a major proliferation risk. The squeezing of advanced technology transfers to India in the 1990s forced the country to re-evaluate the costs of nuclear ambiguity. So long as India remained an undeclared nuclear weapons state, it seemed to have no prospect of gaining access to strategic technologies. Thus the Indian nuclear debate had to consider the trade-off between the pain of punishment that would inevitably follow an Indian test and cumulative costs of technology denial over the last quarter of a century. If the former was politically manageable and could be limited, why suffer agonizing permanent denial of technologies? The need to once again demonstrate India's nuclear capability and transform itself into a declared nuclear weapons power was reinforced by the perception that the international nuclear order was closing in on New Delhi. India saw the indefinite extension of the NPT in 1995 as a permanent legitimization of the possession of nuclear weapons by a few states; the treaty's objective for the total elimination of nuclear weapons was an increasingly unrealistic one. The NPT extension fundamentally altered India's own attitude to the ongoing negotiations on the Comprehensive Test Ban Treaty.

New Delhi had long supported the idea of the CTBT as an important and integral step towards disarmament. As its drafting proceeded, it became clear to India that the treaty was driven more by non-proliferation concerns than those relating to disarmament. The political objective was to limit the capabilities of the threshold states like India to anything other than crude nuclear weapons. The CTBT shook the Indian nuclear debate out of its long stupor and forced into the open the question of testing. There was a growing sense that the CTBT would forever close an Indian option to test—whether India joined the treaty or not. It also raised doubts about the long-standing policy of keeping Indian nuclear option open or ambiguous. China's insistence that the CTBT would not come into force without India's signature and the incorporation of this provision into the treaty despite India's objections reinforced India's unease.

The CTBT resulted in the emergence of two schools of thought within the strategic community: one argued that India could live without testing and build a reasonably credible deterrent, and the other suggested that India's deterrent would not be credible without testing. The latter view was held particularly by the technical community; it insisted that to develop warheads for missiles as well as to create a significant database for future nuclear weapons research, it was necessary to conduct at least a limited number of tests. Confronted with this choice, all the Indian governments during the 1990s toyed with the idea of testing. Narasimha Rao's government came close to testing nuclear weapons in late 1995, and the two United Front governments from 1996 to 1998 looked at the option, but all three backed off with the understanding that the political and economic costs of testing would be inordinately high. The BJP government, however, was willing to risk this and may have calculated that the long-term gains (and perhaps immediate domestic ones) could outweigh the near-term political and economic costs of testing. Its calculation turned out to be right.

Towards Nuclear Pragmatism
Although India acquired nuclear weapons in defiance of the United States and the international order, the challenge of coming to terms with them was at the centre of India's post-Pokhran diplomacy. India's ability to engage the United States after Pokhran-II was rooted in the national confidence that came with the decision to bring its nuclear weapons out of the closet. In the past India was wary of any engagement with other powers fearing that such a dialogue would rob the nation of its nuclear potential, but now it was sanguine that there was no way of rolling back what it already had. With that confidence India was prepared to deal with the outside world on nuclear issues in a productive manner. The declaration of the possession of nuclear weapons also gave India room to rework its nuclear diplomacy.

From being a protestor against discrimination in the nuclear order, India was now transforming itself into a nation that was ready to support the existing order and calling for its incremental reform. The essence of the change in the Indian nuclear policy after Pokhran-II rested in the shift from the past emphasis on disarmament to a new one on pragmatic arms control. The former called for a total abolition of nuclear weapons. The latter focussed on the challenge of reducing the nuclear threat in the short term.

While India has continued to emphasize nuclear disarmament even after the tests, New Delhi has begun to recognize that the pursuit of the goal of total nuclear disarmament can at best be normative. It is not an achievable policy objective in the near term, given the current global nuclear politics. Although disarmament must remain the higher goal for which India needs to strive, the immediate aim of New Delhi after Pokhran-II has been finding a modus vivendi with the global nuclear order and participating in the many nuclear arms control agreements that seek partial rather than total solutions to the nuclear problem. The exclusive emphasis on total disarmament had become a mantra and prevented India from becoming part of any nuclear arms control arrangement, even when it might have been to its national advantage. All that was to change in the wake of Pokhran-II. These changes, however, came from withering criticism from the supporters of the traditional nuclear policy—on the Left as well as the Congress party.[9]

The Indian government quickly recognized that the nuclear tests had fundamentally changed the parameters of India's approach to the CTBT. It was reflected in the unilateral moratorium on testing it had imposed on itself when announcing the tests and an offer to negotiate with the great powers on finding a way to become a party to the CTBT, principally as a means to find reconciliation with the global non-proliferation regime and to signal it had no intent to build a large nuclear arsenal. Yet India also insisted that its accession to the CTBT cannot take place in a political vacuum and must involve reciprocal concessions from the great powers. For the first time India was seeking to use its participation in arms control treaties as a bargaining chip. Gone was the perception that signing a nuclear treaty would be tantamount to yielding to international pressure. It was ready for trade-offs on arms control. As part of the new approach to global arms control, India has also offered to participate in the negotiation of a FMCT.

Even as New Delhi recast its nuclear policy towards greater pragmatism, there were strong objections in the domestic political spectrum to signing a treaty that India had rejected less than two years ago. Although a major domestic debate ensued at the end of 1999 in which some, in the name of realism, urged signing the CTBT in return for substantive benefits from the United States, the turnaround was too rapid to be accepted broadly in India. The exercise of India's nuclear option was built on whipping up extraordinary popular opposition to the CTBT in 1995 and 1996, and a move to join the very same treaty met with political and intellectual resistance. One line of argument was that India's objections to the CTBT, voiced so vigorously in 1996, remained valid. These include the discriminatory character of the CTBT, the unsatisfactory definition of the scope of the treaty and the absence of a linkage with the total elimination of nuclear weapons. Many of the arguments that India raised in 1996 were in fact secondary to its main concern about the CTBT: by banning nuclear tests, the treaty was robbing India of the discretion to test nuclear weapons in the future. Having the room to test was critical to India's policy of keeping its nuclear option open. Now having conducted the tests and exercised its option, it made little sense for India to continue to oppose the CTBT.

The central question for nuclear India in relation to the CTBT was this: does India need to conduct more tests to have a credible and reliable arsenal? R. Chidambaram, the chairman of the Atomic Energy Commission, publicly asserted that there was no need to conduct any more tests. Having reviewed the data from the five nuclear tests, he believed that India could now build a variety of nuclear weapons, and maintain safety and cope with new developments by sustaining an advanced research programme in nuclear weapons.[10] The CTBT permitted such nuclear weapons research, and as a signatory to the CTBT, India could take full advantage of this loophole. Once the scientific community indicated that India could live with the CTBT, opponents shifted their arguments to such problems as verification. To suggest that India should not sign the CTBT because of the extensive verification provisions of the treaty has little rational basis. India had earlier accepted very intrusive verification under the Chemical Weapons Convention, and during the negotiation of the CTBT draft in 1996, India and China worked hard to limit the process and nature of inspections and did not oppose the regime that was eventually agreed upon. More fundamentally, the argument on verification implies that India will not sign any nuclear arms control treaty.

The arguments against the CTBT after the tests were largely based on the inertia of old thinking on nuclear issues. Nuclear paranoia persisted, however, and presented arguments in terms of national sovereignty and prevented the government from clinching a quick deal with the United States on the CTBT. Although the BJP-led government initiated a campaign to get public opinion behind signing the CTBT, it could not successfully conclude it. As in the case of the CTBT, sections of the government also began to look at the FMCT in a practical way. The critical question for India in relation to the FMCT or a moratorium on cessation of the production of nuclear material prior to the treaty was the following: how much plutonium does India need for its nuclear arsenal? The answer, in turn, would depend upon a national determination of the nature of its minimum deterrent. If New Delhi decided that it had enough material to build that minimum deterrent, it could even join an immediate moratorium. If it believed it needed to produce some more material in the coming years, it could wait until the multilateral FMCT is negotiated and comes into force.

While the tension on these treaties between the pragmatists and traditionalists remained unresolved, the immediacy of the problem for India was removed by the US Senate's rejection of the CTBT at the end of 1999. Pressures from the Clinton administration on India to sign the CTBT began to weaken; India, in any case, was in compliance with the spirit of the CTBT through its unilateral moratorium. India's pragmatic approach to arms control continued in a number of other ways. It began to endorse nuclear weapon-free zones in various regions, in particular one in South-East Asia and Africa. India had supported such zones as a non-nuclear weapons power in other regions, but the idea eventually travelled to the subcontinent, with Pakistan as well as various peace movements supporting it. Since the idea came into conflict with preserving India's nuclear option, New Delhi rejected such a zone for the subcontinent. In supporting those zones now, India was signalling its own responsible role as a nuclear weapons power and was ready to extend security guarantees to non-nuclear weapon states. The Indian support to nuclear weapon-free zones might not have had immediate operational significance, but it signalled a fundamental change in India's philosophical attitude to nuclear issues.

Equally important was India's increasing willingness to strengthen national laws on export of sensitive technologies and materials. Previously it had emphasized that the right of technology transfers should not be curbed in the name of non-proliferation. While India continues to insist it needs to have better access to advanced technologies, it has been willing to underscore the importance of preventing sophisticated arms from falling into the hands of the so-called states of concern. Here again there was a subtle change in attitude. In another important shift, India also endorsed the objectives of the Non-Proliferation Treaty. In a formal statement before the Indian Parliament on 9 May 2000, the foreign minister, Jaswant Singh, expounded on the new Indian approach to the treaty. The occasion was the Review Conference of the treaty under way in New York. Singh explained, 'Though not a party to the NPT, India's policies have been consistent with the key provisions of NPT that apply to nuclear weapon states.'[11] After a quarter century of fulminating against the NPT, here was India claiming itself a nuclear weapons power and touting its record in respecting the treaty's objectives.

During the 1990s, India also moved towards a recognition of the importance of establishing military confidence-building measures (CBMs) with Pakistan to promote nuclear stability between the two nations. This transition in India's nuclear policy was captured by the draft nuclear doctrine that India issued in August 1999. The last sentences of the draft state:

> Nuclear arms control measures shall be sought as part of national security policy to reduce potential threats and to protect our own capability and its effectiveness. In view of the very high destructive potential of nuclear weapons, appropriate nuclear risk reduction and confidence building measures shall be sought, negotiated and instituted.[12]

For a Western audience reared on deterrence and arms control, the above statements might sound self-evident, but in the context of the Indian debate that was centred around normative considerations, acknowledging that arms control is part of security policy and recognizing the need to institute nuclear confidence-building measures was a substantial move forward.

The new support for arms control and nuclear confidence building was built on the incremental evolution of attitudes during the 1990s amidst an intense exposure of the Indian strategic community to the unending track-two initiatives that brought former diplomats, retired generals and other intellectuals from both countries to discuss bilateral relations. These contacts were funded by non-governmental foundations in the United States and encouraged by the American administrations with a view to promote nuclear dialogue and CBMs in the subcontinent. By June 1997, when India and Pakistan had agreed on a structured dialogue, they had put peace and security, including CBMs, at the top of their bilateral agenda. After the two governments agreed, in September 1998, to initiate talks after a period of tension following the nuclear tests, the first formal discussion of nuclear and conventional CBMs followed in October 1998.[13] This was further consolidated in the memorandum of understanding (MoU) on CBMs that the Indian and Pakistani Foreign Secretaries signed during Vajpayee's visit to Lahore in February 1999.[14] At the inconclusive conversation at Agra in July 2001, it is believed that the resumption of the negotiations on nuclear and other CBMs was among the many understandings arrived at between the leaders of India and Pakistan.

India's readiness to negotiate CBMs to stabilize its nuclear relationship with Pakistan has also involved another important intellectual leap. Throughout the 1990s, many in India were concerned that the CBMs were part of some American plot to roll back Indian nuclear and missile capabilities. These measures were seen as the first steps on a slippery slope of denuclearization. The Indian strategic community vigorously objected to the United States' constant refrains on the potential for a nuclear war in the subcontinent and Kashmir as the most dangerous nuclear flashpoint in the world. The typical Indian argument then was that India and Pakistan were capable of managing their own affairs and that they did not need American intervention to promote stability in the subcontinent.

Warming Up to Missile Defence
The decision in May 1998 to end its nuclear ambiguity has allowed India to define a more responsible Indian approach to arms control treaties at the global level, establish a new readiness to accept internationally mandated restriction of its strategic programmes, recognize proliferation of weapons of mass destruction as an important international security problem,

raise standards of implementing controls on the spread of sensitive technologies and accept the need for a credible regime of nuclear and conventional military CBMs in the subcontinent to reduce the danger of a nuclear war. India has overcome the past intellectual resistance to the idea of arms control that is limited in scope and aims at a small range of security objectives. New Delhi is no longer the permanent dissident in the global nuclear debate. Now it is ready to contribute constructively in building global and regional arms control regimes.

Ironically, even as India moved quickly after the nuclear tests to find a lasting accommodation with the international system, it began to discover that the old nuclear order was on its last legs. The American post-cold war debate on nuclear strategy appears to have been finally clinched in favour of a more radical view that questioned the value of the traditional arms control framework. The Bush administration was determined to tear up the Anti-Ballistic Missile (ABM) Treaty, build a missile defence system and explore non-traditional means to deal with the threat of weapons of mass destruction in the hands of the so-called rogue states and terrorist organizations. Somewhat counter-intuitively, the advent of the Bush administration offered an entirely unexpected parallelism of interests between Washington and New Delhi.

The Bush administration's attempt to recast the global nuclear strategic framework opened the door for building cooperation between India and the United States in the area of nuclear weapons. India was among the first to back at least parts of President Bush's controversial national missile defence initiative unveiled on 1 May 2001. Stating that the administration's ideas are an attempt 'to transform the strategic parameters on which the Cold War security architecture was built', India declared that 'there is a strategic and technological inevitability in stepping away from a world that is held hostage by the doctrine of [mutual assured destruction] MAD to a cooperative, defensive transition that is underpinned by further [nuclear] cuts and a de-alert of nuclear forces.'[15]

India's surprising support of the missile defence project was based on a number of political expectations. The decision involved considerations of its strategic relations with the United States and Russia as well as its security concerns in relation to China and Pakistan. First, a new strategic framework might open the door to addressing India's long-standing problem with the global nuclear order and India's place in it. India's inability to test nuclear weapons before 1 January 1968 made it impossible for the country to be accepted as a legitimate nuclear weapons power. Its efforts to find a modus vivendi with the NPT system in the late 1990s were indeed real, but that process remained unfinished business during the Clinton administration. While the Clinton White House was willing to live with India's nuclear weapons, it was not ready to lift the restrictions on technology transfer that apply to India under the NPT. The Bush administration's attempts to rework the global nuclear order were seen by some in India as providing an opportunity for India to become part of the making of a new system of nuclear rules. Unlike Russia and China, India had no stakes in the survival of the ABM Treaty. In welcoming the demise of the treaty, the cornerstone of post-cold war global arms control, India of course had to take into account the sensitivities of its long-standing partner, Russia. India, unlike the Europeans and the American Democrats, bet that Moscow would ultimately accommodate Washington rather than confront it on the question of missile defence. India's assessment turned out to be correct as Russia eventually looked for a compromise with Washington on missile defence. While rushing to support the Bush administration, India could not afford to hurt Russia's sensitivities. India sought to assuage Russia by suggesting that the transition towards missile defence must be through cooperation and consultation between Washington and Moscow, not through American unilateralism.

Second, there was a view in India that the American movement towards missile defence might open up the exploration of new solutions to one of the problems that had significantly complicated India's security environment over the last two decades—the proliferation of nuclear weapons and missiles in its neighbourhood. India believed it has been the biggest victim of Chinese proliferation of nuclear weapons to Pakistan in the 1980s and missile technology in the 1990s. For years India protested about Chinese nuclear and missile technology, but it could make no impression on Beijing, which either insisted that it was within the bounds of its treaty commitments or flatly denied such charges. US plans for missile defence have created space for India to put pressure on China, on both its own nuclear arsenal as well as its perceived policy of balancing India through weapons of mass destruction (WMD) transfers to Pakistan.

It has often been argued that the US missile defence programme would lead to an expanded Chinese nuclear arsenal and that India would be forced to respond in kind. New Delhi, however, has no desire to match China weapon for weapon; it is more interested in breaking out of the current political box that it has been trapped into vis-à-vis China and Pakistan. While India has taken out modest nuclear insurance, missile defence might offer at least a conceptual way out of its current security dilemmas by complicating the nuclear calculus of both China and Pakistan. Even before the Bush administration unveiled its plans for missile defence, India was engaged in an effort to obtain theatre missile defence technology from Israel. It is also exploring cooperation with the United States, and the Pentagon has offered to make an evaluation of India's missile defence requirements.

Finally, having recognized the proliferation of WMDs as a serious threat to its own national security, India is deeply concerned about the spread of nuclear weapons to states or groups of terrorists who do not abide by the traditional rules of nuclear deterrence. India's own experience with Pakistan's nuclear blackmail and Islamabad's strategy of using the nuclear balance to foment terrorism across the border makes New Delhi empathetic to arguments that there are forces that cannot be deterred by traditional means. In addition, there is the concern that Pakistan might become a failed state or that nuclear weapons might fall into the hands of extremist forces in that country. Those concerns reinforce India's interest in not only defence but also counter-proliferation. The term *counter-proliferation*, as opposed to the more traditional *non-proliferation*, refers to the importance of having military capabilities to deal with an environment in which there is proliferation of WMDs. The belief is that the legal instruments under the non-proliferation regime might not be adequate to deal with the threat of the spread of WMDs. At the end of their joint Defence Policy Group meeting on 3 and 4 December 2001 in New Delhi, India and the United States pointed to 'the contribution that missile defenses could make to enhance strategic stability and to discourage the proliferation of ballistic missiles with weapons of mass destruction.'[16] They noted that 'both India and the United States have been the targets of terrorism', called for a new emphasis for cooperation on 'counter terrorism initiatives' and recognized the value of 'joint counter-proliferation efforts'.[17]

India's nuclear policy has come a long way. After inconclusive attempts to reconcile with the US non-proliferation policy and global nuclear order following its nuclear tests during the Clinton years, India seized the opportunities opened by the Bush administration's comprehensive overhaul of the notions of arms control and nuclear deterrence. India, which could not be accommodated in the old nuclear order, had nothing to lose in its deconstruction and perhaps could gain something from the rules of the nuclear game being drafted by the Bush administration.

The Nuclear Fulcrum of New Foreign Policy
Beyond the changes in India's approach to arms control itself, India's new nuclear policy had the important effect of redefining the framework of key bilateral relations. Analysts recall the fears that were expressed following the nuclear tests in May

1998—India would be isolated, it would not be able to bear the brunt of economic sanctions, and the Kashmir issue would be internationalized. The results of India's post-Pokhran diplomacy have been counter-intuitive. Thanks to the nuclear tests, India's relationship with the United States stood transformed by the turn of the century. Although the United States did impose sanctions, it also began to treat India more seriously than ever before. The sustained nuclear dialogue between India and the United States on nuclear issues facilitated a significant improvement in bilateral relations and substantially altered the political context of the arms control debate within India.

Instead of letting nuclear differences define the relationship, the two sides have chosen to put in place a broader engagement that will help manage the nuclear divergence in a mature manner. The broader engagement included the recognition of the prospect of a natural alliance between the two democracies; the initiation of security cooperation, for example in the area of counterterrorism; and a readiness to expand the framework of the dialogue between the two states beyond the traditional confines of the subcontinent. The new approach in the final years of the Clinton administration has helped accelerate India's evolution towards accepting the utility of arms control, but the nuclear dialogue between India and the United States remained unfinished. Although the US could not overcome the objections of its non-proliferation community to acknowledge the reality of India's nuclear weapons and normalizing relations with New Delhi, the Bush administration was prepared to deepen the bilateral engagement and reset the parameters of the nuclear debate with India by unconditionally lifting the nuclear sanctions of October 2000. The post-Pokhran US sanctions lasted barely three and a half years and have hardly had an effect on Indian economy. When the United States began to deal with India after its nuclear test and recognized that there was no way of rolling back its capabilities, New Delhi's brief international isolation evaporated. Once the United States—the biting dog—made its peace with nuclear India, the barking dogs (some of the more sanctimonious US allies like Australia, Canada and Japan as well as some of the North European countries) that Washington had let loose on India fell in line. The US allies in Europe and Asia followed the American lead on renewing the engagement with India without a reference to it joining the CTBT. More significantly, as the Bush administration began the controversial effort to restructure the global nuclear order, it found India an unexpected ally.

On the key question of Kashmir, India's nuclear tests certainly brought greater international focus and attention to the problem. The heightened tensions between India and Pakistan after May 1998—despite being interspersed with peace initiatives from Vajpayee—seemed to prove the assertions of the Western strategic analysts about the danger of a nuclear flashpoint in the subcontinent. But the intervention that did take place from the United States in the Indo-Pakistani relationship after May 1998 tended to work decisively in favour of India.

During the Kargil crisis, the US pushed Pakistan into withdrawing unconditionally and unilaterally from across the Line of Control (LoC). After 13 December the American diplomatic pressure and the full-scale Indian military mobilization were critical factors in Musharraf's now celebrated speech on 12 January 2002, in which he promised to end cross-border terrorism and launch Pakistan on a new national course. The American pressure on Pakistan to give up support to cross-border terrorism on a permanent basis intensified after the 14 May 2002 terrorist incident at Kaluchak in Jammu and Kashmir. Instead of rejecting the arguments of a nuclear flashpoint in Kashmir, India successfully turned the concept on its head. In raising the fears of a war that could turn nuclear in the summer of 2002, India drew the attention of the international community to the threat of cross-border terrorism in Pakistan and forced it to pressure Islamabad to make commitments to end the menace. The much feared internationalization of the Kashmir dispute following the nuclear tests of May 1998 did happen, but it helped India to reframe the questions on Kashmir towards a greater emphasis on cross-border terrorism and away from self-determination for the Kashmiris.[18]

More fundamentally, the nuclear tests and the post-Pokhran diplomacy changed the way the Indian elite began to think about external relations and diplomacy. The political will to defy the United States and the wisdom to find reconciliation inevitably brought a new maturity and self-assurance to India's foreign policy. It had exorcized the well-known Indian penchant to substitute pious-sounding slogans for effective action. India's post-Pokhran diplomacy ended India's extended reluctance to discuss difficult national security issues with major powers. The self-perception as an emerging great power armed with nuclear weapons allowed India to negotiate and bargain with great powers on the basis of national interest, without the sense of diffidence that had permeated its earlier thinking. To be sure, the rapid alteration of the benchmarks of the traditional debate on nuclear and foreign policies tended to unhinge the old consensus within the nation on the conduct of external relations. The effective handling of the nuclear transition, however, facilitated a rejigging of the internal intellectual balance in favour of realists and pragmatists and ended the long-standing dominance of so-called Nehruvians and traditional Left-of-centre internationalists over the foreign policy discourse.[19]

India's extended and exciting nuclear debate of the 1990s also brought to the surface a new stream of hyperrealists to launch an unhindered pursuit of power. These analysts who supported India's nuclear tests demanded more. They opposed nuclear negotiations with the United States and other major powers and argued against India joining the CTBT. They sought at once an absolutely unconstrained nuclear weapons programme, and they continue to confront the great powers if they came in their way. They insisted that India take the war across the Line of Control into Pakistan during the Kargil War. India, however, steered the middle path and shunned the old shibboleths but refused to go to the other extreme. In defining its nuclear aspirations to a credible, minimum deterrent, looking for a political rapprochement with the United States and exercising considerable restraint during the Kargil War, India maximized the pay-offs from the nuclear tests.

TWO

Beyond Non-alignment

After the Cold War

The end of the cold war brought into question the central theme of India's foreign and security policies during the first four decades—non-alignment. The collapse of the Soviet Union and the end of a world dominated by two superpowers forced India in its fifth decade of independence to rethink non-alignment and to attempt to find another organizing principle for its external relations. It did not take long for critics of India's foreign policy abroad and at home to mock India's old policy of trying to steer between the all-encompassing competition between East and West, capitalism and socialism, America and Russia. India's initial reactions were defensive and amounted to an insistence that the principle of non-alignment remained valid even after the end of the cold war. In reality, Indian diplomacy throughout the 1990s wrestled hard to come up with alternative ideas to non-alignment. Although India did not formally discard it, the contours of its future foreign policy would bear no resemblance to the idea of non-alignment, which had shaped its image in the world so definitively in the early decades of the republic.

An important distinction must be made between India's foreign policy of non-alignment and the Non-Aligned Movement (NAM). Although the two ideas are related, non-alignment was the defined foreign policy orientation of India from the first days of Independence. The NAM came much later, towards the end of the Nehru years, and developed a dynamic of its own. Although India was one of the founding members of the NAM and its presumed leader, the movement and its politics did not always merge completely with India's own articulation of its national interests. The NAM often complemented India's pursuit of its international objectives but never fully supplanted non-alignment.

The idea of non-alignment figured quite early in Nehru's understanding of how newly independent India should pursue its external relations. In a broadcast on 7 September 1946, Nehru, then vice chairman of the interim government, proclaimed the broad outlines of India's foreign policy. While seeking good relations with all the major powers of the world, Nehru indicated quite clearly that the nation would be averse to taking anyone's side.[1] As independent India stepped out into the world, the alliance that won the Second World War was falling apart, and a cold war between East and West was shaping up. Nehru was determined not to lose India's manoeuvrability by being tied to the apron strings of any major power. Much like the first American President, George Washington, Nehru was deeply suspicious of getting into entangling alliances that could limit India's strategic space, and his emphasis was on avoiding the limitations alliances imposed on nations.

As the world celebrated the end of the cold war and the disappearance of the ideological, political and military rivalry between Washington and Moscow, India had to ask itself, non-alignment between whom? For decades, India had seen itself as the leader of the Third World, an idea that was itself a construct of the cold war. The view that the newly independent nations emerging out of the shadow of decolonization could follow a third way, one different from capitalist West and socialist East, was at the heart of India's choices on its internal development strategy as well as its approach to the world. India believed that political unity within the Third World and collective economic bargaining with the advanced nations were necessary instruments to improve the condition of the developing nations. These ideas formed the keystone of mental architecture of many generations of the Indian elite, who grew up in the era of national movement and the early decades of Independence.

The pursuit of the third way, in the name of non-alignment, became the anchor of India's external relations. The collapse of the second world and its determination to join the first at the turn of the 1990s left the concept of the Third World in a limbo. The universal pressures to globalize in the context of the triumph of capitalism and liberal democracy seemed to have made non-alignment a relic. Nonetheless, it was wrenching for India to give up the concept and its attachment to the Non-Aligned Movement. Much of the Indian intelligentsia continued to articulate the view that India must persist with the notions that originally drove India's enthusiasm for the movement. These included the importance of solidarity with the recently decolonized nations, opposition to power politics and military alliances, democratization of the international order, emphasis on genuine multilateralism, and promotion of global collective security. Yet sustaining these ideas in the utterly changed world was nearly impossible. As India pursued economic reforms and coped with the United States' dominance of the international system, adjustments to its foreign policy inevitably followed. The Indian political class had to step back, review the past and call for definitively new ideas in dealing with the world. Yet given the dynamics of domestic politics in an era of coalition governments and sensing the need to avoid opposition charges that India was deviating from its past foreign policy benchmarks, the governments in the 1990s made little effort to articulate a conscious, new approach to the world. The incremental changes introduced throughout the decade, however, would take India far from the premises of non-alignment.

At the turn of the 1990s, the Congress party, which was the architect of the NAM abroad and state socialism at home during the 1950s, now had the charge to lead India's economic reforms.

Just as it had pursued economic liberalization without critiquing the failure of the earlier policies, the Congress government led by P.V. Narasimha Rao began to adapt to the changed world without a clear rejection of the past. The Narasimha Rao government understood the demands of the new international order on India, but there was no way the Congress, with its reverence of the Nehru dynasty, could come up with an open criticism of non-alignment and make a credible case for change in foreign policy. That would have invited serious political trouble both inside and outside of the Congress party. Yet, in his own low-key manner, it was Narasimha Rao who paved the way for change.

It must be noted, however, that his predecessor, Rajiv Gandhi, had less political inhibition in accepting change, and throughout his five-year rule (1984-89) he sought new ideas on foreign policy and constantly looked for ways to get India out of its diplomatic rut. Gandhi was aware that the NAM was running out of steam in the mid-1980s and looked for ways to rejuvenate it as well as for alternative mechanisms to project India's views on the global stage. On the disarmament front, for example, he enthusiastically backed the five-continent, six-nation initiative that brought together a diverse groups of nations—India, Sweden, Greece, Tanzania, Mexico and Argentina. This group, sponsored by social democratic forces in the West, campaigned against the renewed arms race between the US and the Soviet Union in the 1980s and demanded the drafting of a CTBT and a ban on putting weapons into outer space. In mobilizing world opinion in favour of the economic demands of the developing world, Gandhi looked beyond the NAM and diligently worked to create the Group of 15 (G–15), which brought together key states from the Third World.[2] Despite Gandhi's attempts to innovate, the conditions at home and abroad were not conducive to anything other than a minor tinkering with the non-aligned approach to foreign policy.

Not until 1991 was India compelled to deal with the economic crisis at home and the collapse of the Soviet Union, and then the pressures became irresistible for changing the very premises of India's external relations. The imperatives of economic globalization and reconstruction of Indian foreign policy in a world without the Soviet Union compelled India to unveil a new foreign policy agenda without appearing to reject the old commitments to non-alignment and the NAM. The inertia of non-alignment continued in India's public pronouncements, but more as a matter of routine and without any sense of the old fire. Within the Congress and the Left, however, strong voices were clamouring for the past emphasis on non-alignment and demanding that India remain in the forefront of the attack, if only verbally, on US policies in a unipolar world.

Narasimha Rao would have none of it; his trick was to duck the criticism, refuse to confront the challengers and adapt incrementally to the new foreign policy demands. While there was considerable nostalgia in the Congress party to the well-known moorings of the past, Narasimha Rao navigated the difficult diplomatic waters adroitly, and in the end, he had changed Indian foreign policy by a large measure. The old world of non-alignment was not to be reconstructed.

Nevertheless, the clamour from the Left parties and liberal intelligentsia for the old markers was loud and unremitting. The Leftists, who denounced the economic liberalization of the 1990s, inevitably targeted the foreign policy changes. They saw India departing from the old national consensus on foreign policy. India's new attempts to cosy up to the United States and the West was seen by the Left as giving up on India's independent foreign policy.[3] But the question of independence was ideological and subjective. For the Left, independence in foreign policy was maintaining political distance from the West, and the earlier Indian reliance on Soviet Russia was, of course, progressive and anti-imperialist. Much of the anti-Western as well as the liberal Indian intelligentsia argued that the new approaches to foreign policy meant a sacrifice of the long-standing traditions of Indian foreign policy, in particular non-alignment.

Contrary to perceptions both at home and abroad, there was never a complete national consensus on the policy of non-alignment. That perception was part of national myth making in India. As late as the late 1970s, when the Congress party maintained its uninterrupted hold on national governments, there was repeated questioning of the foreign policy of non-alignment. The Left, for example, was not always enthusiastic about it. In the 1950s and the early 1960s, the Left criticized non-alignment as sitting on the fence in the struggle between good and evil during the cold war. Much like John Foster Dulles, the US Secretary of State during the 1950s, who called non-alignment unacceptable for its refusal to take sides, the Left also accused India of vacillation on the great issues of the day. When Nehru went to the first non-alignment summit in Brioni, Yugoslavia, in 1961, the Left challenged Nehru's emphasis on peace and disarmament as the principal international issues of the moment. It demanded instead that decolonization and anti-imperialism remain the NAM's principal objective. The Left's attitude towards India's non-aligned policy as well as the NAM became more positive only by the 1970s, when the movement took radical overtones and India drew closer to the Soviet Union. It was then that the Left began to attribute an anti-imperialist content to India's foreign policy and saw non-alignment as the principal manifestation of the efforts in the developing world to confront imperialism.

By the late 1970s, the radicalism of the NAM reached its peak. The Left hailed it as part of the changing international correlation of forces in favour of socialism. These were the movement's heady days. The Left saw expansion of the NAM's influence in the 1970s as a reflection of the fundamental contradiction between the national aspirations of the developing world and the imperialist political and economic exploitation of the Third World. If the Left welcomed India's non-alignment for its anti-Western orientation, the Right opposed it for the very same reason. The conservative elements in the Congress as well as in other formations—like the Swatantra Party in the

1960s and the Jan Sangh and its later offshoot, the BJP—were deeply suspicious of the Congress' drift towards left-wing economic populism at home and what they saw as a pro-Soviet orientation abroad. The war for the liberation of Bangladesh in 1971 and the consistent Soviet support for India steadily reduced the domestic criticism of India's close relations with Moscow. Nevertheless, when the Janata Party—a loose conglomeration of non-Congress parties—defeated Indira Gandhi in the 1977 elections, it argued the case for a foreign policy in favour of genuine non-alignment as opposed to one tilted towards the Soviet Union. Once in power, the Janata Party recognized that the strategic necessity of a close relationship with the Soviet Union, and the then-foreign minister, Vajpayee, did little to disrupt the ties with Moscow. The foreign policy of the Janata government confirmed that there was now a broad consensus within the nation on a strong relationship with Moscow, which was based on the imperatives of the regional security environment. But the conservative sections of the Indian political spectrum were never really enamoured with the NAM; they just drifted along with it when in power.

Yet once the cold war ended and India was confronted with a new international context, the foreign policy divisions came back into view. The BJP had far fewer illusions about the relevance of past policy formulations in guiding India's post-cold war foreign policy. In the many parliamentary elections that took place in the 1990s, the BJP made no reference to either non-alignment as the principle feature of India's foreign policy or renewed commitment to the NAM.[4] The Congress party, on the other hand, was far more circumspect, emphasizing the non-aligned roots of India's foreign policy but making a bow to the demands of the new global order. In its manifesto for the general elections of 1998, the Congress party paid 'a great tribute to the foresight and wisdom of Jawaharlal Nehru' for creating a foreign policy framework that 'remains intact in its basics and fundamentals'.[5] At the same time, the manifesto made no reference to either non-alignment or NAM. Instead it went on to argue that in the new situation, 'economics, commerce and trade are the new languages of diplomacy. Our foreign policy and foreign service that has stood us well in the past will be refashioned to suit the contemporary world'.[6] The party at once acknowledged the diplomatic legacy of Nehru and implicitly endorsed the changes introduced by the last Congress government under Narasimha Rao. In power from 1998, the BJP government did not seek to overthrow non-alignment or threaten to walk out of the NAM. It just marginalized the concept of non-alignment as it tried to build on the foundations laid by the Narasimha Rao government for a new foreign policy premised on establishing good relations with the West.

Under the BJP, the immediate focus shifted to coping with the fallout from the nuclear tests of May 1998 and handling a series of crises with Pakistan. Although Vajpayee attended the NAM Summit in Durban, South Africa, in 1998 and offered to host the next summit when Bangladesh backed off from its initial offer in 2001, the movement was not one of his political priorities. Vajpayee's Principal Secretary and National Security Adviser, Brajesh Mishra, summed up the shift in India's attitude towards non-alignment and the NAM when he declared,

> In the post-Nehru period, non-alignment became a mantra just as Gandhiji's non-violent struggle had become the 'moral path'; the fact that these policies were grounded in strict rationality and realpolitik was lost sight of. Escapism was often couched as being principled, and I can safely state that neither Gandhi nor Nehru would have appreciated being made into icons to propagate dogma. There is a new India today that is ready to question these shibboleths and take decisions on the basis of national interest.[7]

Yet the traditional Indian resistance to change appeared to hold back a total rejection of non-alignment. So did the lingering suspicions of American intentions towards India on the Left and the Right, both of whom had strong streaks of anti-Western populism. If the Left was burdened by the logic of anti-imperialism, the Right was saddled with the nativism and antipathy towards Western values.

Although non-alignment and the NAM were moving off the radar screen of the mainstream political establishment in the 1990s, the foreign policy establishment had a different intellectual challenge. The articulation of the principles of non-alignment and the positions that the NAM took on the global stage had acquired a distinct anti-Western tone by the 1980s. This had two dimensions: one was a growing tilt towards the Soviet Union in the conflict between East and West, and the other the formulation of an irreconcilable North-South contradiction that called for a permanent confrontation with the developed world. By no means did the Indian foreign policy establishment share the ideological premises of the Left at home or the radical states in the NAM, despite acquiring an increasingly anti-Western bias. The establishment could and did always rationalize both non-alignment and its activism in the NAM as a sensible power play on the prevailing power politics in the international system in the first decades of Independence. For a country with hardly any real power to exercise in the international system, non-alignment seemed to offer India the best route to promote its diplomatic presence on the world stage. Non-alignment, it was argued by the foreign policy mandarins, gave the nation a voice and a distinct political profile in international politics of the second half of the twentieth century. It also offered India the opportunity to lead the newly decolonized nations in raising their collective demands against the continued dominance of the international system by the former colonial powers of Europe now led by the United States.

India's non-alignment also had a pragmatic economic content, the foreign policy establishment argued. In refusing to align with either bloc, it was believed, India could make considerable economic gains in the all-pervasive rivalry between

East and West. Non-alignment certainly allowed India to become one of the few countries in the world to gain economic assistance from both camps in the international system and to retain the freedom to criticize both the East and West on specific issues. Some of this influence began to subside in the 1980s when aid flows from the West began to decline.

These sorts of rationalizations for non-alignment, however, could no longer be sustained in New Delhi in the aftermath of the cold war. The old economic strategy needed to be modified amidst a new wave of globalization and India's own relative political decline in the world. India had to come to terms with the reality that it was on the losing side of the cold war, the Soviet Union was a footnote in history, and its own finances were in shambles. The Indian foreign policy elite knew the days of non-alignment were over but could not yet figure out if there was an alternative big idea to define India's foreign policy. The challenge of the 1990s for India was to discover ways to go beyond non-alignment to restore India's standing in world affairs. Even as the domestic debate on the national policy of non-alignment moved ahead, India also had to deal with the implications of the marginalization of the NAM.

The Decline of the Non-Aligned Movement
If non-alignment as national policy was essentially about managing India's relations with the great powers and charting the troubled waters of the cold war, the country's self-image as the leader of the Non-Aligned Movement involved broader questions of world order. As India rose out of a prolonged national movement, there were many different conceptions on how India should deal with the world and what kind of international order it should strive for.[8] However, it was Nehru's ideas about the world that ruled the roost in New Delhi. Nehru was by no stretch an idealist or a moralist in his thinking about international relations. While he accepted the realist premises on the struggle for power in the international system and its consequences, he also believed that 'under certain

conditions states can overcome the rigours of anarchy and fashion at least seasons and locales of peace and cooperation'.[9] Nehru also argued that states remain the principal agents of world politics, force and balance of power alone could not be the bases for enduring peace. Nehru believed that it was in the real interests of nations to forge a common set of rules and cooperative institutions. He believed that India could help move the world towards the objective of collective security.

Nehru's followers and successors, however, tended to reduce the sophisticated version of Nehru's world view into a set of formulas that increasingly acquired idealistic and moral overtones. Although Nehru himself was not too enthusiastic about the creation of a bloc of Third World nations, the NAM eventually became a mascot of India's foreign policy. Nehru was the originator of the concept of non-alignment for Indian foreign policy, but he was hesitant about proposals for expanding it into a third bloc apart from both the East and West. India was against the very concept of blocs, so where was the question of creating another one? Enthusiasts in the newly decolonized nations, including India, wanted to transform India's national non-alignment into an international movement, if not a bloc. The newly emerging forces, it was argued by the likes of Indonesia's Sukarno and Ghana's Kwame Nkrumah, must carry forward the struggle against the forces of colonialism to its logical conclusion.

Nehru, however, believed in the reconciliatory nature of India's nationalism. He was determined to engage India's former colonial rulers for mutual benefit. He was not impressed by the champions of the newly-emerging-forces thesis but attended the first NAM Summit in Belgrade in 1961. Nehru also insisted on keeping the focus of the movement on a few key international issues like peace and avoiding the nuclear danger that seemed so real in the United States and Soviet Union's apparent race to Armageddon in the late 1950s and early 1960s.

Nehru's first summit was also his last. If he had attended one of the summits in the late 1970s, he would have been horrified to find the movement's radicalization and anti-Western orientation. Although he would have understood the solidarity among the developing countries, he would have been deeply uncomfortable with the movement's intense ideologization. Nehru's world view had a natural tilt towards the idea of socialism at home, and he would have approved of the quest for a democratic international order, but he had no time for the ideological hatred of the West in the name of anti-imperialism, a sentiment that began to imbue the Non-Aligned Movement by the mid-1970s.

The general radicalism that gripped the movement was aided by at least three factors. First, there was the sense that the West was on decline and the socialist camp of the East was on the rise. The devastating defeat of the United States by a small nation of peasants in Vietnam injected a sense of political elation into the NAM. America's reverse in Vietnam was quickly followed by the defeat and long-delayed Portuguese colonialism from southern Africa, the victory of left-wing Sandinistas in Nicaragua, the triumph of the Saur revolution in Afghanistan led by the Afghan communists, the ouster of the pro-American Shah of Iran and the radicalization of the Arab confrontation with Israel. As America smarted under the worldwide reverses, the perception of an emerging East dramatically strengthened within the NAM. The Soviet Communist Party, reflecting on the changes in the mid-1970s, proclaimed in 1976 that the correlation of forces in the world was turning in favour of the socialist camp. The ideological triumphalism in the NAM was reflected in the dominant perception at the movement's Havana Summit in 1979, where Cuba sought to project the notion that the Soviet Union and the East were the natural allies of the developing world.

The second factor was economic. The ability of the petroleum producers from the developing world to raise the prices of oil fourfold in 1973 transformed the self-perception of the developing world. It showed the possibility of using the strategic dependence of the West on the resources of the developing world to bargain for better prices as well as to set political terms on critical issues like peace in the Middle East. Cooperation within the Third World on resource-related issues and collective bargaining with the former colonial rulers, it was argued, would significantly expand the NAM's political clout in the international system. The nationalization of resource ownership and the ouster of the Western multinational companies from the Third World was considered a natural route to power and prosperity, as an increasing number of developing countries were drawn towards the model of the state-led socialism. State socialism was seen by many in the South as the second liberation of the developing world. If decolonization was about political freedom from colonial masters, state control over the economy was to be about the empowerment of the subjugated masses of the developing world.

The heady mix of left-wing economic populism at home and political radicalism abroad was further spiked with the sense of a diplomatic upper hand for the Third World in the United Nations and other international fora by the mid-1970s. The decolonization that proceeded rapidly in the 1960s had created a numerical majority of the Third World in the United Nations General Assembly. That gave the leadership of the developing world, particularly India, the sense of an opportunity to set the agenda for the world community and challenge the impregnable dominance of the West over international political discourse. The virtual diplomatic arm of the NAM in the United Nations, the Group of 77 (G-77), began to play a powerful role in the UN, virtually dictating terms for the debate on a whole range of issues. The NAM Summit in Lusaka, Zambia, in 1970 gave the clarion call for a new international economic order that demanded a radical reordering of the terms of trade between the West and the developing world and an expansion of the economic sovereignty of the Third World. The Algiers Summit in 1973 called for a new international information order, demanding an end to the Western dominance of information flows across the world.

It appeared that there was not a single aspect of human life that the voice of the new majority in the international system did want to overhaul. The sense of a triumphal confrontation with the West to transform the rules of international politics dominated the diplomatic corps of the more important countries of the NAM, especially India. The new debates in the UN electrified the chattering classes of the developing world. The diplomats of India and other developing countries revelled in the new trench warfare on First Avenue in midtown Manhattan. There was a new self-assurance that their nations were no longer going to remain supplicants in the chanceries of the Western nations but were now ready to dictate terms. The Indian diplomatic corps began to believe that drafting eloquent resolutions in the United Nations and getting them passed against the resistance of a defensive West meant changing the world.

These illusions were challenged in the 1980s by a resurgent West and collapsed when the Soviet Union became a footnote in history at the turn of the 1990s. America moved away from the self-doubts induced by the Vietnam War under the leadership of Ronald Reagan and began to confront both the Soviet Union and the developing world. It dared the Soviet Union into a new nuclear arms race, with a determination to run Moscow to ruin. By making communist China a partner in the war against the Soviet Union, America at once transformed the global geopolitics and divided the left-wing circles all over the world. America, which was seen as retreating everywhere in the developing world in the mid-1970s, adopted a forward policy in the 1980s under the so-called Reagan Doctrine. Instead of combating national liberation movements through techniques of counter-insurgency, under President Reagan the US sponsored insurgencies and national liberation movements in the name of freedom from communist and radical regimes. From Indo-China to Nicaragua, via Afghanistan and southern Africa, the shoe was now on the other foot. The Soviet Union and its radical allies were now on the defensive.

Liberation movement, a term traditionally associated with the left-wing and nationalist movements in the developing world, was appropriated in the 1980s by right-wing forces backed by the United States. The American confrontation with Moscow in the 1980s and the Reagan Doctrine came together in Afghanistan, where the Soviet bear was bled to death in the final phase of the cold war by throwing the jihadis against the communists. America would pay a price later, but the Soviet communists were driven out of Afghanistan. Meanwhile, the Reagan Doctrine had another important effect in deeply dividing the Third World. The traditional focus against the West and the developed world got increasingly blurred in the 1980s amidst the rash of regional conflicts that pitted groups of developing nations against each other in South-East Asia, south-west Asia, the Middle East, southern Africa and Central America. More fundamentally, two decades after decolonization, political oppression and non-democratic governance in most parts of the developing world sharpened the internal conflicts. The growing number of civil wars within the developing nations often saw the intervention by the neighbouring states to defend the presumed interests of ethnic kin or simply to take advantage of the troubles next door. The rise of intrastate and interstate conflicts in the South inevitably undermined the proclaimed unity against the North and reduced the globalism of the Third World to an empty shell.

On the economic front, the grand delusion of the Third World oil producers came to an end in the winter of 1985-86, when oil prices came crashing down. The greatest example of Third World leverage against the West turned into a classic case of how not to push one's luck. The frequent increases in the price of oil made many non-economic resources of hydrocarbons viable and brought new producers into the market. The industrial policies in the West shifted towards energy efficiency, and finally the Organization of the Petroleum Exporting Countries (OPEC) members' attempts to undercut each other by violating production quotas resulted in a glut in the market and brought oil prices to one of their lowest levels since 1973. The story of other resource producers who tried cartelization was even worse. Meanwhile, the state socialist model was increasingly under stress in most developing countries; in contrast, countries of South-East Asia that avoided the temptation of state socialism began to demonstrate a new economic miracle. Those who had adapted to the incipient globalization thrived, and those who were stuck in the mire of economic nationalism and inward-looking policies kept falling behind. If there were soaring hopes within the NAM in the mid-1970s that they would grow by redefining the rules of international economy, by the late 1980s they were being forced to fall in line with the emerging world of globalization and economic liberalization.

At the diplomatic level too, the multilateralism of the NAM at the United Nations was challenged by President Reagan's unilateralism. The US hit back with a vengeance at the NAM majority in the UN by squeezing its funding, refusing to accept the declarations being issued by the majority in the General Assembly and walking out of the United Nations Educational Scientific and Cultural Organization. Within the United States, the UN came to be detested by the conservatives, and attempts by the Clinton administration to renew America's commitment to the United Nations did not succeed. The Third World majority in the mid-1970s began to yield place to a pro-Western dominance by the early 1990s, when a large number of states from Latin America as well as the smaller island states had little interest in NAM's pompous posturing and were willing to go along with the United States on key issues.

On the economic issues, the debate in the UN on the New International Economic Order (NIEO) was paralysed with most countries adjusting to globalization on their own volition or under pressure from multilateral financial institutions. By the mid-1980s what was always evident became crystal clear—the global power on the economic front was vested with the International Monetary Fund and the World Bank in

Washington, and the debate on economic issues at the United Nations in New York was really hot air. As developing countries that quickly accepted economic reforms moved forward, a growing economic differentiation began to take place within the NAM. In other multilateral fora like the General Agreement on Tariffs and Trade (GATT) or the World Trade Organization (WTO), it was clear that there was not much holding the G-77 together. There were far too many regional and sector-specific interests for the developing world to indulge in a collective bashing of the West or engage in collective bargaining with it.

On the political level too the West began to set the agenda for the UN in the post-cold war world. The Clinton administration led the charge with its expansive notion of multilateralism and the use of international institutions and American military force to deal with the manifold crises within the developing world. The UN Secretary General, Kofi Annan, took the initiative to promote the concept of humanitarian intervention to deal with the ethnic strife and failed states within the developing world. Annan argued in 1999 that state sovereignty was not an absolute concept, and if the conditions demanded, the UN should intervene with force in the internal conflicts of the developing world. For the sovereignty-conscious developing world, Annan's agenda was like a red flag for a bull, but the NAM could do very little to counter the new debate on humanitarian intervention. The issue was no longer whether to intervene but when and how to do so, for the new reality in the UN was that the NAM and the Third World were no longer the *demandeurs* but *répondeurs* in the emerging post-cold war debate on managing international security.

The debate, luckily for NAM, was stalled by the second Bush administration, which had no time for the liberal American project of humanitarian intervention and nation building through the United Nations. The Bush administration, however, was neither isolationist nor opposed to the use of American force to meet its national security objectives. It was against wasting American military resources and diplomatic energies in conflicts where the US had little or no definable interests. Although Washington's dramatic intervention in Afghanistan in its war against international terrorism forced the administration to rethink the UN's relevance and the importance of nation building in specific cases, the thrust of a bipartisan American policy towards the UN became clear—multilateralism where convenient, unilateralism where necessary. This muscular American approach to the United Nations has left the NAM and its global agenda in tatters. Politically divided, economically differentiated and ideologically exhausted, the old warhorses of the NAM, including India, have been compelled in the 1990s to rethink the future of the movement, but without much success.

Despite the grudging acknowledgement of its many limitations and failures, New Delhi is unlikely to jettison the NAM. Its formal disavowal of the NAM may not even be necessary. The movement's influence on India's diplomacy steadily eroded in the 1990s as New Delhi sought to reconstruct its foreign policy to meet the requirements of the post-cold war world. As India proclaimed itself a nuclear weapons power and pushed for a seat at the high table of international affairs, the movement's old rhetoric had little value for the new realists running India's foreign policy. India's demand for a role in the management of the international system was not going to be achieved through the role of a trade union leader of the Third World, but through demonstration of its capacity to contribute to the maintenance of international peace and security. Anti-Western political radicalism was no longer a policy option on the external front, although sections of the domestic opinion continued to clamour for it. As India reflected on its role and activism within the NAM, there was very little that India could honestly claim it gained from the movement. India's activism in the NAM no doubt generated considerable political goodwill for New Delhi, but it was largely an intangible element that could hardly be translated into practical benefit.

India's sense of leadership of the NAM rarely provided extra ballast in the pursuit of its core national security interests. Most NAM members were unwilling to take sides in India's wars with Pakistan in 1965, 1971 and 1999 or in India's disputes with China. Few had been ready to back India's attempts to gain the status of a nuclear weapons power, and there was strong resistance from such nations as Egypt and South Africa at the United Nations and the NAM. On the economic front, the G-77 ceased being a vehicle for the promotion of India's economic interests in the international arena. India began to look at fora like the G-15 to project its viewpoint in a more focussed manner. On the diplomatic front, often the radicalism of non-aligned positions limited India's strategic space. For example, as the Middle East radicals pressed for the isolation of Israel in the 1970s, India complied by limiting its own interaction with Tel Aviv. Although India was among the first countries to offer diplomatic recognition to Israel, India's Middle East policy steadily lost political balance. By the late 1990s, it was compelled to look for ways to ease out of the political straitjacket the NAM had become on its external relations. At least a generation of Indian Foreign Service officers grew up believing that multilateral diplomacy in the NAM, the G-77 and the United Nations was the acme of India's skills in international engagement. Defending positions of the NAM became far more important than bilateral relations with key countries—either in the developing or developed world.

The dominance of multilateral diplomacy in Indian foreign policy began to yield place in the late 1990s to the creation of strategic partnerships with pivotal states in the region and beyond. New Delhi was finally beginning to question what multilateral diplomacy could do for India. Previously India asked itself what New Delhi could do for multilateralism. Moving away from the past, abstract battles on defending national sovereignty, promoting anti-imperialism, defending inward-looking economic policies and glossing over unacceptable state practices in the Third World, India began to focus willy-nilly on mobilizing international support on issues of concern for itself—expanding international norms against terrorism and the links between political violence, narcotics trafficking and organized crime. Multilateral diplomacy was finally becoming the servant of India's strategic interest, not its master.

Towards Realignment?

Although Nehru rejected alliances as a vehicle for the pursuit of India's interests in the world and his successors persisted with the line, the political temptations of alignment kept intruding into India's foreign policy calculus. As India began to deal with the complexities of its strategic environment, it inevitably drifted into an alliance of a kind with the Soviet Union. Its prolonged, productive relationship with Moscow had the effect of balancing the American military ties with Pakistan early in the cold war. When a de facto strategic consensus emerged among Pakistan, China and the United States at the turn of the 1970s, India did not hesitate to deepen its relationship with the Soviet Union through a peace and friendship treaty in 1971. This pact served as the linchpin of India's national security policy until the Soviet Union collapsed. All alliances have both positive and negative aspects; they allow individual nation states to increase their strength while imposing a discipline of their own in deferring to the interests of the alliance partner. India began to figure out that alliances could enhance national strength in combination with other major powers.

But there was a problem. Did India's relationship with the Soviet Union deviate from the idea of pure non-alignment? In the vigorous debate that followed the treaty's signing, many in India criticized it as a departure from the principle of non-alignment. The establishment, of course, would not acknowledge that the relationship with the Soviet Union was an alliance for all practical purposes. It would insist that there was no departure from the concept of non-alignment, which did not mean equidistance from the superpowers. India's positions, it was argued, were defined on the merits of the issue. India needed a substantive security relationship with the

Soviet Union to balance the reality of Pakistan's alliances with the United States and China. Like all large nations, India continued to proclaim certain principles as guidelines of its foreign policy while in practice modifying them.

Whatever might have been its emphasis on non-alignment, India had to deal with the hard-nosed realpolitik of the world. As India sought to rework its foreign policy in the world after the Soviet Union, several trends arose in the foreign policy debate. One was an argument to climb on the bandwagon with the United States. Another line called for a policy aimed at balancing the United States, whose dominance created considerable unease in India. Both these approaches, however, called for alliance-like relations with either the United States or its potential competitors. A third course called for an active pursuit of a multipolar world in which India could establish itself as one of the major powers of the international system without recourse to an alliance with any one of them. A fourth and somewhat weaker stream demanded that India continue with the logic of pure non-alignment; all that was needed was to make the NAM more relevant to the new times. All these options were reflected in India's policy during the 1990s. The dominant emphasis, however, remained on building a new partnership with the United States as part of a multidirectional engagement of the major powers.

Barely four months after the nuclear tests in May 1998, to which the United States responded with condemnation and sanctions, Prime Minister Vajpayee declared that India and the United States were 'natural allies'.[10] In a speech in New York, this self-proclaimed head of the NAM talked about the potential for an alliance between the two nations. He examined why the two nations, aptly described as 'estranged democracies',[11] could not work together in the past. Vajpayee blamed America's lack of sensitivity for India's security concerns. This included America's preference for the military dictatorship in Pakistan, its alliance with communist China, its turning a blind eye to the terrorist challenge to the world's largest democracy and its unwillingness to appreciate India's compulsions to acquire nuclear weapons. If those concerns were addressed, Vajpayee hinted, India would be the newest ally of the United States in the twenty-first century.

Vajpayee's speech was simple in its conception but a breathtaking departure from India's traditional foreign policy moorings of non-alignment and anti-American and anti-Western orientation. Not since Nehru sought American help to counter the Chinese invasion of India had New Delhi made such a brazen pitch for an alliance with Washington. Nehru's manoeuvre came at one of India's weakest moments—a perceived defeat at the hands of China. Vajpayee's proposal for an alliance with the US, in contrast, was put forward amidst India's self-confident proclamation of itself as a nuclear power. Indira Gandhi in the 1980s had instinctively understood the importance of balancing India's relations with the Soviet Union and the United States and wanted to correct the excessive tilt towards Moscow by engaging the Reagan administration. As a younger leader, Rajiv Gandhi was less burdened by the anti-Western paranoia of his mother and predecessor and reached out with greater vigour to the United States, but none of his attempts succeeded in redefining the relations between New Delhi and Washington.[12] Vajpayee's call for realizing the natural alliance with the United States could be seen as reflecting the abiding anti-communist, pro-Western orientation of the Jan Sangh and its successor party, the BJP. Although the Jan Sangh in the 1960s and 1970s was critical of the Indian tilt towards the Soviet Union, its own populist and conservative anti-Western sentiments were on the rise in the BJP. The speech in that sense reflected Vajpayee's own sensibilities, rather than those of ideologues in his party or of the foreign policy establishment, which was surprised by the speech.[13]

The American audience at the Asia Society reacted to Vajpayee's speech with scepticism. Here was India that just surprised, shocked and even betrayed the United States by testing nuclear weapons and now claimed itself to be its ally.

Although a nuclear dialogue had started between the two countries after the tests, Vajpayee and his government were still under a cloud in Washington. During his September 1998 visit to New York, his first as India's Prime Minister, Vajpayee did not get a meeting with President Clinton on the margins of the United Nations. More fundamentally, the Clinton administration with its liberal internationalist impulses was de-emphasizing the value of alliances in the post-cold war world. Nevertheless, by the time President Clinton came to India in March 2000 and Vajpayee paid a return visit to the United States in September, the Clinton administration began to refer positively to Vajpayee's formulation of a natural alliance between the two nations, though without appearing to endorse it.[14] Not until the advent of the Bush administration, with its emphasis on realpolitik, did the US seem ready to embrace the idea of a natural alliance. But for the small group of South Asia hands in Washington, the talk of an alliance from India was incredulous. There was nothing in recent history of Indo-US relations to suggest an alliance between New Delhi and Washington was even conceivable, let alone practical.

Even as India drew closer to the United States in a manner that it had never done before, there was considerable unease about building a deeper relationship with the United States. One source of this ambivalence stemmed from the discomfort with the American dominance in world affairs since the end of the cold war. Many in India saw the United States as the most powerful imperial state and believed that its hegemonic tendencies could only harm India's interests. For them, the suggestion that India had no alternative but to engage the United States did not have much appeal. The ideological critics of the United States on the Left were joined by many in the centrist national security establishment on the dangers of American interventionism in the post-cold war world. American diplomatic activism on Jammu and Kashmir and its pressures to roll back the nuclear programme were compounded by the American intervention in the Balkans. India had little time for the complexity of the Western debate on the Balkans in the 1990s and the extreme reluctance with which force was ultimately used in the former Yugoslavia. For the Indian elite who grew up on a steady diet of anti-Americanism, the developments in Yugoslavia were a grist for the anti-imperialist mill. Meanwhile, the new enthusiasm in the United Nations for humanitarian intervention, encouraged by the Clinton administration, added to the fears about the erosion of national sovereignty in the new unipolar world. The United Nations' references to preventive and pre-emptive interventions in the conflict zones of the developing world raised fears in India about an American-led intervention in Kashmir that the international community was increasingly referring to as a nuclear flashpoint.

Preventing world domination by the sole superpower became one of the main themes of Indian foreign policy after the end of the cold war. Strong support for the idea of a multipolar world became the new staple of Indian diplomacy—acquiring a prominent place in India's statements in multilateral fora and in joint statements with major powers that were not part of the Western alliance. France, however, was an exception. Like Russia and China, France turned out to be a major champion of a multipolar world.[15] The idea of a multipolar world certainly clashed with the notion of a natural alliance with the United States, but the duality was real and shaped Indian diplomacy. India at once sought to deepen its ties with the United States and expand its own freedom of action by seeking cooperative action with other second-tier powers in the international system. The calls for a multipolar world and the democratization of international relations seemed in many ways to replace the past emphasis on non-alignment as the core concept of Indian foreign policy.

Non-alignment was the strategy of a weak but ambitious state that refused to be tied down by the discipline of limiting, cold war alliances. The focus on multipolarity reflected the new self-consciousness about India's potential to emerge as a major power in the international system.[16] The economic reforms of the early 1990s created a new hope within the Indian establishment of rapid growth that would be the basis for its becoming a major power in the world. The example of China was vivid. That China could transform itself, within a generation, seemed to suggest that a new status for India in world affairs was achievable. This new self-image as potentially one of the world's largest economies, was a big leap from the previously dominant image of a weak developing country. Although independent India had always had the sense of a manifest destiny, it was only in the 1990s that India seemed able to grasp that destiny. The possibility of India emerging as an important pole—along with the United States, Europe, Russia, China and Japan—informed India's new interest in the quest for a multipolar world.

Despite all its attractions, the idea of such a world was an elusive one. The very imbalance in the global power structure in favour of the United States, which the notion of a multipolar world sought to counter, made it impossible to achieve the objective. As events since 11 September proved and the US confrontation with Saddam Hussein at the end of 2002 confirmed, Washington had the power to set the international agenda, and the rest of the major powers had little ability to challenge it or even modify it in a significant manner.

As India looked to widen the strategic space for itself in the changed world, the notion of a triangular, alliance-like relationship among India, Russia and China was widely debated within the Indian strategic community. This idea had special attraction to those who believed India's interests are impossible to reconcile with those of America. The proposal for a strategic triangle involving the three initially came from Yevgeny Primakov, who served as the foreign minister and later as Prime Minister of Russia in the mid- and late 1990s. The appointment of Primakov to these positions was in part a political response from President Boris Yeltsin to the political backlash in Russia against excessive concessions to the West in the late 1980s and early 1990s. Amidst a growing disillusionment within Russia about the prospect of a productive relationship with the United States, Primakov began to articulate the view that a cooperative triangular relationship among New Delhi, Beijing and Moscow would help balance the domination of the world by one power.[17] Primakov took up the idea with the Indian leaders during his visits to New Delhi in March 1996 and December 1998.

In India there was some support for the notion of a countervailing bloc of nations against the United States. The inveterate critics of the United States on the Left and the orphaned pro-Soviet lobby enthusiastically backed the notion. Some even called for the inclusion of Iran in the grand coalition against the United States, but there was considerable circumspection within the foreign policy establishment. New Delhi understood that while the rhetoric of a countervailing alliance might have some political uses, the centrality of the United States in the new global configuration of power could not be wished away. Any realistic assessment of the international distribution of power suggested that the United States was way ahead of the others in almost all indicators of power. Even if all the other powers joined together, they would still be unable to balance the economic and military might of the United States.

Besides, there was also the structural problem of temptations among each member of the proposed grand alliance using the others to strike a better bargain with the United States. Each member of the proposed strategic triangle knew that the US remained the principal foreign policy priority as well as key source of technology and capital. Every one of them would have preferred to work out a special bilateral relationship with the United States, and the proposed alliance with the other second-tier powers was in essence aimed at increasing its leverage vis-à-vis the United States.

India also knew that China was not enthusiastic about including India in the strategic triangle. Beijing was doubtful about India ever becoming a separate pole in international affairs. It had a very special relationship with the United States and hoped to play the Russia card to improve its bargaining capacity with Washington. In that game India was more of a nuisance than a help, given the uncertain dynamics of Sino-Indian ties. India itself had previously voiced reservations about a Sino-American partnership ending up as a joint hegemony over Asia. When President Clinton travelled to China in June 1998 just weeks after Pokhran-II and joined in the Chinese in criticizing the Indian nuclear tests, India went ballistic. Yet less than two years later, when President Clinton came to India, it was China's turn to worry about a new strategic relationship between New Delhi and Washington. India understood China's aspirations to become the second superpower in the international system. New Delhi suspected that Beijing's support to a multipolar world was only a brief halt on the way to a bipolar world with Beijing as the other pole.

Meanwhile, the renewed efforts between President George W. Bush and Russian President Vladimir Putin to build a new strategic partnership and their convergence of interests in Afghanistan after 11 September raised questions about the political viability of a new alliance against Washington. After the dramatic turn of events on 11 September, China too toned down its criticism of the Bush administration and worked hard to move the Republican Washington away from a hostile attitude towards Beijing and towards a stronger commitment to Sino-US relations. The inevitable tension between the interests of different states within a prospective grand alliance against the US made the union less feasible. Nevertheless, the foreign ministers of Russia, China and India met for the first time in New York on the margins of the UN General Assembly session in September 2002, and all sides were extremely careful to avoid giving even the slightest hint of an anti-American tone to their deliberations.[18]

Even as they recognize both the difficulty and the dangers of confronting the United States, India, like Russia and China, might find it difficult to become a junior partner of the United States. They are too large to fit into an alliance pattern with the

United States à la Europe and Japan. All three will continue to explore the prospects for greater strategic space for themselves, given their discomfort with the American dominance of the world affairs. Deepening economic cooperation among the three is inevitable, and some ad hoc political cooperation is indeed possible. Nevertheless, an alliance of any kind is unlikely to emerge among the three second-ranking powers in the international system, for all three recognize that they cannot advance in opposition to the United States. India's search for strategic space will continue, although it will be within a framework of broad support to the West rather than in an anti-Western framework in which the idea of a strategic triangle was initially conceived.

Finally, the idea of alliances albeit in a very limited form has begun to take root in Indian thinking. Crafting an alliance-like relationship with the United States without giving up its special ties to Russia, exploring deeper relations with the European Union and Japan and managing the complex ties with China became the national strategic objectives. This in itself has not replaced the notion of non-alignment, but it has chipped away at its core.

THREE

Returning to the West

India's Relevance

What does India stand for? As New Delhi seeks a place at the high table of global diplomacy, it is a question that India's international interlocutors in the West keep asking. Why is India so special that the West must make a special effort to have a partnership with New Delhi? India is not demanding a say in the management of the affairs in Asia and the world merely on the fact that it is an ancient civilization, the large size of its population and its potential to emerge as a major economic force. India's claim for a special status is rooted in its ideological claim to being the world's most important democracy. India was reluctant during the cold war to trumpet its virtues as a democratic example to the rest of the Third World, and there was not much of a receptivity to such an argument in the West. The end of the cold war, however, offered one simple truth about India and the West—that they share the basic ideas of European Enlightenment. The shared commitment to Enlightenment values has gained a new prominence since the end of the cold war, and it provides the long-term bond between India and the West. It also increasingly distances New Delhi from the old agenda of the Third World.

The slow pace of this change and the unending arguments between India and the West on nuclear weapons and Kashmir during the 1990s tended to hide the significance of this transformation. The creation of a new partnership with the West became the central preoccupation of the Indian foreign policy in the 1990s. Furthermore, India no longer wanted to remain in the Third World. It was determined to become a developed nation within the first two decades of the twenty-first century. This necessarily called for a fundamental change in political attitudes in India towards the West that were dominated by distrust and hostility in the previous decades. The West too found it easier to do business, both political and economic, with India after the demise of the Soviet Union. One of the great tragedies of the post-cold war history was that India was the only democracy that stood against the West on most political issues during the cold war. India's de facto alliance with the Soviet Union to manage the difficulties in its regional security environment, its commitment to state socialism and its leadership of the Non-Aligned Movement were three factors that reinforced the inherited legacy of anti-colonialism and anti-imperialism. These factors also masked the essential political similarity between India and the West.

The end of the cold war was also an end to the extended civil war within the West—between the ideas of capitalism and socialism, two competing notions about organizing human endeavours. That India drifted towards the losing side of this civil war did not and cannot take away from the fact that India represents the most enduring example of the pursuit of the Enlightenment project outside Europe and North America. As the world's most successful democracy in the South, India represents the triumph of the values of reason, cosmopolitanism, scientific progress and individual freedom against great odds. Some have described the Indian experiment as the third great moment of democracy after the American and French Revolutions.[1] The fact that India held on to the principles of political pluralism and religious tolerance amidst extraordinary challenges is a testament to the fact that freedom and democracy are not just Western values but universal ones that need to be emulated everywhere. At a time when anti-Enlightenment views have gained prominence amidst the emphasis on religious or political totalitarianism as organizing principles for humanity, the importance of the democratic example of India stands out.

It is not that India was not tempted by the authoritarian impulses that so consumed the newly independent nations. The Emergency in India imposed by Indira Gandhi from 1975 to 1977 reflected that impulse most intensely. She justified the Emergency as a necessary move to prevent the Indian Union from being undermined by the pro-imperialist elements of the political spectrum. Individual freedoms and democratic rights may have to be sacrificed, her government argued, for India to continue on its progressive path. A section of the Indian communists and the Soviet Union itself strongly backed the Emergency as part of the struggle against imperialism and retrograde forces at home. As Gandhi's radicalism culminated in the Emergency, India was declared a socialist republic by passing the Forty-second Amendment to the Constitution in 1976 at the peak of the Emergency. Fortunately the Emergency was a brief interlude and might well have inoculated India and its political class against playing the fool with the democratic institutions at home.

Democracy has taken root strong enough to resist the assault from the Right, the latest of which was the attempt in the 1990s to undermine the secular character of the Indian state. The rise of the Hindutva ideology in late twentieth century in India has raised the dangers of majoritarianism in the country. Destruction of the Babri Masjid in Ayodhya by the hordes of Hindu extremists on 6 December 1992 and the butchery of Muslims in Gujarat in early 2002 pointed to an unprecedented threat to the country's principles of secularism, religious tolerance and rule of law. The increased frequency of attacks on the minorities across the nation, the attempt to rewrite text books with a Hindu bias, the temptation to turn the battle against terrorism into a war against the minorities and the communalization of the middle-class mind are all too visible to ignore. Nevertheless, the vigilance of the civil society and the need for the BJP to govern in coalition with other parties have limited the scope and substance of the Hindutva agenda. To be sure the ideologues of the Hindutva dream of creating a mirror image of Pakistan within India, but their ability to realize it remains doubtful despite their many excesses.

The many limitations of Indian democracy are obvious, but with warts and all, it remains a credible model for organizing humanity outside the Euro-Atlantic world.[2] Far more significantly, an inclusive democratic governance that accepts the principles of federalism and respect for the rights of ethnic, religious and linguistic minorities may be better placed than authoritarian structures in managing the growing intrastate conflicts that threaten international peace and security. There can be no better example than India, which has coped with a wide range of internal grievances over the last five decades within a democratic framework.

The cold war ended with the triumph of liberal capitalism and democratic values in Europe. While geopolitical compulsions led India to stay with the Soviet Union right until its bitter end and continue to experiment with state socialism until it was no longer feasible, India's commitment to liberal democracy endured. While the Indian state was in semi-alliance with the Soviet Union, its civil society retained its pro-Western orientation. Even as the Indian intelligentsia thundered against American dominance in world affairs, its children went to the best colleges of Great Britain and the United States. Every political fashion in the West and each cultural trend found its echo in the Indian elite, who soaked up everything from environmental activism to the latest pop music trends. In an abundant flourish since the early 1980s, young Indians began to write in English and establish themselves within the literary trends in the Anglo-American world. Likewise, India's musicians experimented with the fusion of Indian and Western classical and popular traditions. Its scholars dominated the faculties of American universities, and its executives reached the top of Western corporate ladders. As the post-Independence generations of Indians celebrated the spirit of individual freedom and creativity, there was an expansive interaction among the civil societies that preserved a relationship between India and the West, despite the vast political gulf that divided the two sides on the international arena. Moreover, the increasingly assertive Indian diaspora within the Anglo-American world began to create the conditions for greater Western awareness of India and to draw the two political systems together.

India and Democratic Stability

Although Western leaders made a bow throughout the cold war to India's political virtues, the endurance of the Indian democracy had little salience in the relationship between New Delhi and Western embassies. While the Western leaders had to balance their objective of defeating the Soviet Union against their interest in promoting democracy, India tended to underplay its own relevance as the world's largest democracy in the battle for ideas during the cold war. Although the Indian political class has always been proud of its success in sustaining the democratic framework against great odds, over the last half a century it has never really thought through the implications of Indian democracy for the world order. In the immediate aftermath of the cold war too, India and the United States found it difficult to develop the potential of bilateral cooperation around the principle of shared democratic values. It was only in the Clinton administration's fading years that the idea of working together to promote democracy worldwide came up. As the Clinton administration developed the initiative called a Community of Democracies, which would share thoughts on democratic experience, assist the new democracies, and encourage others to follow, it was keen to enlist the support of New Delhi in the new endeavour to promote democracy worldwide.[3]

There was considerable political hesitation before India agreed to join the United States in backing the initiative for a Community of Democracies. Its reluctance was understandable.

As the cold war dynamics overwhelmed the subcontinent, India found itself ranged against the Western democracies on key issues that divided the world. As the US and its allies relentlessly pursued containment of the erstwhile Soviet Union and a comprehensive victory in the all-encompassing civil war within the Western world, the concerns of a fledgling democracy in India never dominated American thinking. India drew considerable American economic assistance from the 1950s to early 1970s as part of an effort to shore up democracies in the American war against communism in Asia, and it was held up as a counterexample to China. The Sino-American rapprochement ended that special value for India as well. Throughout the cold war, India and the US occasionally attempted to build a relationship on the basis of their common democratic values, but nothing came to fruition. Instead, the call for cooperation between the most powerful democracy and the largest one often became a tiresome cliché.

The end of cold war did not immediately lead to an American appreciation of the significance of the Indian democracy. In fact it led to a new American focus on the warts on the face of the Indian democratic experiment. Single-issue groups in the United States, focusing narrowly on either human rights abuses or the practice of religious freedom or a possible link between trade and child labour, tended to concentrate with a new intensity on India's difficulties. At the multilateral level, the American support for greater UN intervention in the developing world's many raging civil wars also raised the alarm bells in India about a potential American political intervention in Kashmir. Likewise, within the United States, the Sikh Khalistani groups and the Kashmiri lobby actively campaigned Congress to pass resolutions against the human rights abuses in the Punjab and Kashmir during the late 1980s and early 1990s. Eventually, of course, India did beat back these efforts with its own intensive lobbying. Only Clinton's visit in March 2000, the first by an American President to India in twenty-two years, brought some emphasis to the shared values of political pluralism. This had particular resonance at a time when Pakistan had just months before reverted to military rule. Clinton's praise of Indian democracy and admonition to Pakistan to change course appeared to deal with the long-standing grievance that India had nursed about America's twisted political priorities in the subcontinent. Clinton's sensitivity to the country's extraordinary diversity and his celebration of India's multicultural tradition put democracy back at the centre of Indo-US relations.[4]

For India, the problem at the end of the cold war was different. Although it has begun to adapt to the changes in the world order, New Delhi had remained unwilling to think of itself as a leading democracy in the world. As the Western world celebrated the triumph of liberal democracy over authoritarian forms of governance at the turn of the 1990s, India was not cheerful about the Soviet Union's collapse. Having developed a huge stake in the strategic alliance with Moscow during the cold war, New Delhi went into deep mourning. The loss of a reliable partner was indeed of greater immediate concern to New Delhi than thinking about the far-reaching, systemic implications of the Soviet demise. As it coped with an uncertain world in 1991, it feared American dominance in a unipolar world more than it enthused for the triumph of democratic principles. The Indian intelligentsia, highly sensitive about any violation of democratic principles at home, seemed utterly insensitive to the international value of political pluralism abroad. The Indian elite, although most intensely Westernized at one level, was also one of the most trenchant critics of the West's cold war foreign policies.

Preventing India from clapping for the triumph of liberal democracy was the deeply held anti-imperialist strain in its foreign policy. The founding fathers of the republic never saw India's interests as being in a fundamental conflict with those of the West, but the imperatives of the cold war and the impossibility of building political cooperation with the US made India steadily drift away from the West. During the cold war it was not just the US that neglected its democratic ideals. India, too, did not emphasize that democracy must be an organizing principle of international affairs. It attached more weight to the anti-Western criterion than the internal democratic credentials of its Eastern and Third World friends. It did not matter to India whether a Third World leader was brutal in his oppression of his own people. So long as he mouthed anti-imperialist slogans and Third World rhetoric, he was an ally in the struggle between North and South.

In the immediate post-cold war American campaigns against human rights abuses worldwide, India found it more convenient to align with China and the Third World bloc than with the West. The inconsistency of Western policies on democracy and human rights left India with no other option. At the annual voting sessions of the United Nations Human Rights Commission in Geneva, India voted against the Western resolutions and gained support from many Third World countries, including China and Iran, to beat back Pakistani resolutions on the human rights situation in Kashmir. Moreover, at the United Nations, India remained opposed to the new international interventionary agenda of Annan and Clinton. India saw defending the sovereignty of the Third World against the new interventionists as more important than defending the values of democracy internationally.

The Clinton administration's Community of Democracies initiative brought democracy back into reckoning in Indo-US relations. At its first meeting in Warsaw in June 2000, India played a prominent role as one of the original members of the convening group and led one of the working groups. A tentative India enjoyed the new attention but was unwilling to step too far out, when other democracies like France and other members of the European Union were sniping at Washington's style of organizing the initiative. Later that year at the United Nations General Assembly, the United States sounded out if India was prepared to lead the caucus of the Community of Democracies at the General Assembly. India, weighed down by its past association with the G-77 and the NAM, a majority of which were not democratic states, was somewhat reluctant to give up old anchors and latch on to uncertain new ones. In another initiative, during Clinton's visit to India, the United States proposed setting up a Centre for Asian Democracy, with all the attendant overtones against China. India again was unwilling to let the idea fly. The United States was trying to discern if India was willing to vote against China, or at least abstain on Beijing's human rights record at the UN Committee on Human Rights in Geneva.

Although India baulked again, the United States was clearly beginning to lend some strategic substance to the promotion of mutually shared democratic values. India was not unaware of the fact that in the international club built around the idea of political pluralism, two of its principal rivals—China and Pakistan—would by definition find it difficult to become members. India, however, was not convinced that Washington was serious either about making democracy a key criterion of American foreign policy or building an enduring strategic partnership with New Delhi. It needed the Bush administration and the dramatic events of 11 September 2001 to inject substantive content to the notion of Indo-US alliance based on democratic values.

In retrospect, it was relatively easy for the United States to deal with the immediate challenges from the 11 September terrorist attacks on New York and Washington. The ouster of the Taliban regime in Afghanistan was easy, but the hunt for Osama bin Laden and his Al Qaeda network proceeded at a much slower pace than anyone had anticipated. The United States is also likely to succeed quickly in draining the swamp in Afghanistan and Pakistan that nurtured the international terror networks. The harder task remains. How does the United States deal with the extraordinary political resentment brewing in large parts of the world against the West in general and the United States in particular? This resentment remains the principal breeding ground for extremism and violence, and dealing with it poses the biggest long-term political challenge for the United States in its war against international terrorism. Three mutually reinforcing elements in the Middle East have spawned the Muslim rage against the United States the world over, particularly in the Middle East; these include authoritarian governments that leave little space for wider participation and inclusiveness in the political structures of the Middle East, the relative decline of the economic fortunes, and the rise of anti-Western ideology in large parts of the region.

The video appeal of Osama bin Laden broadcast on 7 October (the day America started bombing Afghanistan) revealed the fundamental assumptions of the new anti-Enlightenment brigade, namely that the world is divided into two camps—'one of faith where there is no hypocrisy and another of infidelity, from which we hope God will protect us'.[5] Declaring President Bush as the head of the camp of infidels, Bin Laden asked all Muslims to rise in revolt against the American oppression of the 'Muslim nation'. The United States, of course, had no desire to present the war in Afghanistan as one against either Islam or Muslims, but the new ideology of jihad made America painfully aware of the sense of grievance in the Islamic world.

The US was also forced to confront the fact that it needed to do a lot more to win the hearts and minds in the Middle East amidst the unfinished struggle for the modernization and Westernization of the Islamic world. The American historian of the Middle East Bernard Lewis argues that 'fundamentalist leaders are not mistaken in seeing in Western civilization the greatest challenge to the way of life that they wish to retain or restore for their people'.[6] Arguing that Islamic fundamentalists are ultimately struggling against the dramatic changes brought about by secularism and modernism, Lewis further asserts that 'Islamic fundamentalism has given an aim and a form to the otherwise aimless and formless resentment and anger of the Muslim masses at the forces that have devalued their traditional values and, in the final analysis, robbed them of their beliefs, their aspirations, their dignity, and to an increasing extent even their livelihood.'[7]

The rise of anti-Western and anti-Enlightenment ideas is not limited to the Middle East. In the early 1990s, the triumphalism of the East Asian miracle saw the articulation of the thesis of Asian values. Kishore Mahbubani, a diplomat from Singapore, has argued that Asia does not need preaching from the West on democratic governance and political pluralism. He suggested that democracy was a uniquely Western value and could not be transplanted into Asian societies. Asia would find its own way, on the basis of Confucianism, to make political progress. Mahbubani also redeveloped the familiar argument of Western social decline and the resurgence of Asia with the slogan 'Go East, young man'.[8] After a couple of centuries of young men of the East making pilgrimages to the West to absorb the values of a rising civilization, it is now the turn of the West to learn from the East. Mahbubani was articulating the now famous thesis of Lee Kuan Yew that democracy was incompatible with the objectives of rapid economic development and that the political organization in the East must be based on indigenous political cultures. Lee's model of combining authoritarian political governance with liberal capitalism was one that was adopted and enthusiastically endorsed by Deng Xiaoping, who was deeply concerned by the threat to the social order in China by the movement for democracy and the example of the collapse of the Soviet Union.

That the idea of Asian values was a patently self-serving one was evident in the steady advancement of democracy in Asia over the last few years. In addition, the economic crash of 1997 ended the triumphalism in South-East Asia. The ouster of the dictator Suharto in Indonesia by the extended street protests by students in the summer of 1998 suggested the appeal of democracy goes far beyond the Western civilization. Whatever the motivation, the resistance to the universal ideas of freedom and democracy remain rather strong in China and other parts of Asia.

In both eastern and western parts of Asia, there is a huge, new agenda for the United States in promoting the

Enlightenment project. That is the essence of the Bush Doctrine proclaimed by the President in his State of the Union address on 29 January 2002 in the full flush of the military-political triumph in Afghanistan. One of the doctrine's immediate objectives is to defeat international terrorism and the regimes that harbour and nurture it. The other is a promise not to let the 'axis of evil'—North Korea, Iran and Iraq—threaten the world with weapons of mass destruction: 'The United States of America will not permit the world's most dangerous regimes that threaten us with the world's most destructive weapons.'[9] Not so veiled in this doctrine is the determination to induce regime change in key states of concern. The objective of regime change became far more clear in the American confrontation with Iraq later in 2002. But beyond those immediate objectives, President Bush has set for himself the more grandiose goal of relentlessly spreading freedom and democracy in the first years of twenty-first century. Summing up the meaning of 11 September, Bush declared that 'in a single instant, we realized that this will be a decisive decade in the history of liberty . . . . Rarely has the world faced a choice more clear or consequential.'[10]

Scoffing at the many Americans who were warning in the wake of 11 September about the rage against the West in the Arab street, President Bush pointed to the relief that greeted the fall of the Taliban in Kabul. 'Let them look to Afghanistan,' Bush said, 'where the Islamic "street" greeted the fall of tyranny with song and celebration. Let the skeptics look to Islam's own rich history, with its centuries of learning, [*sic*] and tolerance and progress.'[11] He added, 'America will lead by defending liberty and justice because they are right and true and unchanging for all people everywhere.'[12] Bush said, 'No nation owns these aspirations, and no nation is exempt from them.'[13] In setting a new and sweeping agenda for American foreign policy in the coming years, he promised to deliver political change across the world, including the Islamic world, in favour of freedom and democracy. The President insisted that 'we have no intention of imposing our culture [on others],'[14] but added emphatically that 'America will always stand firm for the non-negotiable demands of human dignity: rule of law, limits on the power of the state, respect for women, private property, free speech, equal justice and religious tolerance.'[15] President Bush continued, 'America will take the side of brave men and women who advocate these values around the world, including the Islamic world, because we have a greater objective than eliminating threats and containing resentment. We seek a just and peaceful world beyond the war on terror.'[16]

The Bush Doctrine is a dramatic inversion of the past American policies towards undemocratic and conservative religious forces in Asia. During the cold war, the initial emphasis on preserving and promoting democracy in opposition to communist and left-wing forces gave place to an alliance with anyone ready to join the campaign to defeat the Soviet Union. In the Middle East, the US consciously promoted conservative religious forces and pro-Western military dictatorships to undermine the modernist forces that were drawn by the slogans of socialism and left-wing populism. In East Asia, the US aligned with the Chinese communists to divide the international communist movement and isolate the Russian communists. Assorted dictatorships in East Asia were tolerated in the name of the bigger fight against the Soviet Union. Thus democracy took a back seat in the US policy towards the developing world where it in essence became a contest between 'our sons of bitches' versus 'theirs'.

In the final phase of the cold war, the even more disastrous Reagan Doctrine deliberately promoted extremist forces against the Soviet Union and its allies in the developing world—from the butcher Pol Pot in Cambodia to the mujahedin in Afghanistan. The decision to pit the crusading jihadis against the communists in Afghanistan initially worked brilliantly, but in the end they turned against their sponsors in the United States. The attack on 11 September was the unintended consequence from the American encouragement to anti-

Enlightenment forces. Osama bin Laden was the Reagan Doctrine's most prized child, trained by the CIA to fight the Soviet Union and to mobilize the conservative Arabs in the war against Moscow. After 11 September, the United States had to deal with the consequences of strengthening extremist ideas in the final years of the cold war. The Bush administration's decision to fight to the finish the anti-Western forces is also a significant departure from Clinton's emphasis on promoting democracy. Under the liberal Democrats, the emphasis on democracy was reduced to making laundry lists of human rights violations and other transgressions by various countries and imposing sanctions against them. There was no overarching strategy to challenge either the tyrannical regimes or their policies nor was there a prioritization of the central threats to the ideas of freedom and democracy. The Bush Doctrine lays out a very specific agenda for confronting the worst of these regimes and moves more directly towards the modernization and democratization of the parts of the world that remain resistant to it.

India and the Atlantic Divide

Just as India and the West ended the antagonistic condition they found themselves in during the cold war, India had to deal with an unexpected situation: the deepening divide within the West on key questions of international order. The advent of the Bush administration in Washington at the beginning of 2001 dramatically sharpened the tensions between the United States and its traditional allies in Europe. These differences were reinforced by America's war on international terrorism and its confrontation with Iraq in 2002. Throughout the twentieth century, Europe has been the principal external preoccupation of the United States. In the post-11 September world, Europe has become more of an irritation rather than an enthusiastic associate in America's new war. Europe has always whined about America's unilateralism when Washington acted with force, and it complained about American isolationism when it turned its back, but the carping about American unilateralism has become intense since 11 September. The day after the bombing of the World Trade Centre, there was an outpouring of sympathy in Europe for the United States. A few days later the North Atlantic Treaty Organization (NATO), for the first time in its five decades of its existence, invoked the treaty's provision on collective self-defence. The attack on America was also an attack on Europe. The Americans thanked the Europeans for their support, but insisted politely it was not necessary. The Europeans had little to do, in either Afghanistan or the broader war on terrorism. They did indeed endorse American resolutions in the UN, organized political conferences and joined the peacekeeping and policing functions in Afghanistan, but they secured no real voice in decision making or strategizing about the war on terror.

The European angst deepened as the United States moved towards an uncritical support to Israel in the Middle East and stepped up efforts to oust Saddam Hussein's regime in Iraq. Prior to 11 September, Europeans were shocked by the new determination in Washington to press ahead with controversial plans for missile defence and tear up past multilateral treaties and arrangements from arms control to environmental management. The European anger at American unilateralism reached a crescendo in the wake of the impending war in Iraq. That the mobilization of anti-American sentiment was a decisive factor in the narrow victory that Chancellor Gerhard Schroeder achieved in the German elections in the fall of 2002 showed how far Europe and America have drifted apart. The dramatic reversal of more than five decades of Atlanticism in Germany, one of the most loyal of American allies in Europe, has signalled an imminent geopolitical shift in the Northern Hemisphere. The rising European anxieties on where America was headed have not spared even British Prime Minister Tony Blair, who is struggling to explain his backing of the American confrontation with Iraq to Labour backbenchers as well as the Archbishop of Canterbury.

The European differences with America on Iraq have capped a series of disagreements in the last few years and have covered such wide areas as global environmental policy, the jurisdiction of the International Criminal Court, missile defence, arms control, America's uncritical support of Israel's tough line against the Palestinians and the role of United Nations in the management of international security challenges. The US and Europe have argued before, sometimes passionately, but never have the two sides appeared so far apart. The Bush administration has sharpened the image of American foreign policy in Europe as being too crude in its understanding of the world. The Europeans see Americans as too quick to resort to force in dealing with global problems, impatient with diplomacy and unwilling to abide by the restraints of multilateralism. The Europeans see themselves as more sophisticated in their understanding of the world. Unlike the Americans who prefer coercion, the Europeans emphasize seduction and an indirect approach. The Europeans believe in the efficacy of negotiations and diplomacy, see the use of force as a last resort and emphasize the importance of international law.

Americans, on the other hand, see Europeans pitifully wallowing in a multilateralist illusion. Europe, from Washington's perspective, is too domesticated by the politics of social welfare to focus on the new challenges to international security. Americans see Europeans as being too caught up with procedure to focus on the outcomes of diplomacy. As it prepared for a possible war in Iraq, however, the US found that the Europeans were moving beyond mere protests to resisting American policies on important issues in key international fora. That is the essence of the tectonic movement within the Euro-Atlantic world. As anti-Americanism has risen in Europe, so has the contempt for Europe in America. In the war against terror and against Iraq, the US felt no need to take its allies along. European support was welcome but no longer critical. The conservatives in the Bush administration argued that obtaining the Europeans' solidarity would necessitate a prolonged committee approach to strategy that would constrain the American ability to use decisive force at the appropriate moment. For America, Europe is increasingly an irrelevant behemoth in the new world. Washington also believes that Europeans neither understand the security concerns of the United States after 11 September nor have the political will or the military capacity to confront the new adversaries.

The arguments of the conservatives have been fleshed out more comprehensively by the American analyst Robert Kagan, who asserts that the transatlantic divide is deep, long in development and likely to endure:

> It is time to stop pretending that Europeans and Americans share a common view of the world, or even that they occupy the same world. On the all-important question of power—efficacy of power, the morality of power, desirability of power—American and European perspectives are diverging. Europe is turning away from power, or to put it a little differently, it is moving beyond power into a self-contained world of laws and rules and transnational negotiation and cooperation. It is entering a post-historical paradise of peace and relative prosperity, the realisation of Kant's 'Perpetual Peace'. The United States, meanwhile, remains mired in history, exercising power in the anarchic Hobbesian world where international laws and rules are unreliable and where true security and the defence and promotion of a liberal order still depend on the possession and use of military might. That is why on major strategic and international questions today, Americans are from Mars and Europeans are from Venus: They agree on little and understand one another less and less.[17]

Kagan backs up his argument at three levels, the growing gap in capabilities between America and Europe, the psychology of weakness in Europe and the recent foreign policy experience of the European Union focussed on economic integration.

First, Europe has not lived up to the expectations following the end of the cold war and the Maastricht Treaty that it will emerge as a new superpower promoting global multipolarity. Brussels instead was drawn into the appealing attractions of a 'new Europe' and unwilling to sacrifice social welfare for building new defence capabilities. European capabilities turned out to be inadequate even for the maintenance of peace and security within the corners of the old Continent, let alone projecting it elsewhere in the world. Under the best circumstances, Kagan argues, the 'European role was limited to filling out peacekeeping forces after the United States had, largely on its own, carried out the decisive phases of a military mission and stabilised the situation . . . . [T]he real division of labour consisted of the United States "making the dinner" and the Europeans "doing the dishes".'[18]

The second argument is that the current European emphasis on international law and multilateralism stems from weakness and a consequent unwillingness to confront the new threats to international security from terrorism. It is always the weaker power that hankers after rules and procedures while the stronger one focuses on confronting threats and engineering desirable outcomes. Americans believe it is precisely this weakness that allows greater tolerance or even denial in Europe of the threat from extremism and its supporters. American and European disagreements on how to approach these challenges arise from the basic disparity in power and the will to use it.

The third level of argument from the United States is that Europe's delusions about multilateralism and international law derive from its own regional experience in the last few decades that need not necessarily apply to the rest of the world, let alone being a guide to the future of international relations. European writers like Robert Cooper, a British diplomat and adviser to Tony Blair, have theorized that Europe has evolved into a higher post-modern phase that de-emphasizes the concepts of nation state, national sovereignty and power politics. He identifies three types of states:

First, there are pre-modern states—often former colonies—whose failures have led to a Hobbesian war of all against all: countries such as Somalia and, until recently, Afghanistan. Second, there are post-imperial, postmodern states which no longer think of security primarily in terms of conquest. A third kind are the traditional 'modern' states such as India, Pakistan or China which behave as states always have, following interest, power and raison d'état.

The postmodern system in which we Europeans live does not rely on balance; nor does it emphasise sovereignty or the separation of domestic and foreign affairs. The European Union has become a highly developed system for mutual interference in each other's domestic affairs, right down to beer and sausages. Members of the postmodern world do not consider invading each other. But both the modern and pre-modern zones pose threats to our security.[19]

Not surprisingly Cooper does not include the US in the category of post-modern states but proposes Canada and Japan as possible candidates. Yet the idea that Europe has overcome the impulses of Machtpolitik has become a dominant theme in European thinking about international affairs. The Europeans, the originators of the idea of power politics, now believe that the old Continent has consciously and deliberately left behind what German Foreign Minister Joschka Fischer calls 'the old system of balance with its continued national orientation, constraints of coalition, traditional interest-led politics and the permanent danger of nationalist ideologies and confrontations'.[20] While Americans and Indians might describe this as simplistic idealism, the belief has struck deep roots in Europe. The Europeans have also come to believe that their transcendence of power holds lessons for others, and that they have a civilizing mission in the modern and pre-modern states. Americans are dismissive of the European miracle of collective security and the German lion lying down with the French lamb and their lessons for the rest of the world. They point out that the European miracle was achieved under the protection of US military power, which deterred the Soviet Union for nearly four and a half decades; that European triumphalism about their superior post-modern standing is really a reflection of the fact that the Continent no longer faces either external or internal threats to its security; and that Europe's self-perception of its post-modern orientation is in essence a convenient escape from confronting emerging challenges.

India and the Bush Doctrine

The current European criticisms of American approach to international relations echo many of the arguments that India used to employ in the past. Much like Nehruvian India, Europe is stressing the importance of the normative in international relations. Imbued with a sense of idealism and commitment to the UN Charter and international law, newly independent India stood on the front lines of the cold war arguing against the use or even the threat of use of force to resolve international conflicts. For the West, however, communism was a profound evil that had to be defeated by using all means at its disposal. India insisted that means were as important as ends and that a total confrontation with communism posed a danger to international security. Today Europe has emerged as the main critic of the American war on terrorism. This position should have drawn India and Europe closer on global political issues, but it has not.

At precisely the moment when the Europeans are emboldened to criticize the United States, India believes it cannot jeopardize its budding strategic partnership with it. While Europe is drifting away from America, India appears to be drawing closer to the sole superpower. Not surprisingly, India has been far less critical than Europe of the US policy on Iraq and less insistent on a multilateral route. There is greater convergence today between India and the Republican-led United States on key international issues stretching from support for missile defence and rejection of the CTBT to the importance of limiting the jurisdiction of the International

Criminal Court. As a victim of international terrorism, India is more enthusiastic than Europe about the American war since 11 September. It has also been less critical of the doctrine of pre-emption, for it cannot give up the option of a preventive and pre-emptive war in dealing with the terrorism spawned by a neighbouring country.

India's muted criticism of US policies or enthusiastic support to them is driven neither purely by tactical considerations of improving relations with the United States nor by New Delhi's interest in overcoming the long-standing Indo-US differences over Kashmir and nuclear questions. The unprecedented and unexpected support from New Delhi to the Bush administration's controversial positions are reflective of a new India that is breaking from its past and struggling to find a new set of organizing principles for its foreign and national security policy. The new Indian approach to world affairs comes on top of a steady evolution of Indian security thinking through the 1990s. Just as Europe is moving away from the ideas that shaped its earlier interaction with the world, India's international positions too have evolved amidst fundamental change at home. No wonder then, at the very moment when Europe proclaims that power politics are passé, India is beginning to de-emphasize the notion of collective security and to stress the importance of comprehensive national strength and balance of power. At a time when Europe dismisses the notion of national sovereignty as the basis for dealing with global issues, India is committed to a strong defence of the concept.

New Delhi is also acutely aware of the problems it has had with the Clinton administration's espousal of multilateralism. This type of multilateralism, demanded by liberals in the US and the Europeans, is far wider in scope in terms of the rules and regulations they seek to enforce on India and the rest of the world. The European and liberal American championing of humanitarian intervention and the enthusiasm of UN Secretary General Kofi Annan to promote multilateral diplomatic activism on Kashmir caused deep anxieties in New

Delhi in the late 1990s. India was also upset by the Clinton administration's sponsorship of UNSC Resolution 1172 in the wake of India's nuclear tests in May 1998. Although it has not been articulated in any strong terms, India has greater reason to be worried about the 'new liberal imperialism' championed by the likes of Robert Cooper and other multilateralists than the unilateralism being asserted by the Bush administration. American unilateralism remains a differentiated concept, rooted in geopolitics and the ideas of balance of power and targeting essentially rogue states. India, as the world's largest democracy and the biggest victim of terrorism, has less to fear in an American war against terrorism. It has a lot of apprehensions about the wider indiscriminate effort of the multilateralists to impose standards of behaviour on all states, without considerations to their internal political orientation and the character of the state.

The change in the theatre of warfare since the end of the cold war has induced greater divergence between Indian and European responses to the new American military strategy. While Europe was the principal arena of conflict in the world, India could posture about the problems of deterrence, containment and the cold war. The Europeans, in contrast, emphasized the centrality of defeating totalitarian ideologies. But today with the focus of the new war on terrorism being riveted on the Middle East and South Asia, India is far more sensitive to the complexities of the battle and the importance of imparting a resounding defeat to the forces of extremism and terrorism. No doubt the Middle East lies in the Mediterranean neighbourhood of Europe, which also imports considerable energy from the Persian Gulf. Islamic populations have also become an important minority in Europe today, but India's security is tied up in far more intricate ways with that of the Middle East. India has an important stake in the modernization and political moderation of the Middle East, and it might be more ready to accept the American objective of fundamentally transforming the region as part of the war on terrorism.

Bleeding for more than a decade from the acts of international terrorism on its soil, India naturally saw the opportunities of the new war in resolving its own profound security dilemmas. Few other countries in the world have faced the combined threat from weapons of mass destruction, the rise of religious extremism and the state sponsorship of terrorism that India had to cope with from Pakistan. As a result, it has been easy for India to see the logic of pre-emption and preventive wars that the Bush administration has emphasized in its new national security strategy. New Delhi itself prepared for a massive preventive war against Pakistan after the breathtaking attack on India's Parliament on 13 December, the last straw in Pakistan's strategy to bleed India through a thousand cuts of terrorism. Thus New Delhi has little problem with the US case for finding new approaches to deal with terrorism. India, however, fully understands the very special nature of pre-emptive action against states armed with nuclear weapons but support terrorism. Its coercive diplomacy since 13 December was an attempt to combine judiciously the threat of war with an effort to put international pressure on Islamabad to end its support to cross-border terrorism. India also has a fundamental interest in a regime change in Pakistan, one that would move the nation away from the deadly combination of militarism and religious extremism.

The emerging differences between India and Europe are also rooted in the nature of their position of the international system today. India is a revisionist power, while Europe is a satiated one. This assessment of India will shock supporters of New Delhi who have seen it essentially as a status quo power. The argument is not based on territorial questions because India, of course, has no wish to seek more territory, let alone repossess what it might have lost. It has grown quite accustomed to the notion that it will not be able to regain Pakistan-occupied Kashmir and might even be prepared to settle along the existing Line of Actual Control (LAC) with China. India is revisionist in the sense of its determination to improve its own standing in the global order, if necessary by working to change the rules of the system.

Many Indians believe today that historical circumstances and failures of its past leadership have robbed it of its rightful place at the high table in the international system. Having contributed far more significantly to the two great world wars on the side of victors, India should have been a permanent member of the UNSC. New Delhi, which failed to become a nuclear weapons power in 1968, should be accommodated in the current global order as a nuclear weapons power. As an aspiring power, India is more sympathetic to the American effort to rework the rules of the global game in the wake of the war against terrorism, from which it could benefit. Europe, on the other hand, is a staunch defender of the present order, where one could say it is vastly over-represented. India also has little to lose from a loosening of the alliances that dominated the world for the last six decades since it was not attached to any one of those alliances. As the US seeks to reorder international relations, India stands to gain by participating in the ad hoc coalitions that the US is willing to put together. Such a course opens up greater space for India without tying it down to the discipline of a very rigid alliance with any one power.

The American war on terrorism has opened up a great debate on the future of the international order. The current arguments between Europe and America on the ends and means of this war only signal the beginning of this great debate, not its end. While the US has outlined a strong unilateralist approach, there is no reason to believe that Washington will make no adjustments to its war on terrorism. Nor is it likely that Europe will remain fundamentally opposed to the broad direction of American policy. There will be an intense effort to reduce the differences across the Atlantic. Sections of the European leadership have already endorsed the American approach. Brussels, despite popular European resentment against

America, will have to find a way of working with Washington in the new war against terrorism. Europe cannot opt out of this war. India has a lot at stake in the current war on terrorism, which has the potential to reorder fundamentally its own security environment.

In the new agenda of democratization of Asia that the Bush administration sets for itself, India stands out as an important partner. India is sandwiched between two regions—the Middle East and the Sinic world—that continue to resist the core values of Enlightenment. If the Middle East is an arc of political instability that breeds extremist and anti-modern ideas in western parts of Asia, China with its ultranationalism remains the principal of source of uncertainiy in East Asia and the Pacific. It is within that context that the conservative sections of the American foreign policy establishment envision an arc of democratic stability that could include Turkey, Israel, Russia and India. These old or new friends of the United States could provide the basis for an American strategy that seeks to promote political moderation and economic modernization in large parts of the Middle East. They will also play a key role in getting China to play by the international rules and become part of the global mainstream.[21] While Israel and Turkey are formal allies of the United States and have an interesting strategic partnership themselves, can Russia and India become part of an American project to promote Western values in Asia?

Can India, however, overcome its long-standing distrust of the United States and join it in the next great political enterprise launched by the Bush administration? Can India make the historic choice of aligning with America in a grand global struggle? It is easy for India to talk about a natural alliance as a rhetorical device in publicly thinking about a different future for Indo-US relations. It is entirely another matter to embark upon security cooperation with the United States, which could involve considerable short-term political risks that might be seen as outweighing long-term advantages.

In the short term, Washington's backing of Musharraf's

military regime and its unwillingness to push Pakistan towards a comprehensive overhaul of its society continue to cloud the prospects for unflinching Indian commitment to backing the US policies. Over the long term, India has serious doubts about the constancy of American emphasis on democracy as an important foreign policy objective.

For India, extending the support to the larger objectives of the Bush Doctrine, however, would demand that it walk a longer distance with the United States and comprehensively reject many of the past notions. Further backing of the American policies would require India to look beyond its immediate security interests in combating terrorism to joining the American project to root out all regimes that support extremist tendencies, which might not have a direct bearing on India's immediate interests.

FOUR

The US: A Natural Ally?

Fifty Wasted Years

'Five wasted decades.' So External Affairs Minister Jaswant Singh described independent India's relations with the United States to a small group of reporters on the eve of President Clinton's visit to India.[1] His reflection on the fact that the world's two great democracies found it impossible to engage in any substantive cooperation—either economic or political—in the country's first fifty years evoked a sharp response from the Left parties, who accused the minister of trivializing the long-standing anti-imperialist orientation of Indian foreign policy. Nevertheless, even the most ardent anti-imperialists would be hard-pressed to explain how even communist China had a far stronger and deeper engagement with the United States than India did at the turn of the century. Unlike the Soviet Union and China, India has had no direct clash of interests with America. The United States and China fought a bitter war on the Korean Peninsula during the early 1950s in which thousands of soldiers on both sides were killed. Indian and American soldiers have never looked at each other in anger. Their diplomats, however, have never lost an opportunity for a verbal duel. Moreover, China's policy towards the United States has gone through some wild swings—from war and confrontation up to the 1960s, to a de facto alliance to defeat the Soviet Union from the early 1970s until the end of the cold war.

Since Independence, India and the United States have had a stagnant political relationship. Barring a brief phase from the late 1950s to early 1960s when New Delhi and Washington collaborated against China in Tibet and the US promised military cooperation in dealing with the Chinese aggression, there has been little political engagement of note between the two nations. In the 1950s and early 1960s there also was some interesting American cooperation with India's civilian nuclear and space programmes. American proliferation concerns since the late 1960s, however, choked off the earlier promising trend of interaction in high-technology sectors. Despite occasional efforts in the early 1980s by Indira Gandhi and in the mid-1980s by Rajiv Gandhi, India and the United States remained distant. They focussed more on solving residual problems from an earlier era and managing the fallout from the cold war on bilateral relations. The attempts to cooperate in the areas of high technologies in the mid-1980s never took off. The liberal democratic establishment in the United States, which took a strong interest in India in the 1950s and 1960s with the hope that New Delhi could emerge as a credible alternative to communist China, lost interest once Beijing opened up to Washington in the late 1970s. The American aid flows to India, which were extraordinarily large in the 1950s and 1960s, dried up by the mid-1970s. Moreover, American assistance itself became so controversial in India that it lost much of its initial political significance.

It was only with the end of the cold war that the prospect for a new relationship opened up. As India initiated economic reforms, a commercial component was introduced into the relationship. The US Department of Commerce's 1993 decision to designate India as one of the ten big emerging markets attracted the interest of large American corporations. Although the initially high expectations in the United States about the size of the Indian market and pace of its globalization never materialized, economic ties between the two nations began to acquire substance and lend some depth to bilateral relations. India's advances in the information technology sector opened up a whole new range of possibilities for deepening the commercial ties between the two countries. From a turnover of about $5 billion in bilateral trade in the mid-1980s, the volume tripled to about $15 billion by the end of the 1990s, a paltry sum in comparison to the Sino-US trade of more than a $100 billion. China and the United States also have wider political and military engagements than New Delhi and Washington do. Nevertheless, the expanding economic partnership and hopes for a rapid boost to it in the future gave a dimension to Indo-US relations that did not exist earlier. However, after the initial enthusiasm for the market potential of India in the mid-1990s, the US has been deeply disappointed at the low level of commercial interaction between the two countries and the concern that economics might emerge as a missing element in the growing relationship.[2]

The increasing influence of the Indian community, numbering nearly two million, has had a new, unexpected and strong affect on policy in both Washington and New Delhi. The rising prosperity of the Indian expatriate community in the United States was visible by the mid-1980s but had little impact on the American political system or on Indo-US relations. Rajiv Gandhi first sensed the importance of mobilizing the Indian community in restructuring Indo-US relations and took the initiative to tap into it. The concentration of the Indian communities in a few areas, their growing financial contributions to the electoral funds of members of the US Congress and the two major political parties, and their increasing determination to act together in taking up causes dear to India began to have an effect by the late 1990s. Created in the early 1990s, the India caucus in Congress grew rapidly in membership, and American legislators who had little interest in India before began to support Indian positions and put pressure on the administration to be more accommodating of

New Delhi's political concerns. In the early 1990s, India used to look helpless in the face of intense lobbying efforts by the Pakistanis, Khalistanis and Kashmiris on the Capitol Hill, where they routinely got resolutions criticizing India in the early 1990s on human rights issues. By the mid-1990s the hiring of professional lobbying firms, the activation of the India caucus and the mobilization of the Indian community in putting pressure on the executive branch had a dramatic effect on Indo-US relations. Pakistan-sponsored resolutions began to get defeated by large margins, and by the late 1990s Congress showed very little support for them.

Meanwhile, the American perceptions of the Indian community also began to change significantly by the late 1990s. From being rich but somewhat detached, the Indian community was now getting politically engaged in Washington. The extraordinary presence of the Indian immigrants among the forces of the new economy in the Silicon Valley pointed to a more important ability to create wealth and prosperity in the United States. As President Clinton observed during his visit to India, 'My country has been enriched by the contributions of more than a million Indian Americans, from Vinod Dahm, the father of the Pentium chip . . . to Sabeer Bhatia, creator of the free mail system, Hotmail'.[3]

As the Indian-American community made its mark in the United States, it began to overturn the long-standing negative perceptions of America in their homeland. As the children of its middle class studied in, travelled to and prospered in the US, India gained an awareness of the positive aspects of American society, which helped it transcend both the ignorance of the United States and the long-standing caricature of it as portrayed by the upper-class British prejudice and inherited by the Indian elite. As the Indian political leaders turned to their rich compatriots in the US for political donations as well as help in facilitating economic cooperation with American businesses, non-resident Indians became a veritable bridge between New Delhi and Washington.[4]

As the cold war wound down, there was a great expectation in India that the two countries could now begin afresh at building a viable partnership. Having put the four-decade Soviet-American rivalry that hobbled Indo-US relations behind them, they hoped to embark on a new course. India welcomed the Democrats' return to power in 1993 after a gap of twelve years. It raised hopes in New Delhi that the party's liberal internationalist vision could finally be combined with the dominant Indian world view, centred on the notions of collective security and the primacy of normative principles in the conduct of international relations. Yet the American rediscovery of idealist internationalism in the first term of the Clinton administration pushed the two sides apart. Despite the many positive new factors shaping the relations between them in the 1990s, New Delhi and Washington had to confront the enduring difficulties in structuring a political partnership. Differences over two core issues—nuclear non-proliferation and Kashmir—remained as major obstacles on the road to a rapprochement. Rather than seek an overarching vision of Indo-US relations in the post-cold war world, Washington's approach to India was dominated by the negative focus on these issues.

India also had to engage the Clinton administration within the context of the new unipolar moment in world affairs. American pressures on Kashmir and nuclear issues would have been dismissed with a wave of the hand in New Delhi during the cold war, when India had the Soviet Union's full backing. The emergence of the United States as the sole superpower of the international system, however, dramatically altered the nature of the Indian interaction with Washington on these issues. The changed global power equations made it imperative that building sound relations with the United States became the top priority. At the same time, there was deep discomfort with the new reality of the American dominance of world affairs. Among the Indian chattering classes there was a strong resentment against the new condition, and as the government sought to cope with the difficult international environment, the editorial writers and the political class were continuously suspicious that the Narasimha Rao dispensation would compromise on core national security interests with Washington. The government was already under criticism from sections of its own party as well as from the Left for departing from the traditional economic orientation, and, lacking a majority in the Parliament, it had to be cautious in engaging the United States without yielding too much on nuclear policy and Kashmir. As a result, Narasimha Rao's dealings with the United States saw diplomatic ducking and weaving. Narasimha Rao, however, allowed his domestic weakness to become a strength in dealing with Washington: by letting domestic political pressure and noise build up against compromise on Kashmir and nuclear questions, he bought himself valuable time in dealing with the Clinton administration.

The Clinton administration's early emphasis on the promotion of human rights, non-proliferation and preventive diplomacy fused into activism on Kashmir. Just when the two sides needed to build trust and confidence in each other, US diplomacy on Kashmir and nuclear non-proliferation stirred deep anxieties in India about American intentions and motivations. What from the American viewpoint appeared as an attempt to address the problems of stability in the subcontinent were seen in India as inimical to two of India's core national security interests—its territorial integrity and the preservation of the nuclear option. The US forays in Kashmir appeared to India as an intervention on behalf of Pakistan when Islamabad was determined to take advantage of New Delhi's political troubles in the Kashmir Valley; the American refusal to countenance the brazen Pakistani support of terrorism in Kashmir added insult to Indian injury. Furthermore, the relentless American pressure in the 1990s on India's nuclear and missile programmes and its attempts to cap, reduce and eliminate over a period of time India's strategic programmes suggested that Washington had no desire to accommodate India's political aspirations on the world stage. All the political energies in Indo-US relations were expended in dealing with these two problems but with no real movement forward. It was only at the end of the 1990s, when India first defied the United States on the CTBT and then tested nuclear weapons, that Washington was forced to take a more pragmatic approach to India. Although President Clinton's visit dramatically changed the tone and tenor of American attitude towards India, it was the Bush administration that opened the doors for a long-term strategic relationship between New Delhi and Washington.

Somewhat counter-intuitively the nuclear tests of May 1998 created the basis for ending the discord between India and the US on non-proliferation. So long as India remained undecided about what it wanted to do with nuclear weapons, it was natural that the United States would do everything to prevent India from becoming a nuclear weapons power. Yet once India made up its mind, it was only a matter of time before the US would come back and engage India. The Bush administration's decision in September 2001 to lift the sanctions imposed after the nuclear tests completed that process. India's support of the Bush administration's missile defence initiative in May 2001 put the country on a road towards cooperation with the United States on nuclear non-proliferation issues. The terrorist attacks on New York and Washington in September 2001 and the consequent American war on terrorism has generated the political space for a more positive American engagement in the subcontinent and the Indian acceptance of at least an indirect US role in resolving the differences between India and Pakistan, in particular on Jammu and Kashmir. And that is precisely where the perceived paradigm shift in Indo-US relations began to manifest itself.

Nuclear Defiance and Reconciliation

India's nuclear defiance of the United States from 1996 to 1998 and the reconciliation from 1998 to 2001 are likely to go down in the history of Indian diplomacy as the most complex, daring and successful political manoeuvres the nation ever initiated.

Never had India confronted the dominant discourse of the international system so directly as when it walked out of the CTBT negotiations and then challenged the existing international norms by testing its nuclear weapons in 1998. Nor did India ever undertake a diplomatic effort of the magnitude that it did in getting the dominant power of the international system to accept India's apparent nuclear transgression as a fait accompli. The fear of American reprisals held India back from testing its nuclear weapons in December 1995. When the US government threatened India with sanctions after picking up signals of the impending nuclear test in Pokhran, the Narasimha Rao government backed off, but the Vajpayee government reversed that judgement in May 1998 and went ahead with the tests. The different responses reflected the two divergent schools of thought in India during the 1990s: one believed testing would terribly damage India's relations with the United States, bring international isolation and undermine India's economic reforms, and the other argued testing would compel the United States to take India seriously and was absolutely necessary to transform both India's security condition and the long-term relationship with Washington. The first argument was self-evident, but the second involved a political leap of faith.

The United States reacted with extraordinary anger to the Indian nuclear tests held on 11 and 13 May 1998. Washington felt betrayed by the new BJP-led government. The failure to detect the preparations for the test added to the Clinton administration's sense of shock. Washington held that it was misled by senior officials of the Vajpayee government into believing that India would not rock the boat and that controversial decisions on nuclear policy would be made only after a comprehensive review of the nuclear policy was undertaken. With President Clinton announcing his intent to travel to India later in 1998 as part of a new intensive engagement of the subcontinent by the United States, India's decision was seen as a political slap in the face. Washington also showed more understanding of Pakistan's decision to test after

India, while it held New Delhi responsible for the overt nuclearization of the subcontinent and threatening the international non-proliferation regime.

The Clinton administration imposed mandatory sanctions and mobilized other nations, in particular Japan, to cut economic assistance to India. Although France and Russia were more sympathetic to India, they could not stand in the way of the United States' creation of an international framework in the form of the unanimous United Nations Security Council Resolution 1172 on 11 June 1998. This laid down a full set of markers for India, including signing the Non-Proliferation Treaty and addressing the root cause of Indo-Pakistani tensions—the Kashmir dispute. During his trip to China in June 1998, Clinton announced a new strategic partnership with China and condemned the nuclear proliferation in the subcontinent. The worst fears of those Indians who believed nuclear tests might be counterproductive appeared to come true. India was under US and Japanese sanctions, the UNSC had put in a resolution under Chapter VI. While not mandatory, the demands of UNSC Resolution 1172 provided the basis for further action by the international system. Moreover, the resolution seemed to open the door for the dreaded internationalization of the Kashmir dispute and UN intervention in Kashmir, which Pakistan had long sought. The apparent Sino-American convergence of interests in putting the newly nuclear India down was the last straw.

Within a month of the nuclear tests, however, there was a tentative contact between the US Deputy Secretary of State, Strobe Talbott, and the Deputy Chairman of the Planning Commission, Jaswant Singh. The two agreed to initiate a dialogue to reconcile India's security concerns with the non-proliferation objectives of the United States. Talbott insisted that the US was not exploring a deal that would find a way out of the countries' apparently irreconcilable objectives. Rather the US, he said, was looking for Indian compliance with five benchmarks derived from the UNSC Resolution 1172; these were signing on to the CTBT, joining the negotiations on the FMCT, tightening Indian controls over the exports of sensitive technologies and commodities, adopting non-threatening nuclear weapons posture and lessening Indo-Pakistani tensions through dialogue. Singh also suggested he was not in talks with Talbott to finesse a compromise that would demean India; New Delhi was engaging Washington to make it appreciate India's security concerns.

Singh and Talbott began to meet almost every month until early 1999 and then less frequently until early 2000. While neither side would acknowledge it was in search of compromises, each in fact was. The United States sought legally binding restraints on India's nuclear programme that would limit its size and sophistication. Washington was not willing to end its political opposition to India's nuclear weapons programme, nor would it legitimize it by accepting it as a reality. In return for India's acceptance of limits on its programme, Washington was willing to ease its sanctions. India, on the other hand, was declaring that it had no interest in pursuing an untrammelled nuclear weapons programme; it was interested only in a minimum credible deterrent that would be guided by a no-first-use policy. India was also willing to consider binding constraints on its nuclear programme, but it was unwilling to accept any suggestion of its rollback; in return for its restraint, India wanted an American political acknowledgement of New Delhi as a nuclear weapons power and the removal of all sanctions against India, including those technology restrictions imposed after the first nuclear test of May 1974, not just those that followed Pokhran-II.

The essence of the deal boiled down to an Indian adherence to the CTBT, which was emblematic of the Clinton administration's arms control policies, in return for a substantive easing of US sanctions. In interviews given to the author within a span of a few weeks, Singh and Talbott hinted at how far the two sides had moved towards a nuclear accommodation. Singh, in an interview at the end of 1999, hinted at the possibility of India signing the treaty while holding back on its ratification; he also distanced the government from some of the more expansive plans for the Indian nuclear weapons programme—the Draft Nuclear Doctrine that was issued by the National Security Advisory Board in August 1999.[5] Talbott, on the other hand, suggested that the US, while disagreeing with the Indian decision to go nuclear, would not insist on India joining the NPT and giving up the nuclear weapons programme; it might acknowledge, however, India's right to press ahead with subcritical testing of nuclear weapons, which the CTBT permitted.[6]

After many rounds of dialogue, the countries appeared close to clinching a deal, but in the end they could not do it. In India, the government's efforts to build a consensus on signing the treaty did not take off, thanks to the appearance of a rapid turnaround in the Indian position.[7] Getting the political establishment to agree to sign the CTBT foundered amidst the US Senate's refusal to consider ratifying the treaty. In the United States, there was a strong reluctance within the non-proliferation establishment to lift the many high-technology sanctions that had accumulated since 1974. The arms control community in the US was dead set against being seen as rewarding India for its violation of non-proliferation norms.

Despite the failure to conclude a nuclear understanding, President Clinton chose to go ahead with his visit to India in March 2000 and initiate a political rapprochement with New Delhi. India's campaign with the political establishment in Washington against the policy of not engaging India was beginning to pay off. Clinton himself moved from punishing India for its nuclear transgressions to building a new partnership, despite the continuing differences over the nuclear issue. In his address to the Indian Parliament on 22 March 2000, he offered an extended critique of India's decision to go nuclear, but his tone was respectful and gave the sense of a debate among equals.[8] Furthermore, he unveiled a future vision of Indo-US relations that was appealing and warm. The Clinton magic was such that the entire Indian Parliament, for a long time the deepest sceptic of American intentions towards India, was swooning over the American President. In one speech, Clinton had transformed the atmosphere of Indo-US relations.

While parts of the punitive framework that the US had imposed in May and June 1998 remained in place, the two sides renewed their bilateral engagement across a broad front. Once Clinton signalled America's readiness to engage India, the rest of the world leaders were queuing up to visit New Delhi. India broke out of the nuclear isolation that was imposed upon it after Pokhran-II. That in fact was the biggest contribution of the Singh–Talbott dialogue. While the nuclear differences themselves could not be resolved, the sustained conversation between Singh and Talbott produced a much greater appreciation of each other's security concerns. It was the most intensive bilateral engagement between the two countries in fifty years. Never before had the two nations had such detailed discussions at the high political level over such a long period of time. As Talbott explained, 'We're getting better at disagreeing without being disagreeable with each other. We are developing the kind of mutual confidence—on a personal level, but I think also on a government-to-government level—that is needed to work constructively on sensitive and important issues, including national security, counterterrorism and non-proliferation.'[9] Talbott was referring to the intensive communications between the two governments during the Kargil War and the crisis resulting from the hijacking of the Indian Airlines flight IC 814 from Kathmandu to Kandahar via the United Arab Emirates. In both the situations of great difficulty for India, the United States played a positive role, which created the basis for trust and confidence between the two nations.

As it turned out, the nuclear reconciliation was not to be completed during the Clinton administration. President Clinton transformed the political context of the relationship, but there was no cutting of the Gordian knot of the nuclear differences. Despite the Senate's refusal to ratify the CTBT, the Clinton administration continued to hope for an Indian signature on the treaty. Weighed down by non-proliferation lobby's pressures, the administration insisted until the very end of its term that the full potential of Indo-US relations will not be realized until India has met the nuclear benchmarks. When nuclear differences were set aside, they did not disappear as an obstacle to progress in bilateral relations. Crucial technology sanctions imposed after the tests in 1974 and 1998 remained in place.

The Bush administration understood that there was no way to reverse the nuclear weapons programmes of India and Pakistan. At the political level, President Bush made an early decision to build a long-term strategic partnership with India, one that would go beyond the change of atmosphere introduced by Clinton. The Bush administration promised that it would lift the sanctions imposed on India at the earliest possible opportunity without a reference to the CTBT or the other benchmarks imposed by Clinton. That decision ended, quietly and without great fanfare, the nuclear dispute that so hobbled Indo-US relations during the 1990s. By the time the internal consultations were completed on lifting the sanctions against India, the United States was in the aftermath of 11 September, an event that would further transform the Indo-US relationship.

India also did its bit in shifting around the ideological parameters of the Indo-US engagement. First, it consciously reached out to the Bush administration on an issue of core ideological concern to the Republicans—missile defence. Even before the President announced his missile defence initiative on 1 May, Jaswant Singh, in his meeting at the White House on 6 April 2001, expressed his understanding of the imperatives of the coming transformation of the deterrence calculus in favour of defensive technologies. Those familiar with the meeting say Bush was absolutely delighted at the understanding of his views on missile defence, which were being attacked ferociously in the United States, Russia, Europe and elsewhere.

India's support endeared it to the Republican establishment, and Bush chose to send a special envoy to India to explain his initiative. While India departed from its traditional positions on arms control, it demonstrated to Washington that New Delhi was prepared to extend its political support on controversial issues. The Indian support came despite strong Russian opposition to the Bush proposals; this showed that New Delhi was not going to be tied down by the weight of the past in redefining the relations with Washington. In the same vein, India was also among the first nations to back the American war against terrorism after 11 September and offer full use of its military facilities in pursuit of its military and political objectives in Afghanistan. Together the two Indian positions, while drawing criticism at home, were also defining a new paradigm in India's approach to the United States.

Kashmir: Confrontation to Convergence

If there was one issue other than nuclear non-proliferation that deeply divided India and the United States, it was the American attitude towards the Kashmir question. Much of India's enduring distrust of the United States was rooted in the belief that the American position on Kashmir favoured Pakistan. The Indian foreign policy community held that in the late 1940s and early 1950s, the United States was unfamiliar with the subcontinent and misled by Great Britain into siding with Pakistan on Kashmir. Subsequently, the American compulsions during the cold war for a strategic partnership with Pakistan further skewed the balance. The Anglo-American pressure on India at the UNSC meeting on the Kashmir question deeply troubled New Delhi and forced it to turn towards the Soviet Union, which vetoed these resolutions in India's favour. India was also angered and frustrated by the Anglo-American efforts to mediate the Kashmir dispute when New Delhi turned to them for support in its confrontation with China in 1962. The intense Anglo-American pressure on India to settle the Kashmir dispute with Pakistan from 1962 to 1965 stirred deep political resentments in India. During the 1965 conflict with Pakistan, New Delhi was offended by the suspension of the arms sales relationship and by the American neutrality in the face of Pakistani aggression. After the 1965 war, India turned towards Moscow for mediation at Tashkent. The perception of an American tilt towards Pakistan in the 1971 war convinced India of the irreconcilable nature of the US-Pakistani relationship and India's interests.

The end of the cold war raised the expectations of a new template for Indo-US relations. Two important moves by the Bush administration in 1990 seemed to confirm the possibilities. It confronted Pakistan's nuclear weapons programme in 1990 by imposing sanctions and suspending military cooperation. Furthermore, its declaration in August 1990 that the UN resolutions on Kashmir were no longer relevant appeared to offer the prospect of a restructuring of the triangular relationship among New Delhi, Islamabad and Washington, and this time in India's favour. The apparent decline of Pakistan's strategic importance to the United States after the cold war seemed to create the opportunity to generate a different framework to govern US relations with India and Pakistan. But these hopes were quickly dashed by the Clinton administration in its first term (1993-97), with its renewed diplomatic activism on the Kashmir question.

The questioning of the accession of the state of Jammu and Kashmir to India in 1947 by the new US Assistant Secretary of State for South Asian Affairs, Robin L. Raphel, in October 1993 raised a political storm in New Delhi and brought to the fore all the deeply held suspicions of American intentions for Kashmir and conspiracy theories about Washington's interest in balkanizing India. President Clinton's repeated references through the early 1990s to Kashmir as a nuclear flashpoint and his urging India and Pakistan to end the world's most dangerous military confrontation seemed to suggest an invidious American agenda in the subcontinent. Adding to these fears were his administration's growing support of intervention by the

international community to resolve long-standing conflicts in
the world. At a time when India was trying to change course on
the economic and foreign policy fronts and cope with massive
internal security problems, the American activism on Kashmir
deepened India's distrust of the United States.

The Kargil crisis in the summer of 1999, however, brought
about a paradigm shift in the way India and the United States
engaged each other on Indo-Pakistani disputes, in particular on
the Kashmir question.[10] When India was surprised to discover
Pakistani troops and irregulars positioned across the Line of
Control in May 1999, it had little expectation of any political
support from the United States in reversing this aggression.
Pakistan, on the other hand, might have calculated with some
justification that even a neutral American position would help
it achieve a number of objectives. Based on the record of
international interventions in Indo-Pakistani disputes, Islamabad
might have assessed that Indian military attempts to restore
the status quo ante in the Kargil sector would have brought
demands from the international community for an immediate
ceasefire and bilateral talks. Such demands, based on the fears
of a nuclear conflict, would have helped Pakistan begin talks on
the basis of a changed territorial status quo in Kashmir for the
first time since 1972, when the LoC was confirmed by the two
sides. An American decision to oppose military action by India
by invoking the danger of a nuclear war and to propose talks to
defuse the crisis would have put India in an awkward diplomatic
spot. While India was determined to push the Pakistani forces
back at any cost, a hostile attitude from the United States would
have complicated the international political dimension of its
strategy in Kargil. Instead Washington supported India's military
action and exerted diplomatic pressure on Pakistan to restore
the sanctity of the LoC.

Clinton held Pakistan responsible for nuclear brinkmanship
and demanded that it restore the status quo ante. Washington
argued that, with the nuclearization of the subcontinent, there

was no room for the kind of military antics that Pakistan had initiated in Kargil. The Clinton administration rejected Pakistan's attempt to question the reality of the LoC or to link its withdrawal from Kargil to negotiations with India on the Kashmir dispute. It insisted that Pakistan's withdrawal must be unambiguous and unconditional. The US judged that Pakistan could not be rewarded for its aggression.[11] Besides putting direct pressure on the Pakistani military establishment, the US also mobilized support from Saudi Arabia to nudge Islamabad into swallowing the bitter pill of unilateral withdrawal from Kargil. Moreover, Washington continuously engaged Beijing during the Kargil crisis to limit any Chinese support for Pakistan. As a face-saving measure, President Clinton invited Pakistani Prime Minister Nawaz Sharif to visit Washington on the Fourth of July weekend of 1999 and got him to announce the withdrawal. That the United States did not ask India to do anything except restrain from taking its military activity across the LoC was news that pleasantly surprised India.

Writing about the 'new paradigm' in Indo-US relations, two experienced South Asia hands in Washington, Teresita C. Schaffer and Howard B. Schaffer, argued that

> the explanation is simple: the United States saw the facts as India did, and pursued its own national interests. The fact that these coincided with India's interests is not unique, but illustrates how, in a changing world, both countries need to look for opportunities where their agendas overlap .... Pakistan had started the problem by playing with fire; the remedy seemed clear: push Pakistan hard to end its provocation. India handled the situation with care and restraint; there was no reason to call for the usual reciprocating gesture.[12]

While the explanation was simple, its political significance was large. India could now begin to look at America as a potential partner instead of seeing it as it did in the many previous decades—a force hostile to its interests in the subcontinent.

The extraordinary American diplomatic and political support to India in the Kargil crisis was probably the first instance of security cooperation between the two countries since 1962 when Washington offered to back New Delhi in its war against China. Moreover, this was the first time that the United States supported India in its various conflicts with Pakistan. The crisis saw a rare intensity of communication between the leaders of India and the United States. President Clinton, Secretary of State Madeleine Albright and Deputy Secretary of State Strobe Talbott were on the phone talking to the Indian leadership throughout the Kargil crisis. This was capped by President Clinton's call to Prime Minister Vajpayee as he concluded the final negotiations with Prime Minister Nawaz Sharif. Of greater interest was the reference in this joint statement with Pakistan to the importance of 'respecting the sanctity of the LoC'.[13] This seemed to open the possibility of American support to an eventual final settlement of the Kashmir dispute LoC, which India had long hinted it might accept and Pakistan found it difficult to digest politically. Expanding on this, the Schaffers explain that

> Kargil crystallized a change in thinking, not just in Washington but more broadly in the West, about the troubled India–Pakistan relationship. There emerged from the smoke and fire a rough consensus that the peace of the region would be more secure if the border question were settled along the line which has separated Indian and Pakistani forces for fifty years. There remains considerable international sympathy for the people of the Kashmir valley, who have been largely left out of the debate over Kashmir and whose aspirations to greater autonomy seem reasonable. But the West has no sympathy for Pakistan's desire to detach Kashmir from India. This new consensus is far closer to India's policy than to Pakistan's, and may give Indian policymakers an opportunity to reexamine their diplomatic strategy.[14]

The shift in American thinking on Kashmir was hinted at more obliquely by Secretary of State Albright on the eve of President Clinton's visit to India. In a speech to the Asia Society on 14 March 2000, she reaffirmed that 'tangible steps must be taken to respect the Line of Control. For so long as this simple principle is violated, the people of Kashmir have no real hope of peace.'[15] She also reaffirmed American opposition to changing the territorial status quo in Kashmir through the use of force:

> The conflict over Kashmir has been fundamentally transformed. For nations must not attempt to change borders or zones of occupation through armed force. And now that they have exploded nuclear devices, India and Pakistan have all the more reason to avoid an armed conflict, and all the more reason to restart a discussion on ways to build confidence and prevent escalation.[16]

Clinton further developed the new approach during his visit to the region. In his speeches, statements and interviews, he distanced the United States from the concept of self-determination for Kashmiris, renewed the argument that there can be no military solution to the dispute and emphasized the importance of a peaceful dialogue between the two nations. In his powerful appeal to the people of Pakistan urging them to adopt the path of moderation and discard the obsession over Kashmir, Clinton warned that 'this era does not reward people who struggle in vain to redraw borders with blood'.[17] In an elaboration of the new American views on Kashmir, he made it absolutely clear, probably for the first time by an American President, that the US had no desire to see a disintegration of India in the name of Kashmiri self-determination:

> Our policy is first, respect the Line of Control. Second, do not promote violence by the third parties in Kashmir. Third, negotiate. And, fourth, with respect to India, that there's not a military solution to Kashmir's problems by India either—that the Kashmiris deserve

to have their own concerns addressed on the merits. But I don't think that an ethnically diverse country like India can't exist any more. I don't agree with that.[18]

Clinton's policy on Kashmir had come full circle. From appearing to question the accession of Jammu and Kashmir in late 1993, he came to reject the idea of self-determination while encouraging India to address the grievances of the Kashmiris and suggesting that the Line of Control might have the basis for an eventual settlement of the long-standing dispute between the two nations. On the diplomatic front, Clinton helped broker a ceasefire between the two armed forces in July 2000 and got it formalized at the end of 2000, when Vajpayee announced a unilateral cessation of hostilities against the militants in Jammu and Kashmir. It also encouraged the resumption of the dialogue between India and Pakistan that was suspended by New Delhi after Kargil. While Clinton transformed the context of its approach to the Kashmir question in fundamental ways, he would not, however, squarely face up to the problem of Pakistan's active support of cross-border terrorism in Kashmir.

That had to wait until the dramatic events of 11 September and America's subsequent war on terrorism, the 13 December attack on the Indian Parliament House and India's biggest military mobilization since Independence. Immediately after 11 September, India's expectations soared on the prospect of a final American confrontation with the sources of international terrorism in Pakistan that were now threatening the United States itself. But the US, as it turned out, also needed Pakistan's support in ousting the Taliban from power in Afghanistan and pursuing Al Qaeda. As Washington mobilized support from Islamabad, there was a deep disappointment in India that Pakistan was back at the top of the US political agenda for the region. But for many in New Delhi, the worst fears of a renewed US-Pakistani alliance began to resurface. Those Indians who questioned the BJP-led government's extraordinary political investment in improving relations with the United States could now argue with some credibility that India was barking up the wrong tree and that Washington was never about to give up its special relationship with Islamabad. Pakistan's return to the United States' affections at such a crucial moment seemed to bring the triangular relationship between New Delhi, Islamabad and Washington back to the very frustrating square one.

At the next level there was a deep apprehension in New Delhi that Pakistan would be able to insulate its own support of terrorism in Kashmir from the broader declared objectives of the American war on terrorism. Put another way, there was near certainty in New Delhi that the US, in order to keep Musharraf happy, would pursue double standards in its fight against terrorism. There was a strong sense that the United States would only be interested in pursuing those terrorists threatening its security and not those tormenting India. Since the sources of Indian threats were in Pakistan, the US would be unwilling to counter them. Finally at the highest level, a mood of pessimism began to cloud the thinking on the future of Indo-US relations. The sense that more than a decade of political effort to restructure the relationship with the United States had been blown away by the developments since 11 September.

Whether it had a conscious strategy or not, Washington was determined not to undermine its new relationship with India even as it reached out to Pakistan. President Bush consistently sought to assure India that there would be no double standards in battling terrorism. At the same time, however, he insisted that there would be priorities in dealing with the challenge. He also promised that once the immediate threat in Afghanistan has been addressed, the Indian concerns on terrorism would be dealt with. On their own, these assurances had limited credibility. It was Washington's response to a series of major terrorist incidents in India after 11 September that convinced New Delhi that there will be no US double standards on terrorism. These incidents—on 1 October 2001 in Srinagar, on 13 December 2001 at the Parliament House in New Delhi, on 14 May 2002 at Kaluchak in Jammu and Kashmir and the Indian threat to go to war against Pakistan in the summer of 2002—forced the United States into new activism to restrain Pakistan from supporting terrorism in India.

As a result, the US formally acknowledged for the first time the link between Kashmiri terrorist groups operating in Pakistan and the state, put pressure on Musharraf to proclaim that Pakistani soil will not be used to export terror to any part of the world, and obtained formal commitments from Pakistan to end all cross-border infiltration and not disrupt the impending elections for the Jammu and Kashmir Assembly. Despite the demands from Pakistan that India engage in talks on Kashmir immediately, Bush backed India's broad negotiating position that the creation of an appropriate environment free of violence must precede talks. The American decision to confront Pakistan on the question of its support to Kashmiri terrorism has been a big gain for India, despite the doubts about Musharraf's ability and willingness to honour the commitments he made to Washington on ending cross-border terrorism.

In the end, the US successfully defused the military crisis between India and Pakistan in the first half of 2002, but it could not get Musharraf to abide by his promises to end cross-border terrorism. The US seemed unwilling to confront Pakistan on the commitments it had given to the international community. While India was satisfied that its threat to go to war against Pakistan after 13 December did help mobilize American pressure on Pakistan to end cross-border infiltration, it was disappointed that it was not decisive enough.[19] Nevertheless, the US diplomacy during the 2002 crisis altered both the American perspective on Kashmir as well as the nature of the triangular relationship. Kashmir, once one of the most contentious issues between India and the United States, emerged as an arena of tacit cooperation in the post-11 September period. The US became India's principal interlocutor with Pakistan. It acknowledged Pakistan's responsibility to end terrorism emanating from its soil and extracted promises from Islamabad to end cross-border infiltration. The Bush administration also offered sensors and other technologies to strengthen India's capabilities to monitor the Line of Control effectively and prevent infiltration across it.

Moreover, the crisis shaped important changes in the American perceptions of the Kashmir problem. As the six-yearly elections to the assembly of Jammu and Kashmir came up amidst renewed American attempts to defuse Indo-Pakistani tensions, the American policy went through a significant evolution. For years now the US has said that India and Pakistan should resolve the problem of Kashmir through a bilateral dialogue that takes into account the wishes of the Kashmiri people, but there was considerable ambiguity in the American position on how to ascertain the sentiments of the Kashimiris. Would it be through a referendum or a plebiscite? Must it be under international auspices? The US would not say. On the eve of Secretary of State Colin Powell's visit in July 2002, the Bush administration ruled out a plebiscite as an option. In New Delhi, Powell himself acknowledged that the elections to the assembly in Jammu and Kashmir could be the vehicle for an assessment of the wishes of the people in the state. In his extensive remarks to the American press after his visit to India and Pakistan in July 2002, Powell stated that, while there were questions about the participation of certain groups, the elections in Kashmir were 'one step forward in a process of determining the will of the Kashmiri people'.[20]

Having obtained assurances from the Indian government that it would hold free and fair elections in Kashmir, US diplomats in India kept nudging the leading dissident organization in the Valley, the Hurriyat, to participate. The US mission took an active part in observing the elections and was quick to assert that the polls were by and large free and fair. The Bush administration condemned the violence from various terrorist groups based in Pakistan aimed at disrupting the elections. The US continued to insist that free and fair elections alone would not be enough to resolve the Kashmir dispute,

and it required negotiations between India and Pakistan. At the
same time the Bush administration backed New Delhi's position
that negotiations between India and Pakistan must wait until
an appropriate environment is created by the latter's ending
cross-border infiltration.[21] Indications from Washington after
11 September were also that the US was no longer interested
in the independence of Jammu and Kashmir. Such an outcome
would only create a fragile state and potential haven for Islamic
extremists. In his visit to Kashmir after the elections there,
Ambassador Robert D. Blackwill departed from the practice
of the 1990s to meet the Hurriyat leaders in Srinagar and
reinforced the message that India saw the newly elected
government in Kashmir as a legitimate representative of the
people.[22]

As the United States recast its approach to Kashmir in the
summer of 2002, India itself began to discard many of its long-
held suspicions of American intentions on Kashmir. Boosted
by the unexpected American diplomatic support during the
Kargil War, India was creative in using the concerns in
Washington about a nuclear flashpoint in Kashmir. After years
of vehemently rejecting any role for the United States in
resolving its disputes with Pakistan, in particular Jammu and
Kashmir, India was now bold enough to entice the United States
to apply pressure on Pakistan and to redefine its own political
line on Kashmir. The Indian military mobilization after 13
December was partly aimed at getting the United States to
confront the sources of Kashmir-related terrorism in Pakistan,
and India succeeded to an extent. India, which traditionally
rejected roles for outsiders in the Kashmir dispute, consciously
signalled its willingness to let Delhi-based diplomats, including
American embassy staff, serve as international observers—if
only in their individual capacity to see for themselves the Indian
determination to hold elections in an open and transparent
manner. With that one stroke, India turned a leaf in the tragic
electoral book in Kashmir that saw many rigged elections in
the past and brought a new international legitimacy to the state

government in Kashmir, constituted within the political framework of the Indian Union.

Further, the triangular diplomacy involving India, Pakistan and the United States in the military crisis after 13 December saw the crystallization of India's willingness to accept a larger American role in the resolution of the Kashmir dispute. The Bush administration, on the other hand, recognized that despite its ideological resistance to getting tangled in the Kashmir dispute, the time might have come to contemplate a greater role for Washington in its resolution. Washington seemed ready to move from crisis management to conflict resolution.

Internationalization of the Kashmir dispute and *third-party mediation* were phrases that had sent the Indian political class into a rage for decades. Discarding that political baggage, India was beginning to suggest it was ready to accept a discreet American role in promoting a reasonable settlement of the Kashmir dispute with Pakistan. Formal mediation was still political taboo, and a table for three on Kashmir would invite the wrath of the Indian polity. The BJP-led government was suggesting it might be prepared to accept a behind-the-scenes American role. In an interview in *Newsweek* in June 2002, Vajpayee insisted that there was no question of India accepting mediation on Kashmir by the international community, but it was prepared to accept a facilitation by the United States.[23] The simple play on semantics demonstrated how far India had moved in its thinking on Kashmir and the US role in it. Privately, Vajpayee's top aides were wondering, if the United States could deliver Pakistan on a settlement of the Kashmir dispute along the Line of Control and complete the partition of the state, why should India have any objections to such an outcome? Washington seemed to be asking the same question. US sources were also suggesting that conversion of the LoC into a border between India and Pakistan plus a substantive autonomy for the state of Jammu and Kashmir must be the principal elements of a final settlement. While neither side would go public with these premises, for the fear of inviting Pakistani rejection, an unstated parallelism between the interests of India and the US in Kashmir began to emerge.

Pakistan and Beyond

Liberating its relationship with the United States from the Pakistan factor has long been one of the central aims of India's grand strategy, but it remained elusive throughout the cold war. The attempts by India and the United States to develop a relationship by skirting Pakistan could never have succeeded in the cold war, thanks to the logic of America's geopolitical compulsions in the region. India faced two direct challenges from the US-Pakistani relationship—American security cooperation with Pakistan and its approach on the disputes between the two regional rivals. Indians never ceased to protest during the cold war about the American preference for dictatorships in Pakistan (and later China) rather than a democratic India. New Delhi was also offended that the only American engagement with India aimed at limiting the damage to the US relationship with Pakistan, and it was upset that Washington had no larger vision for the potential for a broad-based relationship between the two countries. India also complained that the US policy put India into the small box of the subcontinent, instead of recognizing India's larger aspirations for a role in Asia and beyond. Breaking out of this constraining framework and removing the hyphen in the US relations with subcontinental rivals were among the principal objectives of New Delhi in its engagement of Washington in the 1990s. At the end of a roller coaster ride with the US on issues relating to Pakistan during that decade, a different paradigm seemed to be at hand.

By the time President Clinton came to India in March 2000, it was the United States' declared policy that it no longer wished to treat India and Pakistan as Siamese twins. Moreover, Washington would pursue its relations with both on their own merits. The fact that he spent five days in India and barely five hours in Pakistan seemed to reflect new American priorities.

India as an emerging power, an important economic partner and a potentially larger player in the world stood in contrast to the growing American perception of Pakistan as a failing state. Beyond the changing relative importance of India and Pakistan, Clinton's visit also appeared to define a radically different engagement with the two nations. With India, the US focussed on a positive agenda of cooperation on regional and global issues, but with Pakistan it had a negative one, of coping with terrorism emanating from its soil and preventing it from becoming a failed state.

The new South Asian differentiation introduced by the Clinton administration was pursued with greater vigour by the Bush administration that took charge in January 2001. By the fall of 2001, the Bush administration seemed all set to further downgrade the relationship with Pakistan and make India the centrepiece of its policy towards the subcontinent. But 11 September changed all that. As Pakistan returned to the strategic affections of the United States, the extended effort by India during the 1990s appeared to have come to nought. The Bush administration's promises after 11 September to avoid double standards in its war on terrorism and its pressure on Pakistan to stop cross-border infiltration went some distance to address the Indian concerns, but in the end they could not satisfy India. Bush prevented the triangular relationship among India, the US and Pakistan from returning to the old paradigm of the 1950s and 1980s, but he could not remove Pakistan as a complicating factor in Indo-US relations after 11 September. Nevertheless, mitigating the situation were two important themes of the Bush administration's approach to India. One was the commitment to treat India as part of a larger framework of Asian balance of power, the other a determination to inject substantive content into the bilateral relations.

During his election campaign, Bush and his advisers promised to continue the new engagement of India initiated by Clinton, but within a new global framework. The Bush ideologues placed India in the context of America's relations with major powers—which were described as a declining Russia, a rising China and an emerging India. The strong impulse in the Bush foreign policy team to rethink the China policy appeared to give a new importance to the relationship with India. Explaining then-candidate George W. Bush's foreign policy priorities, his future National Security Adviser Condoleezza Rice asserted:

> China's success in controlling the balance of power depends in large part on America's reaction to the challenge. The United States must deepen its cooperation with Japan and South Korea and maintain its commitment to a robust military presence in the region. It should pay closer attention to India's role in the regional balance. There is a strong tendency conceptually to connect India with Pakistan and to think only of Kashmir or the nuclear competition between the two states. But India is an element in China's calculation, and it should be in America's, too. India is not a great power yet, but it has the potential to emerge as one.[24]

In the early months of 2001, Bush and his foreign policy aides rejected the earlier notion of China as a strategic partner and began to call it a potential competitor, raising the prospect of a new American policy aimed at balancing China and placing some weight on India's strategic role in Asia. The events of 11 September, however, forced the Bush administration to abandon the incipient hostility towards China, as its attention was riveted on the war against terrorism and confronting Iraq in the Persian Gulf. As Sino-US relations began to improve significantly after 11 September, the China factor too seemed to disappear from the US calculus on India. Nevertheless, the deep suspicion of China remained among the ideologues of the Bush administration, and consequently a continuing emphasis on Indian role in stabilizing Asia.

In its first comprehensive articulation of its world view in September 2002, the Bush White House put India for the first time in the category of great powers and suggested an Indian role in Asian balance of power and contrasted a positive approach towards India with a more critical one towards China. It also listed India after its NATO allies and Russia and ahead of China. On India, the Bush administration stated:

> The United States has undertaken a transformation in its bilateral relationship with India based on a conviction that US interests require a strong relationship with India. We are the two largest democracies, committed to political freedom protected by representative government. India is moving toward greater economic freedom as well. We have a common interest in the free flow of commerce, including through the vital sea lanes of the Indian Ocean. Finally, we share an interest in fighting terrorism and in creating a strategically stable Asia.[25]

The new stress on India's role in Asian balance of power was also articulated by Ambassador Blackwill. In a speech in late 2002, he proclaimed:

> [P]eace within Asia—a peace that helps perpetuate Asian prosperity—remains an objective that a transformed US–India relationship will help advance. Within a fellowship of democratic nations, the United States and India would benefit from an Asian environment free from inter-state conflict—including among the region's great powers—open to trade and commerce, and respectful of human rights and personal freedoms . . . .

> Achieving this objective requires the United States to particularly strengthen political, economic, and military-to-military relations with those Asian states that share our democratic values and national interests. That spells India. A strong US–India partnership contributing to the construction of a peaceful and prosperous Asia binds the resources of the world's most powerful and most populous democracies in support of freedom, political moderation, and economic and technological development.[26]

While both India and the United States were working on improving relations with China, neither would explicitly declare China a common enemy or propose that they would work together to contain Beijing. Nevertheless, concerns on China, expressed in more modest terms of stability and Asian balance, have clearly emerged as new themes for the first time since the early 1960s in the policy discourse on Indo-US relations. The Bush administration also initiated more broad-based consultations and exchanges of information with the Indian government on issues relating to China.

Working together to maintain peace and stability in the Indian Ocean was another theme that would begin to figure in the relations between the two countries. This was highlighted at the very beginning of the Bush administration. At his confirmation hearings, Colin Powell put the relationship with India not in the context of China but in that of the Indian Ocean and Pakistan:

> We must deal more wisely with the world's largest democracy. Soon to be the most populous country in the world, India has the potential to help keep the peace in the vast Indian Ocean area and its periphery. We need to work harder and more consistently to assist India in this endeavour, while not neglecting our friends in Pakistan.[27]

For decades, India and the United States saw themselves as antagonists in the Indian Ocean region. They renewed naval contacts in the mid- to late 1980s under Indira and Rajiv Gandhi. India offered and then withdrew military cooperation to the United States during the Gulf war. There were regular naval exercises during the 1990s, until they were suspended after the nuclear tests. Despite these contacts, the prospect of Indo-US naval cooperation in Indian Ocean seemed somewhat far-fetched, yet in the changed context of regional security at the turn of the millennium, it no longer appeared impossible. The new convergence of interests in the Indian Ocean was reflected in India's decision to provide naval escort to American military assets transiting the Malacca Straits during Operation Enduring Freedom in Afghanistan in the summer of 2002.

Even as a larger framework of strategic cooperation that transcended Pakistan began to present itself for Indian and American decision makers, the outlook for bilateral relations expanded considerably in the early years of the Bush administration. One important new element was renewed defence cooperation, including India's likely purchase of arms and military equipment from the United States. The credit for exploring the acquisition of American military technology, despite the entrenched scepticism in the establishment goes to Rajiv Gandhi. As a result of his initiative, India and the US began limited defence technological cooperation in the late 1980s. It did not go anywhere during the 1990s when India curtailed its defence purchases radically, and the Clinton administration was loath to sell arms to tension-prone regions like the subcontinent. In any case, even the minimal Indo-US cooperation in defence did not survive the nuclear tests. The Bush administration, which lifted the sanctions imposed by Clinton after May 1998, cleared the ground for renewed defence cooperation. Besides upgradation of the scope and substance of Indo-US military contacts and exercises, the Bush administration was prepared to sell weapon systems, and India was ready to buy them. A number of systems including aircraft, naval ships and missiles were under discussion at the end of 2001.

The meeting of the Defence Policy Group in New Delhi in December 2001 outlined the emerging defence cooperation:

> The two delegations underscored the importance of a stable, long-term defense supply relationship as part of the overall strategic cooperation between India and the United States. Since the waiver of sanctions, a number of applications for export licenses have been approved by the US Departments of State and Defense and are in the process of notification to Congress. These include

licenses such as that related to weapon locating radars. The US also agreed to expeditious review of India's acquisition priorities, including engine and systems for Light Combat Aircraft, radars, multi-mission maritime aircraft, components for jet trainer and high performance jet engines. To assist this licensing and sales process in the future, the two sides have resolved to establish a separate Security Cooperation Group to manage the defense supply relationship between India and the United States.[28]

Further, as India began to consider the privatization of its defence production, Indian and American companies began to look at the prospects for collaboration.

Beyond defence, the Bush administration also opened up bilateral interaction across a broad spectrum of issues. The cooperation on counterterrorism that began under the Clinton administration was expanded in the Bush years amidst a new focus on the war against international terrorism. This involved more intensive cooperation on law enforcement, weapons of mass destruction-related terrorism, cyber-terrorism and white-collar crime, among other areas. There were also institutionalized consultations on missile defence. During his visit to the US in December 2002, National Security Adviser Brajesh Mishra obtained a political commitment from the Bush administration to expand cooperation in the trinity of areas of great interest to India—civil nuclear energy, commercial space applications and high-technology trade.

In the early years of the new century, Indo-US relations were transformed beyond recognition. The differences on the nuclear proliferation were brought down to manageable levels, and the prolonged confrontation over Kashmir was yielding place to more trust and cooperation. While India and the United States could not shake off Pakistan from the inherited baggage of their bilateral ties, a wider framework for strategic cooperation and a deepening bilateral relationship have created a new hope that the two nations can now travel together. India and the United States are some distance away from being allies in a traditional sense, but the areas of agreement and common endeavour have begun to replace the negative agenda of the earlier wasted decades.

FIVE

Reviving the Russian Connection

The Trauma of the Soviet Collapse

Following the nuclear tests of May 1998 and the sharp international condemnation, one of the first stops on Brajesh Mishra's damage limitation tour was Moscow. A huge surprise awaited Mishra who, as the Principal Secretary to Prime Minister Vajpayee, was responsible for organizing the nuclear tests and handling the immediate post-Pokhran diplomacy. Russian Foreign Minister Yevgeny Primakov launched into a lengthy harangue on the negative consequences of Indian nuclear tests, and as Mishra squirmed with unease, the thought of getting up to end the meeting might have crossed his mind. Mishra is believed to have said that this was not the kind of reaction he had hoped from India's traditional friend and strategic partner. Although he might have expected a monologue on the virtues of non-proliferation from Madeleine Albright, Primakov's American counterpart, Mishra had come to Moscow looking for a Russian understanding of India's concerns that led to the nuclear tests, not a lecture.[1]

There was no doubt that the Russian establishment, from President Boris Yeltsin downward, was furious with the Indian tests. There was as much egg on the face of the Russian intelligence agencies—and Primakov was the former head of the KGB—as there was on the American CIA for having missed India's preparations for the tests. Great powers and their intelligence establishments hate major surprises. Moscow also felt hurt that its Indian friends had not informed the Russian leadership of the impending tests. The Russian leaders, who believed that they had a special relationship with India, got only a letter similar to that which Prime Minister Vajpayee sent to President Clinton and other world leaders explaining the Indian decision to test. Nevertheless, the Russian anger did not last. After the initial private criticism, Russia, along with France, worked hard within the club of major powers—the P-5, G-8 and the United Nations Security Council—to limit the collective international action against India. But the message from Russia after Pokhran-II was clear: India could not take Russia for granted, and it would have to work hard to gain Russian support and keep it informed on issues of mutually vital concern. Preserving the relationship with Russia at levels that preceded the collapse of the Soviet Union and deepening this rapport in the changed international context were two of the biggest challenges Indian diplomacy faced in the 1990s. Moscow severely tested India's policy suppleness and its envoys' individual skills. New Delhi can take considerable pride in salvaging the core of the Indo-Russian relationship from the ashes of the cold war.

Nothing was as traumatic for the Indian leadership and its foreign policy elite as the collapse of the Soviet Union. India's initial reaction to the rise of Mikhail Gorbachev in the Soviet Union was enthusiastic. India hypothesized that a young dynamic leader keen on revitalizing his country would also want to strengthen Indo-Soviet relations. The bonhomie between Gorbachev and Rajiv Gandhi was seen as lending a new vigour to bilateral ties, but as the full implications of Gorbachev's reforms at home and the new foreign policy thinking abroad became visible by the late 1980s, the enthusiasm turned into deep dismay across the political spectrum. For the traditional Left, Gorbachev's internal policies were increasingly seen as an attempt to dismantle communism in the Soviet Union and his external policies as an appeasement of the United States and other Western powers. These views were widely shared within the Indian intelligentsia. The foreign policy elite viewed with alarm the whole range of moves that Gorbachev was making on the diplomatic front. These included unilateral concessions on nuclear arms control, attempts to improve relations with the US at any cost, a new rapprochement with China and a departure from traditional positions on Afghanistan and Cambodia. The withdrawal from Afghanistan made it abundantly clear that the Soviet Union had begun to retrench, and quickly, under Gorbachev.

Every one of these moves undermined India's key assumptions about international and regional security. The country was slow to grasp the significance of the changes under way in Moscow. It was fashionable in New Delhi to decry Gorbachev's policies in the late 1980s, and when the coup against him unfolded in early August 1991, New Delhi could not hide its glee. Even the normally unflappable Narasimha Rao said that Gorbachev's fall was due to his attempts at too radical a reform at too fast a pace.[2] The coup was short-lived, but neither the Soviet Union nor Gorbachev would survive it for long. In the debate that followed in Parliament, Jaswant Singh, the BJP leader who would become external affairs minister, accused the Narasimha Rao government of 'blinkered timidity and ineptitude' in dealing with historic changes in Moscow and attacked the official Indian response to the coup for being 'glued in yesterday's clichés'.[3] While the Indian Right revelled in the Soviet Union's dissolution, the communist Left and the socialists in the Congress party went into deep mourning.

J.N. Dixit, who took over as India's Foreign Secretary at the end of 1991, called the initial handling of the changes in Soviet Union as one of the 'significant foreign policy aberrations' during the five-year tenure of P.V. Narasimha Rao (1991-96).[4] Narasimha Rao's statement criticizing Gorbachev and the liberal forces in Moscow, Dixit says, was based on 'somewhat slanted assessments of our diplomatic mission in Moscow' and the prognosis that 'the communists might come back to power'.[5] The problem was perhaps deeper, a collective refusal of the Indian elite to accept the inevitable collapse of the communist order in Moscow even weeks before it actually happened. This had an interesting diplomatic consequence. Yeltsin, on the rise in the new Russia, had indicated his desire to come to India as his first destination abroad, and he reaffirmed his commitment to maintain Indo-Russian relations on the same footing as Indo-Soviet relations. According to Dixit, 'Our response to his suggestion was inhibited and reluctant,' and it took quite an effort to get Narasimha Rao to invite him to India.[6] The unwillingness to come to terms with the new Russia created a political distance between Moscow and New Delhi for a long time.

The nostalgia for the old order in Moscow and hopes for its return were enduring within the Indian establishment during the early 1990s. Although the Indian attitudes and hopes were unrealistic, they had a strong basis within the political establishment, for the depth of positive feelings towards the Soviet Union in India was extraordinary. Built over three decades of partnership during the cold war, New Delhi's ties to Moscow had solid foundations in ideological, political and security considerations. At the ideological level, the strong influence of left-wing radicalism on the national movement gave the Soviet Union a special place in the evolution of the Indian world view. While the communists saw Moscow as the guiding centre of world revolution, the Soviet experience in rapid economic development was worthy of emulation to large sections of the Left and Centre of the Indian political spectrum. Soviet support for the building of the Indian public sector was seen as Moscow's enduring commitment to help India develop in a self-reliant manner. The Soviet opposition to the West also fit in with India's anti-imperialist struggle in the first part of the twentieth century. The ideas of non-alignment and Third Worldism in India ran parallel, if not entirely coincidental, with the Soviet world view during the cold war. Although officially India never backed the argument that the Soviet Union was a natural ally of the developing world in its battles with the West, it was a view that was widely held by the Indian intelligentsia.

Although there was a tradition of anti-communism within Indian politics, it was rooted among conservative sections of the Indian society, which did not exercise too much intellectual influence in the first decades of the republic. The base of liberal and ideologically pro-Western elements was extremely narrow. The split in the international communist movement, arising from the Sino-Soviet divide in the early 1960s, brought into being a left-wing force that was also opposed to Moscow. The Right challenged the socialist economic orientation initiated by Nehru and his closeness to the communists. Later, as Indira Gandhi successfully moved India towards left-wing populism, anti-Soviet elements—both conservative and radical—were marginalized. The outflanking of the anti-Soviet attitudes was also achieved amidst the popular sense that the Soviet Union was the only reliable ally India had in the international system. The dynamics of the US-Soviet cold war and the Sino-Soviet conflict relentlessly moved New Delhi and Moscow into a close embrace.

In the 1950s, as Moscow saw the value of cultivating India, it extended unstinting support to New Delhi in its difficulties with Pakistan over Kashmir. At a time when the Anglo-Americans were seen as manipulating the issue in Pakistan's favour, the Soviets' valuable support in the United Nations Security Council remained a defining feature of Indian perceptions of them. For a short while in the mid-1960s, they began to adopt a more balanced approach towards India and Pakistan and became the promoter of a peace process between the two after the 1965 war. In the late 1960s, the Soviet Union also began an active economic engagement of Pakistan. This phase did not last too long. Moscow chose a strategic alignment with India through the 1971 Treaty of Peace and Friendship, ended its flirtation with Pakistan and backed India in the war for the liberation of Bangladesh. For the next decade and a half, the Indo-Soviet political partnership flourished. The widespread national acceptance of the strategic significance of the Soviet connection was demonstrated in the attitude of the Janata government that came to power by ousting Indira Gandhi in the 1977 elections. The Janata Party, in which many anti-Soviet and anti-communist forces like the Jan Sangh gained new prominence, had been critical of the Indo-Soviet treaty, New Delhi's political tilt towards Moscow and the presumed dilution of the principle of non-alignment. Nevertheless, within months after coming to power, the Janata government, with its foreign minister, Atal Bihari Vajpayee, saw very little that could be tinkered with in the relationship.

The Soviet connection was as significant in the management of the rivalry with China as it was in coping with Western support to Pakistan for Kashmir. The Sino-Soviet rift coinciding with the Sino-Indian conflict reinforced the bonds between New Delhi and Moscow during the early 1960s. Moscow moved from a position of support of Beijing to a careful neutrality in the Sino-Indian conflict that erupted into a brief war at the end of 1962. The triangular relationship among New Delhi, Beijing and Moscow was an extremely dynamic one from the late 1950s, and every single bilateral relationship within that triangle affected the other two and the shaping of the triangle itself. By the early 1970s Sino-Soviet and Sino-Indian political hostility deepened, and the Indo-Soviet de facto alliance was cemented. Meanwhile, Sino-US relations took off in the 1970s, and a full normalization of bilateral relations was achieved by the end of the decade. It was also the period when Indo-US ties began to dissipate. A new and enduring balance had been established in the subcontinent—the US, China and Pakistan on one side and the Soviet Union and India on the other. The Soviet intervention in Afghanistan in December 1979 and the massive international mobilization of forces against it by the United States deepened the divide in the region, and New Delhi found itself in a tight geopolitical link with Moscow.

The special relationship between India and the Soviet Union was strengthened by a deepening arms transfer relationship.

The first significant project of military sales was the Mig 21, which came amidst heightening tensions between India and China as well as between Moscow and Beijing. Although Soviet arms sales to India were initiated in the mid- to late 1950s, the Mig 21 was the first supply of high-end combat equipment to India. The fact that the Soviet Union had refused to sell the Mig 21 to China demonstrated the new political calculus that was binding New Delhi and Moscow. India's dismal experience with the US military assistance during the 1962 war with China and Washington's reluctance to meet the arms requirements of India after the war began to make the Soviet Union an extremely valued source of military supplies. India's very British armed forces soon overcame their initial resistance to accepting the Soviet equipment, and the Soviet Union acquired a dominant role in meeting the requirements of the Indian Navy, Air Force and the Army. Briefly in the late 1970s there was some talk about too much dependence on the Soviet Union and the need to diversify the sources of supply. That phase, however, did not last long. Although India bought the Jaguar and Mirage aircraft and HDW submarines from Great Britain, France and Germany respectively, Western Europe was not a real substitute for the Soviet military connection. In the 1980s, as the US resumed arms supplies to Pakistan and as China began to raise the level of military engagement with Islamabad, the Indo-Soviet military relationship deepened. By the time the Soviet Union broke up in 1991, it was meeting nearly 80 per cent of India's defence needs.

The last two decades of the Soviet Union also saw the establishment of cooperation between New Delhi and Moscow in sensitive high-technology areas. The Indian nuclear and space programmes were entirely Western-oriented in their initial phases. Built by Homi Bhabha and Vikram Sarabhai with their excellent connections to the Western scientific establishments, there was little or no interaction between the Indian nuclear and space establishments and their Soviet counterparts. Yet in the 1970s and 1980s, as the West began to impose restrictions on technological cooperation with India after Pokhran-I, India began to look to Moscow. The Soviet supply of heavy water in the mid-1970s to the Indo-Canadian reactors in Rajasthan was the first instance of bilateral cooperation in the atomic energy field between New Delhi and Moscow. The Soviet Union's less restrictive approach to nuclear transfers and its reluctance to isolate India on the non-proliferation question opened the door for the consideration of a Soviet role in India's civilian nuclear power programme in the early 1980s. The two countries signed an agreement to build two nuclear power reactors at Kudankulam, during Gorbachev's visit to New Delhi in 1988. In addition, cooperation in the space sector began to take off in the 1980s with the Indian use of Russian launch facilities, and it culminated in an agreement to cooperate in the development of Indian geo-stationary launch capabilities.

By the mid-1980s India and the Soviet Union had created a very productive relationship across a wide range of areas. The intensity of bilateral cooperation between Moscow and New Delhi as well as their broad convergence of political interests made the Soviet connection a very special one, unlike any other. Although the people-to-people relations between the Soviet Union and India never reached the levels of engagement between the Indian and the Anglo-American civil societies, there was extraordinary warmth between the two nations. Given the expansive size of state sectors in both, interaction between the professional elites in the defence, scientific and industrial levels was intense. The Indian political class indeed became Slavophile, even as its children went in droves to the West. The quest for the expansion of national capabilities in India and the consistent Soviet support for it took place on a foundation of deep political empathy between the two elites. It is not that New Delhi and Moscow did not have differences or disagreements, but these did not come in the way of building a productive partnership.

The story of Indo-Russian relations, it is often said, is also the story of Indian foreign policy. Precisely for that reason, the collapse of the Soviet Union was so difficult for the Indian political establishment to digest. Despite its misgivings about the turn of events in Moscow in the late 1980s, India had no option but to find ways to deal with the new realities in the post-Soviet Russia and preserve the core elements of the traditional relationship in the new context.

Salvaging the Relationship

The collapse of the Soviet Union also coincided with a powerful internal imperative in India for a radical reorientation. Both countries were compelled to confront new economic choices. For Russia, it was a sweeping revolutionary change. For India, it was no less painful to restructure its economy under the pressures of globalization. At the turn of the 1990s, both nations also had the difficult task of rethinking their foreign policy priorities and coming to terms with the fact that the West had won the cold war. As they embarked on their respective journeys, it was by no means clear that they would be working together. In the immediate aftermath of the collapse of the Soviet Union, the Indo-Russian relationship appeared to have little chance of surviving at the top of the two nations' diplomatic agendas. The first reactions in both capitals amounted to downgrading each other's importance.

Russian diplomacy under the stewardship of Andrei Kozyrev, the Russian foreign minister whom India found difficult to deal with, seemed to acquire an intense pro-Western orientation. He identified three concentric circles of Russian foreign policy: the West; the immediate neighbourhood or the near-abroad, constituting the former Soviet republics; and the rest of the world. Entente and intense engagement with the West to join the so-called club of civilized nations was at the top of Kozyrev's diplomatic agenda. In his pursuit of its de-ideologized foreign policy, he had little time for the past relationship with India. The Yeltsin establishment had not forgotten the ambivalent Indian reaction to the August coup.

On the Indian side, the debate was dominated by two views.

One wallowed in nostalgia for the glorious days of the Soviet Union and kept up the hopes that the old order would return to Moscow; for them, Yeltsin's was a passing parade, not an enduring reflection of the historic rupture in Russia. The other was dismissive of Russia; this school argued that Russia was a declining power and increasingly aligned with the West and hence was of no consequence for New Delhi. It was inevitable that the relations between New Delhi and Moscow would turn frosty in the early 1990s. Nevertheless, both foreign policy establishments had strong proponents of salvaging the ties from the debris of the cold war. Key diplomatic functionaries on both sides had confidence in the future of the Indo-Russian relationship, but they were realistic enough to see that it had to be built on new premises. Their challenge was to get their own establishments to recognize the enduring mutuality of interests between New Delhi and Moscow. Equally daunting was the challenge of coping with the immediate complications that arose from the collapse of the Soviet Union.

By the time Yeltsin visited India in January 1993, the two sides had succeeded in imparting a sense of order to the chaos that Indo-Russian relations had witnessed in the immediate aftermath of the Soviet Union's demise. It was relatively easy to replace the 1971 Indo-Soviet Treaty of Peace, Friendship and Cooperation—that symbol of de facto alliance between New Delhi and Moscow for two decades—with a new document that reflected the changed realities. Neither nation wanted to be seen as pursuing such an alliance, yet it was also important to proclaim the continuing convergence of interests between the two countries. The word *peace* in the title of the new document was dropped, as was the famous Article IX of the earlier treaty. Article IX, the kernel of the old arrangement, read as follows:

> In the event of either party being subject to an attack or a threat thereof, the High Contracting Parties shall immediately enter into mutual consultations in order to remove such a threat and to take

appropriate effective measures to ensure peace and the security of their countries.

Article III, however, was the operative part of the new treaty and stated that

the High Contracting Parties shall hold regular consultations with each other at various levels on all important issues affecting the interests of both the parties. In case of a situation which in the opinion of the High Contracting Parties, constituted a threat to peace or breach of peace, they would immediately contact each other for coordination of their positions in the interest of eliminating the threat or re-establishing peace. Neither Party shall take any actions which might pose a threat or impair the security of the other Party.[7]

Although coming up with a successor document to the original treaty was seen as an important political and diplomatic objective, the two countries were in fact proclaiming that the context of the relationship had changed. Both countries were already set on improving their relationships with the West. Moreover, the original treaty was beginning to lose much of its salience by the early 1980s. Although India supported the Soviet intervention in Afghanistan, it was not very enthusiastic about it. In private conversations with the Soviet leaders, New Delhi underlined the unfortunate consequences of the intervention. Moreover, Moscow had not consulted New Delhi before taking action. Recognizing the costs of being identified with Moscow in Afghanistan, Indira Gandhi refused to celebrate the tenth anniversary of the treaty in 1981 and avoided visiting Moscow for the festivities. She had already begun the effort to engage the United States and inject some balance into India's external relations.

Far more important than the treaty was the resolution of the rupee–rouble imbroglio and the move towards trade in hard currency. India agreed to repay its outstanding rouble debt to Russia in rupees over a period of twelve years. The total amount India would pay back between 1993 and 2005 would be Rs 36,000 crores. The money would be returned through goods bought by Russian entrepreneurs in India, through investment in Russian projects in India or simply through directly selling the Indian rupee in Russian stock exchanges. There was strong criticism in India that it had agreed to far too generous terms in resolving the issue. The exchange rate on which the total amount fixed (six rupees to one rouble) was by no means realistic, and as the Russian economy entered the capitalist waters, the rouble's value plummeted. The argument in New Delhi, however, was that the value of the past relationship between the two sides could not be assessed purely in terms of current exchanges, and the focus was on getting a reasonable settlement that suited the interests of both sides.

Managing the arms supply relationship was yet another immediate challenge. During Yeltsin's visit, the two sides agreed to streamline the supply of spares for the Russian military equipment that dominated Indian stores, but managing the supplies on the ground amidst the institutional chaos of Russia was entirely another matter. During the Soviet years, the supply of arms and spares was on a point-to-point basis. Now India had to deal with the specific production units directly. With frequent changes in the organizational structure and lines of authority in Russia, securing the arms relationship in the early 1990s was a nightmare. India adopted the method of triangular MoUs with the production units and the controlling ministries to keep the supplies running. Further complicating the problem was the fact that the break up of the Soviet Union left many defence production units under the control of other independent republics.

The new ties between the United States and Russia and Washington's pressures on Russia to limit its advanced technology transfers to non-nuclear nations severely tested the cooperation between New Delhi and Moscow. On the nuclear front, Russia agreed in 1992 to abide by the new guidelines of the Nuclear Suppliers Group (NSG) on technology transfers to non-NPT states. These guidelines called for full-scope safeguards—that is, international monitoring of all the nuclear facilities—from the recipient countries. India, which had a weapons-oriented nuclear programme, was in no position to accept these guidelines. The understanding between Moscow and New Delhi on the transfer of two civilian nuclear reactors for Kudankulam, however, was exempted from these provisions.

It was in the area of space technology that problems arose. Since 1993 the Clinton administration insisted that the Russian agreement to supply cryogenic engines and technology for the Indian launch vehicle programme violated the rules of the Missile Technology Control Regime (MTCR). India and Russia tried in vain to convince the US that the transfer was only for a civilian space programme. Amidst relentless pressure from Washington, Yeltsin finally cancelled the parts of the cryogenic contract with India that dealt with the transfer of technology, but he went ahead with the transfer of seven cryogenic engine blocks to India. New Delhi was disappointed but not bitter. It also was prepared to accept that Moscow had done all it could to help boost India's launch vehicle programme.[8]

By the mid-1990s, however, matters had come full circle. As the romance with the West began to wear off in Moscow and the demands rose at home for a more assertive foreign policy, Russia once again began to look towards to its old relationships and tried to revitalize them. This new approach from Russia came in handy for India, which was waiting for such an opportunity. The arms supply relationship took off in the mid-1990s as Russia offered a full range of advanced weapons systems for India. Not only weapon systems but also transfers of technology were on offer. India and Russia were no longer looking at a buyer–seller relationship of arms but at joint development of technologies and systems and marketing them abroad under the Long-term Integrated Military Technical Cooperation Agreement of 1994. Initially meant for six years, this deal was extended in 1998 to 2010. Renewed defence cooperation covered the full spectrum—from the consideration of the *Admiral Gorshkov* aircraft carrier to the development and production of the cruise missile *Brahmos*. Other major items included the purchase and production of the Su-30, development of avionics for the Indian light combat aircraft, advanced air defence missiles, upgradation of old MiG aircraft, joint development of military and civilian transport aircraft and multiple-launch rocket systems, to name a few. At the turn of the millennium, Indo-Russian defence cooperation never looked better.

When Putin visited India in October 2000, his proclamation that India and Russia were once again strategic partners had a ring of truth. The rise of a powerful and purposeful leader in Russia brought considerable cheer to the Indo-Russian relations. No one had shed tears at the departure of Yeltsin, whose tenure was a period of extreme uncertainty for the bilateral relationship. Putin, who brought a measure of order, stability and economic progress at home, was also determined to pursue Russia's interests abroad with some consistency. Within the region that India and Russia shared was a renewed convergence of geopolitical interests. The common threats of religious extremism and terrorism, identified six years earlier by Yeltsin and Narasimha Rao during the latter's visit to Moscow, were no longer merely theoretical. The rise of the Taliban in Afghanistan made these threats real for both nations. Although India had faced the threat of terrorism for more than a decade, Russia had to deal with spectacular terrorist attacks on vulnerable urban targets. Moreover, the Russian wound in Chechnya kept bleeding Moscow much like Kashmir was draining Indian energies. With the sources of this threat leading to Afghanistan and Pakistan, it was inevitable that New Delhi and Moscow would draw closer.[9]

As the Taliban, backed by Pakistan, began to expand its territorial control over much of Afghanistan in the late 1990s, the Northern Alliance, led by Commander Ahmad Shah Masood, was holed up in the Panjsher Valley and on its last legs. The consolidation of the Taliban in Afghanistan, India feared, would end the regime's international isolation and lead to increased pressure by the Kashmiri militants. Russia feared that strengthening the Taliban would encourage the forces of extremism to cross the Amu Darya and undermine the regimes on Russia's southern borders and boost the Muslim rebels fighting in Chechnya. Russian forces were already guarding the frontiers of Tajikistan with Afghanistan, and the Taliban's consolidation would have accentuated the threats to the Russian security to the south. Beating back the Taliban became an urgent imperative for New Delhi and Moscow, and so together with Teheran, they began a coordinated effort to strengthen the Northern Alliance militarily. When the United States moved towards a war against the Taliban in Afghanistan after 11 September, Russia and India overrode the traditional domestic constituencies opposed to cooperation with the United States and were among the first countries to back Washington. As the global war on terrorism unfolded, New Delhi and Moscow stepped up bilateral cooperation in countering terrorism. During Putin's visit to New Delhi in December 2002, the two sides declared that 'as victims of terrorism having its roots in our common neighbourhood, we have particular interest in putting an end to this common threat through preventive and deterrent measures nationally and bilaterally'.[10]

Putin's emergence in Russia also heralded a positive phase in bilateral relations. Conceding the past neglect of India in the 1990s, Putin now pointed to an old Russian saying, 'One old friend is better than two new ones'.[11] Russia's new assertiveness in the global arena and its reluctance to toe the American line on issues of interest to it opened the door for an expansive new phase in cooperation with India on strategic technologies. Russia began to shed its reserve, seen immediately after the Indian nuclear tests, and move towards a rapid expansion of engagement in atomic energy and missile-related areas. In the mid-1990s, Russia revived the idea of the Kudankulam nuclear project. Likewise, since Putin's visit in 2000, Moscow renewed its interest in helping New Delhi boost its civilian atomic energy programme. Although the Russian supply of additional reactors beyond the original two would clash with Moscow's commitments under the NSG guidelines, the Putin administration was willing to consider it. Moscow drew criticism from the Western member states of the NSG for its decision in 2001 to supply enriched uranium fuel to India. Besides justifying the sale of enriched uranium to India as consistent with the NSG rules, Russia, along with France, argued that the restrictions against nuclear technology transfers to India must be relaxed.

The Russian policy on nuclear cooperation with India was based on the premise that India was already a nuclear weapons power and denying it advanced technologies in the name of preventing proliferation of nuclear weapons made no sense. To illustrate this judgement, Putin visited the Bhabha Atomic Research Centre (BARC) at Trombay, the heart of Indian nuclear weapons programme. His visit to BARC was the first by any top political leader of a nuclear weapons state, and it occurred less than two and a half years after India proclaimed itself as a state in possession of nuclear weapons. Furthermore, during Putin's visit the two countries announced a protocol on nuclear cooperation. Despite its best efforts along with those of France to change the international rules of nuclear commerce against India, Russia did not succeed. It had informed India in mid-2002 that New Delhi had to find a way of getting the Americans on board. A wink and nod from the US would be necessary.

During his visit to New Delhi at the end of 2002, Putin reaffirmed the Russian commitment to expand nuclear cooperation with India by selling additional nuclear reactors, but he said that this will have to take place

within the framework of our international obligations in the nuclear field . . . . We also believe that the rules and regulations of this framework require improvement. We have discussed our [nuclear] cooperation with India in detail. We are ready, prepared and willing to develop relations with India, including in the nuclear field.[12]

India was also pleased that Putin made a significant distinction between the Indian and Pakistani nuclear weapons programmes. On the eve of his visit to New Delhi, Putin expressed concern at the danger of Pakistani weapons falling into the hands of terrorists.[13] In effect he was calling for a tightening of the restrictions against nuclear transfers to countries like Pakistan while urging their liberalization in favour of India. Since the nuclear tests, India struggled to differentiate itself from Pakistan and seek a special exemption of the NSG rules on nuclear transfers for itself. Putin was effectively endorsing the Indian case.

There has been speculation that the Indo-Russian cooperation extends beyond civilian areas to the military application of nuclear energy.[14] Russia is believed to be assisting India to build a nuclear reactor for its nuclear submarine, providing a nuclear submarine on a three-year lease and also supplying India with 300-kilometre range Klub class cruise missiles that can be launched under water. These transfers could place in India's hands a sea-based deterrent and a sophisticated nuclear arsenal 'with a full-fledged triad of nuclear weapons'.[15] While much of the expansive nuclear cooperation in both civil and military fields had to be consolidated, the Indo-Russian relationship has progressed to a new phase of strategic significance.

Future Challenges
The Indo-Russian relationship survived the difficulties of the 1990s. Notwithstanding the fundamental changes in both countries and considerable doubts in their establishments about the future of the relationship, they re-established their strategic partnership. The upbeat mood characterizing Indo-Russian relations after the advent of Putin, however, has not dispelled all the imponderables in place. The unpredictability in the

evolution of Russian and Indian relations with the other major powers—in particular the United States and China—and the changing dynamics of Russian relations with Pakistan have left shadows over the Indo-Russian entente. In announcing their new strategic partnership, both countries were conscious that they must operate in a radically altered international context. Building a special relationship with the United States has been at the top of their agendas, and neither side wants to project their partnership as being directed at the United States, China or even Pakistan. At the same time, both countries emphasize the importance of the creation of a multipolar world that would give them some additional political space in the international structure dominated by the United States.

Striking this balance was at the centre of the declaration on strategic partnership signed during Putin's visit to India in October 2000. The declaration 'envisages the elevation of their multifaceted ties to an even higher and qualitatively new level, while imparting them with a specially close and dynamic character'.[16] Furthermore, it states that the Indo-Russian strategic partnership 'is not directed against any other State or group of States, and does not seek to create a military-political alliance'.[17] On the eve of his visit, Putin also expressed an understanding of India's quest for improved relations with the United States since the end of the cold war:

> The collapse of the Soviet Union changed the ideological foundation of our state. The communist ideology no longer dominates in Russia and our priorities have changed. Russia today does not see the US either as an enemy or an opponent. For Russia, today, the US—one of the world's major nations—is a partner. We have different views when it comes to the resolution of certain conflicts. We are in favour of a multipolar world, of respect for sovereignty and territorial integrity. We are holding discussions with our American partners on many of the issues. So, we welcome the fact that India is developing its relations with all countries, including the US.[18]

Sections of the Indian establishment see Putin's Russia returning to the old mode of confrontation with Washington. Such an assessment overlooks the fundamental transition in Russia's world view during the 1990s. Putin appears to have made a strategic choice that Russia's future lies in integrating with the West. Unlike the early post-Soviet decision makers, Putin's Kremlin will not simply cede ground but will bargain intensely on every issue to secure its position in world affairs. This new approach was visible in Putin's refusal to confront the United States after it announced plans in May 2001 to build the controversial national missile defence system. Likewise, after two years of intense campaigning against American plans to scrap the Anti-Ballistic Missile Treaty, Putin opted for quiet but intense negotiations with the United States on new agreements for strategic stability. Putin also avoided a confrontation with the United States on the expansion of the North Atlantic Treaty to Russian borders. The change in the Russian attitude was even visible in the way Russia reacted to the events of 11 September and after. Sensing a new moment in world affairs, Putin grabbed the opportunity to extend solid support to the American war on terrorism by overruling sceptics at home. Not only did Putin offer military cooperation with the United States, but he also winked at Washington's establishment of military bases in Central Asia, a possibility that had long worried Moscow.

Putin's new approach struck a political resonance in Washington. The Bush administration, which came to power in 2001 with quite a bit of the old baggage about the Russian threat, quickly embraced Russia as a potential ally. The frequent meetings between Bush and Putin during 2001-02 produced a new agreement on nuclear arms reductions and a plan for restructuring the relationship between offence and defence in the calculus of nuclear deterrence. More fundamentally, it has identified a full range of international issues—from combating international terrorism to the management of the international oil markets—on which the two sides could cooperate. Within

Europe, Russia was given a vote along with a voice in NATO's deliberations. On the key issue of trade relations, Washington agreed to drop some of the long-standing legislation that curbed bilateral commerce with Russia and to support Moscow's bid to join the World Trade Organization.

The new ties between Washington and Moscow mark the end of the last historic rivalry in the Euro-Atlantic world. For nearly four centuries, the rivalries among the Euro-Atlantic powers were the fundamental driver of international politics. The US-Russian rivalry throughout the twentieth century— except for a brief but intense cooperation during the Second World War—is now history. The irreversible integration of Russia into the West does not mean an end to their differences, but they are unlikely to degenerate into antagonism and confrontation.

The Indian government demonstrated some intuitive sense of this new stability when it supported American plans for missile defence while being fully aware of the Russian opposition to them. External Affairs Minister Jaswant Singh assessed on 1 May 2001 that Russia, despite its stated position, would not confront the US on the issue. Singh had an animated conversation on the subject with the Russian foreign minister, Igor Ivanov, when he arrived in New Delhi just hours after India announced its support. In the end the two sides agreed that they must maintain contact on the subject and that the transition to a new nuclear order, which India was very keen on, must be achieved in a peaceful and consultative manner.[19] The Indian gamble on Russia's stance on missile defence paid off.

New Delhi will constantly be tempted to join the Russians in their tactical campaigns against specific American policies, aimed at improving their own strategic bargaining position vis-à-vis Washington. Although the traditionalists in Indian foreign policy establishment would love to return to an old-style posturing against the US regardless of the outcomes, India has begun to resist that temptation and decide its positions on the basis of individual merit. For a pattern has emerged in Putin's engagement of the United States: put up stiff resistance on key issues, bargain hard and settle for a reasonable compromise. The expanding cooperation between Russia and the United States has given India more space, and there are also areas where all the three countries agree.

India is also likely to face complications from the changing Russian relations with two of its key neighbours—China and Pakistan. Although India's own relations with China have improved since the late 1980s, the pace of Sino-Russian rapprochement has been far faster in the 1990s. Given the uncertainties in the Sino-Indian relationship, the deepening of the Sino-Russian strategic partnership is of concern to India. Amidst its own internal debate on the prospects for a strategic triangle involving Russia, China and India, New Delhi has not paid enough attention to the dramatic expansion of the Sino-Russian relationship in the 1990s culminating in the signing of a strategic partnership agreement in July 2001. The density of Sino-Russian contacts—in economic, political and strategic terms—has slowly begun to overshadow that of the Indo-Russian relationship. With its better economic standing, China has been more adept than India at taking advantage of the Russian situation in the 1990s. While China was building a new relationship, India was trying to salvage the old one. The intensification of Sino-Russian ties includes military and technical cooperation and reported transfers of Russian technologies in the nuclear weapons and missile fields. India can only hope that geography and history as well as the Russian desire for integration into the West will impose some limitations on the partnership between Moscow and Beijing. While Russia has sought to play the China card in its attempts to improve both its international standing and the leverages in Washington, Moscow remains distrustful of Beijing.

Of more immediate concern to India has been Moscow's continued effort during the 1990s to renew its ties with Pakistan. The logic of the new international situation and Russian attempts to reconsider the old Soviet positions made it inevitable that post-Soviet Russia would take a fresh look at its South Asian policy. In the early 1990s, a strong view in Moscow demanded an end to the asymmetry in Russian relations with India and Pakistan. As India tried to revitalize its ties with the US and China—the cold war allies of Pakistan—Islamabad also made a consistent effort to encourage Moscow to take a more balanced approach to the subcontinent and end its tilt towards New Delhi. Political contacts between the civilian leadership of Pakistan and the new Russian establishment intensified, and they agreed to more political consultations and expanded economic relations, which had withered since the late 1960s. Technological contacts expanded in the space field too; for example, Russia agreed to launch Pakistan's satellites. Facing a cut-off in military cooperation with the United States in the 1990s, Pakistan also explored the possibility of purchasing arms and equipment from Russia.[20]

A number of factors, however, prevented the two from making progress. India applied intense diplomatic pressure on Russia to avoid moving too quickly towards a normalization of relations with Pakistan. New Delhi was dead set against Moscow initiating any arms transfers to Islamabad, and these Indian interventions turned out to be reasonably successful. Russia also had to calculate the potential losses on the Indian front in the event of a rapprochement with Pakistan. Furthermore, the political chaos in Russia and the instabilities in Pakistan during the 1990s prevented Russia from unveiling a comprehensive policy of engaging Pakistan. The situation in Afghanistan and Pakistan's support of extremist groups, including those operating in Chechnya, also proved to be major obstacles to the improvement of relations between Moscow and Islamabad. But the nature of the new security threats to Russia such as terrorism, narcotics trafficking and religious extremism from its southern borders has also encouraged some in Moscow to engage Pakistan in addressing these challenges. Given Pakistan's inability to deliver on these threats, it has been difficult to construct a solid relationship.

Nevertheless, under Putin's dispensation, Moscow appears to have made a strategic decision to bring some balance into its ties with New Delhi and Islamabad, because Moscow found the context of the great power relations with the subcontinental rivals unacceptable. While the US was expanding its leverages in both India and Pakistan and China was increasing its profile in India despite an expansive all-weather friendship with Pakistan, Russia found itself tilted towards India and with no standing in Pakistan. In an important signal, barely a couple of weeks before his visit to India in October 2000, Putin dispatched a special envoy to Pakistan. Although the visit was apparently meant to deal with the Russian difficulties arising from Afghanistan, it signalled a new strategy in Moscow. Throughout his visit to India, Putin refrained from saying anything on Indo-Pakistani relations or Kashmir that would be offensive to Pakistan. While emphasizing the importance of the war against terrorism, Putin avoided blaming Pakistan directly for cross-border terrorism in Kashmir and called for an Indo-Pakistani dialogue. In his address to the Indian Parliament, Putin said,

> We know at present what is going on in Kashmir. We share your concern about outbreaks of violence there. The fact that the Kashmir issue has not been settled, has been making the relations between India and Pakistan tense, worst over the last three decades. The issue can be resolved on a bilateral basis, on the basis of a compromise and on an unconditional respect for the Line of Control. Any foreign interference should be stopped.[21]

The new Russian approach came into sharp relief at an international conference in Almaty, Kazakhstan, where the three heads of government were represented. President Putin gave an impression in his meeting with General Musharraf that he might be prepared to mediate between India and Pakistan on Kashmir and wants to invite the Indian and Pakistani leaders to Moscow to promote a peace process. India had to move quickly to disabuse the Russians of any Indian interest in such a mediation.[22] Nevertheless, a new aspect of Russian policy towards South Asia stood out—Putin's interest in a balanced policy towards South Asia and an affirmation of its international responsibilities for the maintenance of peace and international security. This revised stand was also evidenced by a series of Russian statements during the Indo-Pakistani military confrontation after 13 December in which Moscow did not demand unambiguously that Pakistan put an end to cross-border terrorism before a dialogue could begin, a position that India would have liked to see. Unlike the Bush administration which backed India's line on negotiating with Pakistan, Moscow's focus has been on talks for a resolution of the conflict in Kashmir.[23]

India cannot operate on the premise that Russia will never build a political relationship with Pakistan. Nor can India hope for uncritical and total Russian support for every aspect of India's line on Kashmir and Pakistan. That phase in Indo-Russian relations may be over. Russia is in no position to ignore the geo-strategic importance of Pakistan—one of the world's largest countries and one armed with nuclear weapons and weilding some influence on Russia's southern borders. The Russian oil companies, now privatized and looking for opportunities worldwide, have begun to explore expanded energy cooperation with Pakistan.[24] Russia has apparently assured India that while it is set to engage Pakistan, its relations with India will always be on a stronger footing. Part of this assurance is apparently about a clear commitment that Moscow will not transfer arms to Pakistan. During his visit to India in December 2002, Putin again walked the tightrope on issues relating to the tensions between New Delhi and Islamabad. While he focussed on the imperative of a bilateral dialogue between India and Pakistan, the Indo-Russian joint statement issued at the end of the visit seemed to reflect the Indian position in full when it underlined the 'importance of Islamabad implementing in full its obligations and promises to prevent the infiltration of terrorists across the Line of Control . . . as a prerequisite for the renewal of peaceful dialogue between the two countries.'[25] While Putin was cautious, India was quite happy to focus on the joint statement's unambiguous formulation.

While the new dynamism in Russian relations with Pakistan, China and the US begins to inject some complexity into the ties between New Delhi and Moscow, India should be more worried about the stagnation in the economic and social ties between the two nations. India and Russia have managed to revive the cooperation in the military, technical and advanced technology sectors, but that is no substitute for a revitalized, broad-based economic and commercial engagement. Indo-Russian trade, minus arms, quickly declined from $5.5 billion in 1989 and stagnated at around $1.5 billion at the turn of the century. If the rupee–rouble trade of about $1 billion is taken out, the actual commercial flows do not amount to more than half a billion dollars. This pittance stands well below India's trade with Bangladesh or Sri Lanka. If the economic foundation of Indo-Russian ties begins to wobble, it might be difficult to sustain the larger relationship. Although there have been some high-profile projects like the Indian investment in the Sakhalin oil field in Siberia,[26] trade and investment flows between the two have become marginal.

The Indian private sector has been too timid explore the Russian market and take advantage of Russia's economic revival at the turn of the millennium. During Putin's visit to India at the end of 2002, the two sides began to explore the possibility of using Indian debt repayments to fund Russian investments in India, but India's long-term challenge is to rebuild the brand image of its products. As an observer of Indo-Russian relations says:

> Indian goods will need to compete for market space, unlike in the Soviet days when they were probably the only products available from a non-socialist country. This exercise should also address the damage done to the image of Indian brands by unscrupulous traders in the early 1990s when under the rupee-rouble trade, sub-standard products were supplied in an attempt to make a quick

buck. There is need for Indian businessmen, particularly the big business houses, to consider moving away from pure trade to investment in Russia.[27]

Besides adapting to the new economic conditions in Russia, the Indian establishment also needs to arrest the rapid decline in the contacts between the two civil societies. The old intensive state-sponsored interaction across a broad spectrum has fallen rapidly in the 1990s. Unless there is a conscious attempt to restore those links through private funding, the new political elites in Russia and India could begin to drift apart. For at least three generations, these elites have grown with a clear and positive view to the other, but as both look towards the West, they might begin to ignore each other.

SIX

Emulating China

Between Resentment and Rapprochement

Reacting to India's nuclear tests of May 1988, Chinese President Jiang Zemin expressed befuddlement at India citing China's nuclear arsenal as a reason for its defiance of the world. He recalled his happy visit to India and productive conversations with its leaders, and he wondered why they would want to resurrect the bogey of a Chinese threat.[1] For months after the tests, Chinese interlocutors would say that their leadership was offended by the Indian assertions immediately before and after the nuclear tests. India was equally surprised by China's intensely negative reaction. After all, China had nuclear weapons since 1964, and it had assisted Pakistan in acquiring them and undermined India's security condition in the 1980s and 1990s. Why was the pot calling the kettle black?[2]

In the 1990s India seemed to overcome the trauma of the 1962 war with China slowly and tried to normalize bilateral relations. The decade also exposed the fragility of the Sino-Indian normalization and the mutual wariness that underlay it. India's reference to the 1962 war with China in the letters it had sent out to international leaders explaining its tests showed the depth of scar on India's political psyche.

Nonetheless, India cannot run away from China. All the key issues of India's foreign policy—the incipient strategic partnership with the United States, its future role in the Asia, its military and political balance with Pakistan or the stabilization of the subcontinent—are intimately tied to the nature of its relationship with China. Handling the ties with Beijing is likely to be the biggest political challenge for Indian foreign policy in the coming decades.

Can India find a way to deal with China that is not encumbered by the self-doubt or romanticism that marked its past efforts? New Delhi is better placed at the turn of the twenty-first century than ever before to define a new course with its northern neighbour. The nuclear tests of May 1998, the improved economic performance of the 1990s and the positive evolution of India's relations with the United States in the changed international and regional context after the cold war have given India an opportunity for a realistic and productive engagement with China in the coming decades.

Prime Minister Rajiv Gandhi's historic visit to China in December 1988 ended the extended period of stasis in bilateral relations since 1962 and created a new political basis for bilateral relations. India restored full diplomatic relations with China in July 1976 and agreed to initiate discussions on the boundary dispute in 1981, but New Delhi refused to normalize relations with Beijing until after they had settled the boundary question. Moreover, the border talks were going nowhere. Gandhi recognized that the inflexible policy towards China had deepened India's security dilemmas within the region and constrained its relations with the major powers, and he boldly tried to overcome the huge political resistance and bureaucratic inertia in the Indian establishment to improve relations. The only earlier attempt to engage China was by Vajpayee, who despite the deep antagonism towards China among the right-wing Hindu nationalists, gambled on the prospects of a rapprochement with Beijing when he travelled there in February 1979. The controversial end to that visit, amidst the Chinese invasion of Vietnam, made it that much more risky for any other leader to attempt the same. Yet choosing to end India's unrealistic China policy, Gandhi moved towards a normalization of relations with China and found a framework to accelerate the negotiations on the boundary dispute at the same time. One factor that drove him was the judgement that India has willingly allowed a two-front problem to persist on its borders since 1962. Renewed military tensions on the disputed boundary with China during the mid-1980s necessitated an effort to bring peace and tranquillity on at least one front. Gandhi also saw the importance of creating an opening with China at a time when Beijing's relations with the West, Russia and Pakistan were getting stronger.

Gandhi's visit to Beijing reduced the salience of the boundary dispute in bilateral relations. During his visit, the two sides agreed to define a new mechanism, the Joint Working Group, to resolve the boundary dispute and move ahead with cooperation elsewhere. High-level political contacts intensified with the visit of Prime Minister Li Peng to India 1991 and Prime Minister Narasimha Rao to Beijing in 1993. President R. Venkataraman travelled to Beijing in 1992 and President Jiang to India at the end of 1996. The two sides agreed to maintain peace on the disputed border, and as part of that process they agreed to implement two sets of confidence-building measures in 1993 and 1996.[3] Although the agreements could not be implemented, because of the undesignated nature of the LAC,[4] the boundary itself became relatively quiet without the military tensions that were seen as late as 1986-87.[5] There was also the one-time nuclear cooperation between India and China, when the latter agreed in 1993-94 to supply low-enriched uranium fuel to the Tarapur reactors, built with American assistance in the 1960s.

One of the important diplomatic gains from the rapprochement with China was the broad shift in the Chinese position on Kashmir through the 1990s from an aggressively pro-Pakistani position on self-determination for Kashmiris in the 1970s to an emphasis on Indo-Pakistani bilateralism in the 1990s. Jiang himself told the Pakistani Senate in December 1996 that if the Kashmir issue could not be resolved immediately, then it should be put on the back burner and South Asia should concentrate on economic cooperation. Coming amidst an intensified Pakistani campaign to internationalize the Kashmir dispute, China's new position appeared to please India and surprise Pakistan. Although the evolution of the Chinese position on Kashmir satisfied New Delhi, it was uneasy at the implicit suggestion that Beijing was ready for a partnership with 'south Asia as a whole'.[6] This seemed to indicate that New Delhi was only one of Beijing's partners in the region.

Another element of Jiang's speech was a call for Sino-South Asian cooperation against hegemony, suggesting the need for the region to work along with China in opposing American domination.[7] Resisting US hegemony became a constant theme in Sino-Indian relations in the 1990s. Although improving its relations with the United States was its top priority, New Delhi went along with the slogan partly as an insurance against the uncertainty in Indo-US relations in the early 1990s. In India's and China's search for common political ground on the international arena, each was banking on the other side's problems with the United States. This cooperation was not entirely abstract. On a whole range of issues, from the question of global carbon emissions to resisting the US promotion of human rights, democratic India and communist China found it convenient to oppose the interventionist approaches of the Clinton administration. At the United Nations Commission on Human Rights in Geneva, India voted against Western attempts to condemn the human rights practices in China, and Beijing in turn put pressure on Pakistan to withdraw its condemnation of Indian human rights abuses in Kashmir.

Opposition to hegemonism at the global level, however, was not a strong enough force to overcome the regional security divide between India and China. The mutual distrust was reflected in the chill in bilateral relations that followed India's nuclear tests in May 1998. Although not in any way connected to the tests, they were preceded by a series of outbursts against China by the defence minister, George Fernandes. Given his sympathies for the movement for Tibetan independence and his long anti-China record, Fernandes's assessment that China was a bigger threat than Pakistan to national security began to

disturb China.[8] Beijing reacted in a relatively muted manner—
by expressing grave concern—after the first round of tests
announced by India on 11 May. Yet by the time the second
round took place on 13 May, Beijing condemned them and
noted that India had 'maliciously accused China of posing a
nuclear threat to India', which it called 'utterly groundless'.[9]
What intervened was a letter by Prime Minister Vajpayee to
President Clinton that justified the decision on the basis of the
threat from China. Vajpayee wrote:

> I have been deeply concerned at the deteriorating security
> environment, especially the nuclear environment, faced by India
> for some years past. We have an overt nuclear weapon state on our
> borders, a state which committed armed aggression against India
> in 1962. Although our relations with that country have improved
> in the last decade or so, an atmosphere of distrust persists mainly
> due to the unresolved border problem. To add to the distrust that
> country has materially helped another armed neighbour of ours to
> become a covert nuclear weapons state. At the hands of this bitter
> neighbour we have suffered three aggressions in the last 50 years.[10]

The letter, written in confidence to President Clinton and a
few other leaders, was leaked by Washington, an act which
embarrassed India and pushed the Sino-Indian relations into a
freeze. The missive was strongly criticized at home for wantonly
undermining the relations with China that were on the upward
curve over the previous two decades. New Delhi was also
accused of being daft in trying to raise the China bogey with
the United States at a time when Washington was all set to
proclaim Beijing a strategic partner, which indeed happened in
June 1998 when Clinton visited China and issued a strong joint
statement with the Chinese leaders on preventing nuclear
proliferation in the subcontinent. Instead of separating the US
from China, the letter appeared to push Washington and Beijing
together in their opposition to Indian nuclear tests.

There was speculation in New Delhi about who was

responsible for this controversial letter. In the weeks after Pokhran-II, there was no full-time Cabinet minister in charge of external affairs. It was a post held by Vajpayee himself. Many of the immediate statements issued immediately after the nuclear tests were believed to have been drafted under the supervision of the Principal Secretary to the Prime Minister, Brajesh Mishra.

Mishra was unapologetic about the letter, which did not achieve the immediate objective of distancing Washington from Beijing. Nevertheless, it did tap a small but growing sentiment in the US that India could be a potential nuclear rival to China. Mishra, a former Foreign Service officer who had served in Beijing and is known for his plain speaking, had Vajpayee's confidence and is known to have been one of the driving forces behind the nuclear tests. The letter captured the essence of India's concerns with China despite the decade-long improvement in relations between the two nations. It reminded the world that despite the focus on Indo-Pakistani tensions as the principal driver of India's nuclear programme, the original impulse of India's nuclear weapons debate was the first Chinese test in 1964 that followed so soon after the 1962 debacle. It also put four-square the Indian anger against the Chinese aid to Pakistan's nuclear weapons programme in the 1980s and its missile programme in the 1990s.

For more than a decade, India resented that China helped Pakistan neutralize the superior Indian military capabilities with nuclear weapons as part of a strategy of boxing New Delhi within the subcontinent. In its own efforts to improve relations with China since 1988, India appeared hesitant to broach New Delhi's strong concerns on Beijing's nuclear and missile assistance to Pakistan in the higher level political engagement between the two nations. China hands in the Ministry of External Affairs had no real explanation for the Indian political leadership's reluctance to broach the unpleasant but extremely important national security concern face to face with Beijing. Officially China issued bland denials on the question of its support of Pakistan's nuclear and missile programmes. The long-simmering frustration had to boil over, as it did in Vajpayee's letter. After the nuclear tests, China finally dropped its reluctance to engage India on nuclear issues, both global and regional. A formal annual security dialogue that started in March 2000 provided a forum for India to raise its concerns on China's nuclear and missile cooperation with Pakistan as well as broader questions of nuclear arms control.[11]

Although China took strong umbrage at Vajpayee's letter, it was a matter of time before the two sides began the painful process of re-engaging each other. New Delhi downplayed the significance of the letter and reaffirmed its commitment to maintain good relations with China. Beijing insisted that India must make the first move, asserting that 'he who tied the knot should untie it'.[12] At his meeting with the Chinese foreign minister in Manila at the Asian Regional Forum in July 1998, Jaswant Singh, the then-deputy chairman of the Planning Commission, told reporters accompanying him he insisted that 'it takes two hands to untie any knot'.[13] Nevertheless, India was determined to limit the damage to Sino-Indian relations. Brajesh Mishra issued a statement to mollify the Chinese sentiments at the end of October 1998 declaring that India did not see China as a threat nor did it have any intention of pursuing a nuclear arms race with China.

A series of high-level exchanges set the tone for normalization of bilateral relations. External Affairs Minister Jaswant Singh visited China in July 1999, President K.R. Narayanan went in May 2000, and Brajesh Mishra made an unannounced visit to Beijing at the end of 2000. In the other direction, Foreign Minister Tang Jiaxuan came to India in July 2000 followed by Chairman of the National People's Congress Li Peng in January 2001 and Premier Zhu Rongji in February 2002. Although it may have had to meet Chinese conditions for normalization of bilateral relations, India was quite pleased to have redefined, through its overt nuclear posture the psychological framework of bilateral relations with China. The sense of inferiority complex that dominated India since 1962 was doused by India acquiring nuclear parity of a sort and normalizing relations with China without too much of a political cost.

Nevertheless, the nuclear developments at the end of the 1990s brought into full relief the relationship's enduring challenges. India's worries about the relationship between China and Pakistan reflected its larger concern about China's intentions in India's own backyard. Also in view were the apprehensions in both the capitals about the relationship of the other with the sole superpower, the United States. If Clinton's visit to Beijing in June 1998 alarmed New Delhi about the prospect of a Sino-American condominium, or joint hegemony, over the subcontinent, warming relations between India and the United States in the new century raised the apprehensions in Beijing about New Delhi joining the American containment plans against China. Besides the global flux that was generating concerns in both capitals and the clashing interests in the region, all the difficulties in bilateral relations— the boundary dispute, China's concerns about India's policy towards Tibet, India's frustration at China's reluctance to formally recognize Sikkim as part of India, and New Delhi's anxieties about the strategic nexus between Islamabad and Beijing remained to be addressed.

From Envy to Emulation
As China's standing in world affairs expanded by leaps and bounds in the last two decades of the twentieth century, India was increasingly dismayed at its own steady marginalization in the international system. In all the new comparisons between the two Asian neighbours who entered the modern world at around the same time, India appeared to fall behind in every single indicator of national power and social prosperity. India's friends abroad and its adversaries were despondent that New Delhi lagged behind China in terms of flows of investment and trade even after a decade of reforms. While many in India

and abroad argued that India was no longer in a position to catch up with China, restoring the balance with China became an unstated national strategic objective for India during the 1990s. The principal means of achieving parity with China was to emulate it rather than suffer forever from political envy.

India's nuclear diplomatic strategy in the 1990s was similar to China's in the 1960s. Both had to break out of the emerging international constraints on their nuclear ambitions and adopt a moral posture that would help legitimize their attempts to join the nuclear club. After denouncing the global nuclear order as discriminatory and hegemonic, both eventually sought to gain a modus vivendi with the international regime. As Beijing prepared to conduct its first atomic tests in 1964, the 1963 agreement between United States and Russia to end nuclear testing in the atmosphere got in the way. While much of the world, including India, welcomed the Partial Test Ban Treaty (PTBT), the Chinese communists denounced it as a plot by the US and the Soviet Union to maintain their global hegemony. The Chinese argument against nuclear arms control, on ideological grounds, continued against the NPT of 1968 despite the fact that the treaty preserved Beijing's position as a recognized nuclear weapons state. But in the 1980s as China joined the global mainstream, it ended its long-standing opposition to arms control regimes. It joined various treaties including the PTBT and the NPT by the early 1990s.

Just as China was entering the global nuclear order, India had to step up its traditional opposition to various arms control treaties that constrained its own freedom of action. While China took nearly two decades to reconcile with the international nuclear order, India had to do it in less than two years. Having declared itself a nuclear weapons power, New Delhi agreed to respect the spirit of the CTBT and also extended support to the NPT in a bid to demonstrate its position as a responsible nuclear power. The emphasis on no-first-use of nuclear weapons by both Beijing and New Delhi could be seen as part of the attempt to differentiate themselves from the Western nuclear powers and retain the high moral ground even as they acquired nuclear weapons.

India's nuclear doctrine also reflected some of China's pragmatism. As they declared themselves nuclear weapons powers, both countries consciously sought to avoid the impression that they wanted to engage in a nuclear arms race. Although China demonstrated its nuclear capability in October 1964, it wisely refused to follow the road taken by United States and Russia in building a large arsenal. Just as China proclaimed its faith in a minimum nuclear deterrent, India too decided fairly quickly after the tests that it does not have to embark on a huge nuclear weapons programme. Like China, India viewed nuclear weapons as political instruments. Both saw them more as strategic insurance against extreme threats and a symbol of their own aspirations in the international system rather than as weapons usable in a war. Although China might be tempted to veer away from the ideas of minimum deterrence following the renewed American bid to build a missile defence system, India is likely to focus on a modest nuclear capability for the foreseeable future.

Although acquiring psychological nuclear parity with China was an important concern for the Indian governments in the last decade of the twentieth century, the long-term competition with China, New Delhi understood, lay in accelerating the pace of India's economic growth. In just one generation, China's reforms have produced one of the world's largest economies, and on that basis China has become the second most powerful country in the international system. A decade after the launch of reforms, India remains mired in self-doubt. It is hesitant to make a clean break with the past and seek power and prosperity as China has done.

The Indian political class justifies the slow pace of reforms in the name of democracy and the difficulty of generating consensus on complex policy issues. Many Indian analysts argue that the absence of political pluralism in China makes it easy for the communist party to press ahead with necessary but unpopular reforms. Democracy or the lack of it can only explain a small part of the reality in China and India. China might not have a democratic system, but it has a thriving political culture. The communist leadership manages many competing interests within the party and outside it, and Chinese politics in the last two decades have been about defining the pace and direction of its reforms. The Chinese communists reconciled the demands of economic change with the opposition from sectoral interests and bent ideology to fit the policy requirements. They buried past slogans and invented new ones to suit present realities. Equally important has been the unfinished Chinese debate about the tension between modernization and Westernization and finding the right relationship between China and the West.

The very same issues are at the heart of the politics of reform in India. Yet the outcomes have been very different. The Chinese leadership, following the debacle of the cultural revolution, acknowledged by the end of the 1970s the need for the unadulterated modernization of China by drawing closer to the West. Despite the ravages from decades of state-led socialism, India continues to pretend that the old order works. In India economic reforms had to be undertaken at a juncture when the old anti-Western mindsets on the Left remain persistent and anti-modernist forces on the Right have been on the ascent. Indian leaders have preferred to tinker with the old order and undertake reform by stealth rather than with bold conviction.

Although India's reforms have been slow in comparison to China's, there is a strong view in India and abroad that the internal changes in the 1990s have given New Delhi at least a chance to stay in the economic race with China. India's own intensifying globalization has given a basis for New Delhi to advance steadily in the coming decades, even if it cannot maintain the scorching pace of the Chinese reforms. The diplomatic and political gains from the expanding economic size have already become visible for India in the 1990s. This centrist view of India's potential to make a mark vis-à-vis China is flanked by two extreme ideas: one suggests that India has no real chance of catching up with China, and the other purports that the Indian tortoise will ultimately win the economic race against the Chinese hare. The argument is that while China has moved rapidly ahead on the economic front, it has huge internal political problems that could explode at some point in the not too distant future. India, on the other hand, has moved slowly while strengthening its democratic political infrastructure.

On the diplomatic front too, India's new foreign policy in the 1990s seemed to take after China's realism. India's toning down of the earlier rhetoric on non-alignment and reluctance to put itself in front of the battle against the United States and the West was very similar to China's de-ideologization of its foreign policy during the Dengist phase. Deng advised his foreign policymakers 'keep a cool head, maintain a low profile and never take the lead'. This simple slogan summed up the twenty-eight-character strategy, which Deng raised after the Tiananmen incidents of 1989 when China faced economic sanctions from the West and the disintegration of communism in Russia and East Europe. The twenty-eight characters of Deng's slogan had seven phrases: watch and analyse (developments) calmly, secure (our own) positions, handle (changes) with confidence, conceal (our) capacities, be good at keeping a low profile, never become the leader and make some contributions.[14]

Deng's advice held equally well for India at the turn of the 1990s. Whether or not Narasimha Rao heard Deng's dictum, India's post-cold war foreign policy followed the pattern prescribed by the Chinese leader. Of particular significance was Deng's proposition not to get deluded by a false sense of leadership of the developing world. In his talk to the leading members of the Central Committee of the Communist Party of China in 1990, Deng outlined his strategy:

> Some developing countries would like China to become the leader of the Third World. But we absolutely cannot do that—this is one

of our basic state policies. We can't afford to do it and besides, we aren't strong enough. There is nothing to be gained by playing that role; we would only lose most of our initiative . . . . We do not fear any one, but we should not give offense to anyone either.[15]

Although Narasimha Rao never made such a speech, his counsel for himself in the first half of the 1990s could not have been very different. Focusing on economic modernization and keeping a low international political profile became the central themes of India's foreign policy after the cold war.

India also emulated China in reaching out to the United States in the 1990s. 'Doing a China on China' is what Venu Rajamony, the political counsellor in the Indian mission in Beijing from 1999 to 2002, called India's wooing of the United States in a manner similar to Deng's structuring of an alliance with Washington at the turn of the 1980s.[16] He points to the emerging concerns in China on the potential threat from improving Indo-US relations. 'In China's perception, India, by virtue of its geo-political situation, naval capabilities, unresolved bilateral disputes and history of hostility with China, is an ideal country for the United States to have on its side in the eventuality of any conflict' with China.[17] Rajamony also suggests that a number of factors contributed to a fundamental reassessment of India in Beijing at the turn of the century, and these include 'a) India's nuclear tests b) India's success in multidirectional diplomacy, including in particular with the United States c) China's need for India to be a partner in the building of a multi-polar world d) the decline of Pakistan as an asset and e) India's recent economic success.'[18] For a country that was virtually written off by Beijing as an unlikely rival, India surprised China in the late 1990s.

Managing Regional Competition
Although a sense of equanimity has come to settle upon the various bilateral disputes between India and China, their competition for influence in South Asia remains a major source

Prime Minister Rajiv Gandhi in conversation with Deng Xiaoping during his historic visit to Beijing, December 1988. This visit opened doors for a renewed engagement between the Asian giants.

Prime Minister P.V. Narasimha Rao with Russian President Boris Yeltsin in New Delhi, January 1993, when the two sides began to salvage the bilateral relationship after the collapse of the Soviet Union.

US President Bill Clinton and Narasimha Rao at the White House, May 1994, when they were attempting to narrow differences on the nuclear and Kashmir questions.

Indian envoy Arundhati Ghose at the CTBT talks in Geneva, August 1996. Her refusal to sign the treaty marked the transformation of India's nuclear objectives in the 1990s.

Chinese President Jiang Zemin with External Affairs Minster I.K. Gujral, President S.D. Sharma and Prime Minister H.D. Deve Gowda in New Delhi, November 1996. The bilateral relations soured after the May 1995 nuclear tests.

Prime Minister of Bangladesh Sheikh Hasina with Deve Gowda and Gujral and Foreign Minister of Bangladesh Abdul Samad Azad in New Delhi, December 1996. The visit launched a positive phase in Indo-Bangla relations.

Prime Minister Atal Bihari Vajpayee at the Pokhran nuclear test site, May 1998. India's declaration of itself as a nuclear weapons power was a defining moment in its new foreign policy.

US Deputy Secretary of State Strobe Talbott and External Affairs Minister Jaswant Singh during nuclear talks in New Delhi, August 1998. Their many rounds of talks turned out to be the first substantive dialogue on security issues between the two nations.

Vajpayee on his arrival in Pakistan, February 1999. Also seen are (from left to right) Indian film star Dev Anand, Pakistani Prime Minister Nawaz Sharif, Jaswant Singh and National Security Adviser Brajesh Mishra. The expectations raised by this famous bus journey collapsed within weeks, as India discovered Pakistan's aggression in the Kargil sector.

Indian soldiers during the Kargil War, June 1999. In the war India gained international support for its nuclear restraint. The world also pressured Pakistan to respect the sanctity of the LoC.

Vajpayee meeting the Prime Minister of Nepal, G.P. Koirala, in New York, September 2000. The two leaders struggled to manage the growing complexity in bilateral ties.

President Vladimir Putin with the chairman of the Atomic Energy Commission, R. Chidambaram, at the Bhabha Atomic Research Centre, Trombay, November 2000. This visit signalled Russia's acceptance of India as a nuclear weapons power and Moscow's readiness to transfer sensitive technologies to India.

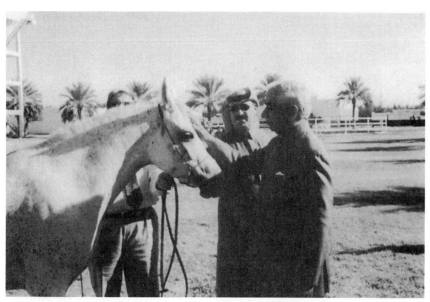

Jaswant Singh at Saudi Crown Prince Abdullah's horse farm near Riyadh, January 2001. This was the first visit by an Indian external affairs minister to the desert kingdom.

Vajpayee with US Deputy Secretary of State Richard Armitage in New Delhi, May 2001. Armitage visited after the unexpected Indian support to the Bush administration's controversial missile defence plan.

Vajpayee with Pakistan's President General Pervez Musharraf at Agra, July 2001. Also seen are Commerce Minister Murasoli Maran and Home Minister L.K. Advani. It was a summit that raised hopes for peace and shattered them, all in one weekend.

Vajpayee and US President George W. Bush in New York, September 2002. The meeting helped consolidate the forward movement in bilateral relations.

of bilateral tension and uncertainty in the region as a whole. More specifically, the expanding political influence of China in the subcontinent, and in particular its strategic relationship with Pakistan, has been an important concern for New Delhi in the last two decades of the twentieth century.

China scholar John W. Garver argues that the overlapping spheres of influence sought by India and China in South and South-East Asia has been a fundamental source of tension between the two Asian giants, each with its own exalted sense of its place in the world and Asia. While India believes that the subcontinent and its environs are its natural security zone, China believes that it cannot let India exercise dominance on its southern borders. Garver asserts that the Indian perception of the Chinese policies in the subcontinent amounts to a 'strategic encirclement', while Beijing sees its polices as being aimed at preventing 'Indian hegemony' in the subcontinent.[19] Garver narrates the steady advances China has made in the subcontinent in the teeth of Indian opposition. He notes that India's ability to maintain primacy in its own security zone in the subcontinent has tended to decline. The rise of Chinese influence in the subcontinent and its environs over the last two decades—in the form of deepening strategic relations with Pakistan; a new position in Myanmar; and expanding links with Nepal, Bangladesh and Sri Lanka—has taken place at a time of increasing complexity of India's own relations with its immediate neighbours in the subcontinent.

India's position is not as hopeless as Garver makes it out to be. In coping with the strategic challenge from China, India cannot hope to restore the status quo ante but must find new ways of managing it. In the age of globalization and economic integration, the proposition that dominated Indian thinking for five decades—to maintain exclusive relationships with its smaller neighbours like Bhutan, Nepal, Sri Lanka and Bangladesh and retain a veto over their relationships with the other great powers cannot be sustained. The quest for a new approach to the neighbours has been at the centre of the Indian foreign policy debate throughout the 1990s and was most explicitly articulated in the form of the Gujral Doctrine in the mid-1990s. India is increasingly conscious of the need to modernize the traditional special relationships with Bhutan and Nepal and find ways to sort out the many outstanding issues with its neighbours even if it demands walking more than half the distance. Although the debate on how to deal with the neighbours has been inconclusive, the new international trends might in fact facilitate the integration of the region under Indian primacy.

Thus the question of whether India should try to keep China out of the geopolitics of the region or accommodate its rise in the subcontinent is inaccurately framed. On the economic front, New Delhi cannot prevent increased Chinese presence in the subcontinent, including India. China is racing to become the second largest economy in the world and has joined the World Trade Organization. Hence all the South Asian nations will find it inevitable and mutually beneficial to expand their economic engagement with China. The political challenge for India is not to stop Chinese economic presence in the subcontinent but to increase its own commercial integration with its neighbours. The liberalization of all the South Asian economies under the pressure of globalization has given India a historic opportunity to integrate the smaller economies of the subcontinent into its own. While China could contribute to the economic development of the region, the geographic conditions are in favour of an integration with India.

A confident India could in fact leverage China's growing economic presence to achieve its own objective of regional integration in South Asia. But the old fears of China persist in the security establishment that has tended to block Chinese initiatives for transregional economic integration. India has been reluctant to support China's Kunming proposals that call for greater economic cooperation between eastern India, south-west China, Myanmar and Bangladesh. During President Narayanan's visit to Kunming in June 2000, the provincial authorities formally made a presentation to him on the subject and sought India's support to this idea of economic cooperation between the eastern part of the subcontinent and China.[20] While optimists see this as a potentially useful instrument to develop India's north-eastern regions and help integrate northern Myanmar and Bangladesh into a single economic zone, the pessimists see it as a Chinese plot to swamp the sensitive Indian North-East. While avoiding economic integration with China, India is pushing ahead with its own ideas for regional economic cooperation without Chinese presence. In the late 1990s it began to take steps to raise its profile in Myanmar, competing with China on a small scale to build roads and take up other strategic projects.[21]

India has also been trying to promote the Bangladesh-India-Myanmar-Sri Lanka-Thailand Economic Cooperation (BIMST-EC) that started in 1997. But BIMST-EC as a transregional organization linking the subcontinent with South-East Asia has not really taken off because of the economic crisis in South-East Asia. In 2000, India undertook the Ganga–Mekong project, a new initiative that calls for greater cultural and economic cooperation between the countries of the Ganga and Mekong Basins.[22] The proposal, however, leaves out China, through which the Mekong runs, and Bangladesh, where the Ganges ends. It includes India and five South-East Asian nations, Myanmar, Thailand, Laos, Cambodia and Vietnam. The first meeting of the initiative took place at the level of foreign ministers at Vientiane, Laos, in November 2000 and outlined a broad range of cooperation—first in tourism, culture and education and later in the transport and infrastructure sectors.[23]

Despite the Indian claims that the proposal was not aimed against China, which was developing its own Mekong Basin initiative with Indo-China, the sense of a Sino-Indian rivalry has dominated the perception of Indian initiatives for transregional cooperation. In the immediate term, India is not an economic rival to China in South-East Asia, but more rapid internal development in the coming years and a bolder regional policy could position India to engage China in healthy commercial competition without generating political antagonism.

Managing the growing Chinese political influence in the subcontinent appears a bigger challenge, yet here again the answer may not lie in holding on to the old ways of doing business with India's smaller neighbours. In the changed world, India cannot successfully exercise a veto over the relations of its neighbours with the major powers and China in particular.

Despite the considerable advances, China's relationships remain less than threatening. With its smaller neighbours, India's challenge lies less in confronting China than in modernizing and transforming New Delhi's own ties with them. That task is worth doing on its own merit and not as an imperative of coping with the growing Chinese influence in the region. For India's neighbours too, while Chinese political support is welcome, the resolution of their internal and external security problems remains intimately tied to Indian policies. There is no escaping that geographic reality. Further, the international context of India's relations with its smaller neighbours has been transformed—in the past both the United States and China sought to chip away at Indian and Russian influence in the subcontinent. An emerging Sino-American rivalry and an Indo-US entente could alter the dynamics of the region.

The Sino-Pakistani relationship remains in a category of its own. China's active assistance in making Pakistan a nuclear weapons and missile power, eroding Indian conventional superiority over Pakistan and giving Islamabad the freedom to engage in low-intensity conflict against New Delhi have been the most negative developments from the Indian perspective. That China allowed Pakistan to gain nuclear parity with India will remain a long-standing Indian grievance, and it is made that much more worse by the reality that it could not constrain China in any manner. The only pressure to modify Chinese strategic support to Pakistan has come in the 1990s from the United States, which tried to get China to abide by its non-proliferation commitments, but with limited effect. India's own hopes that the positive evolution of Sino-Indian relations in the 1990s would encourage China to change its approach on nuclear and missile issues to Pakistan were not realized. The resultant bitterness came out in Vajpayee's letter to Clinton. Optimists in India as well as some Chinese academics have often pointed out that the Chinese nuclear and missile transfers were a spillover from its cold war approach to the region, and they will continue to be limited as Sino-Indian relations improve and as India's economic and political weight in the Chinese calculus increases. Nonetheless, officials have continued to defend these sales as part of 'normal military trade' between nations and similar to India's own military acquisitions from Russia.[24] While China will neither acknowledge nor apologize for its past nuclear liaison, for India the real question is about the future nuclear and missile transfers to Pakistan.

In handling this threat, India seems to have dealt itself a new card—missile defence. India's surprising support to President Bush's plans for missile defence was partly rooted in the desperate quest to counter Chinese nuclear and missile proliferation in its neighbourhood. Until the reassertion of American interest in missile defence, India had no option but to lodge weak protests in Beijing. The prospects for an effective future missile defence over the long term and political and strategic cooperation with the United States in the near term offer India an opportunity to change the dynamics of Sino-Pakistani nuclear nexus, which have bothered India for nearly two decades.

Unlike in the area of nuclear and missile cooperation, China's stand on Indo-Pakistani issues underwent some adjustment in the 1990s. President Jiang's call to put Kashmir on the back burner during his visit to the subcontinent in 1996 was seen as the culmination of Chinese reassessment of its approach to Indo-Pakistani tensions. Although there were some modifications to this in China's immediate post-Pokhran reactions, its neutrality in the Kargil conflict between India and

Pakistan in the summer of 1999, its reluctance to bail out Nawaz
Sharif from his misadventure and its endorsement of the Indian
position that the Line of Control must be respected have been
seen in India as another indicator of Beijing's intent to pursue
a more balanced policy in the subcontinent.[25] Sceptics, however,
suggest that if Pakistan continues to become relatively weaker
than India, Beijing might have a strong interest in stepping up
its support to Islamabad to prevent this outcome as well as
increased Pakistani dependence on the United States.

Pessimists in India see basic limits to India's ability to drive
a wedge between China and Pakistan or even neutralize China
in the Indo-Pakistani conflicts. The perceived Chinese
neutrality in Kargil conflict is seen by some as the lack of any
other credible policy option for Beijing. An overt support to
Pakistan's unjustifiable aggression in Kargil would have
deepened Indian hostility towards China and irreparably
damaged the relations. Even indirect support to Pakistan in the
form of an immediate ceasefire would have been seen in India
as a way of legitimizing the aggression. Such calls would have
been untenable in any case, given the American pressure on
Pakistan to withdraw unconditionally and unambiguously from
across the Line of Control. Some have seen Beijing's approach
to the Kargil conflict not as a favour to India but as the projection
of a China that 'stands above' the subcontinental rivalries and
plays a constructive role along with the United States in
managing them. India recognizes that the Chinese standing in
the world, in Asia and in its own neighbourhood has dramatically
expanded in the last two decades of the twentieth century, but
it is not a trend that India wants to let go uncontested. At the
turn of the century, India is ready to contest China's new-found
gains in the region without initiating a fully-fledged confrontation.

Towards a Pragmatic China Policy

The many-faceted emulation of its neighbour to the North in
the 1990s has begun to alter the framework that has governed
Sino-Indian relations during the 1980s and 1990s and generated

a variety of policy options for India in coping with the rise of China. The nuclear tests of May 1998 have given India the long-sought nuclear equivalence, if not parity, with China. To be sure, India is some distance away from acquiring operational parity in terms of longer-range nuclear delivery systems. As India's Agni missile programme continues to move forward, it is a matter of a few years before the country will have a deployable and credible nuclear deterrent against China. India's nuclear tests have not made any significant immediate impact on the nuclear doctrine and force structure of China, but further advances in India's nuclear and missile programme will eventually force Beijing to factor India's nuclear weapons into its strategic calculus. Indian movement towards deployment of longer-range missiles could end Beijing's traditional dismissal of India's nuclear and great power aspirations. Coupled with the nuclear tests has been India's massive plans for military modernization based on a deepening military industrial cooperation with Russia; sourcing high-technology weapons from Israel, including systems that were denied to China; and likely acquisition of force multipliers from the United States, such as the P-3 Orion aircraft. Because India has never had such diverse sources of advanced weapons as it had since the turn of the century, China will have to deal with a significant military power on its borders in the future.

India's great power diplomacy since the Pokhran tests has positioned the country in an advantageous situation in Asia for the first time since the 1950s. Its expanding engagement with the United States and its ability to retain a partnership with Russia has given it significant strategic space. Much like China in the 1980s when there was all-round improvement in China's relations with the major powers, India has enjoyed a quiet revival of ties with the constellation of great powers in the late 1990s. India's search for a 'natural alliance' with the United States has introduced new dynamism into the triangular relationship among New Delhi, Washington and Beijing. Occurring at a moment when Sino-US relations have entered into an uncertain phase, India's warming ties with the United States have forced Beijing to reconsider its own relations with New Delhi. An expanding Indo-US relationship has been accompanied by a higher Indian profile in South-East Asia, where many nations see New Delhi as a natural partner in maintaining the balance of power in the region. Although India remains concerned about China's expanding influence in the subcontinent, New Delhi is rediscovering its potential to develop a strategic profile in China's backyard. India's deepening of strategic ties with Vietnam and its growing military diplomacy in the region, including naval exercises in South China Sea and its initiation of military cooperation with Japan, reflect the new trend of Indian assertiveness. In the past, India's intervention in Indo-China and South-East Asia was tied to its relationship with the Soviet Union and was resisted by many pro-Western regimes. In the future it will be part of a cooperative effort with the United States and, consequently, far more credible and acceptable. Yet it is unlikely that India will wantonly confront China and become a front-line state in a potential American containment of Beijing. In the immediate future, India is likely to pursue simultaneous improvement in relations with both countries.

An important change in Indian policy towards China was its relationship with Taiwan. Until 1991, India had a One China Policy that was incredible in its utter lack of pragmatism. If India's policy of not recognizing Taiwan as the legitimate representative of Chinese people in 1949 was understandable, New Delhi's refusal to deal at all with Taipei made little sense. It looked even more incredible as the US and its allies recognized the People's Republic of China in the late 1970s and found a framework in which to deal with Taiwan without diplomatic recognition. India, however, refused, despite the expanding Cross Straits links between China and Taiwan in the 1980s. It was only in 1991, when India began to look around desperately to manage its balance of payments crisis that New Delhi turned towards Taiwan. As part of a new pragmatism that began to dawn on Indian foreign policy, India chose to deal with Taiwan directly by setting up the India-Taipei Association in 1994. It began to post senior Foreign Service officers to head the mission after 'retiring' them from the service.[26] By the turn of the century India was discovering the confidence to post regular Foreign Service officers to the second-rung jobs in the mission in Taiwan. Future heads of the Indian mission could be serving Indian Foreign Service officers.

Through the 1990s trade links between India and Taiwan grew steadily.[27] Yet New Delhi went to great lengths to avoid giving any political offence to Beijing by keeping its activities in Taiwan on a very low key, avoiding posting officers who had been to China and severely restricting senior officials of the government, let alone ministers, from travelling to Taiwan. There is disappointment in Taiwan that India is hypersensitive to Chinese concerns and has not been willing to develop political relations along the lines of many other countries in Asia that have faced no serious objections from Beijing. Taiwan is keen on all-round development of bilateral relations—including economic partnership, high-level political contact and even strategic ties. Taiwanese officials and academics are direct in wanting to know why India is unwilling to cooperate with them in advanced technology areas when China has hurt India so badly by assisting Pakistan with nuclear weapons and missiles. Although some anti-China elements in India have often urged New Delhi to play the Taiwan card, New Delhi is likely to remain extremely cautious in the development of ties with Taipei. Having established ties with Taiwan, India might want to give them a strategic dimension, but only under extreme provocation from China. Meanwhile, Beijing has begun to demand from New Delhi unambiguous formal assertions that Taiwan is an integral and inseparable part of China.

The last decade of the twentieth century has created the basis for a rapid expansion of Sino-Indian economic relations. Trade between the two countries has grown by leaps and bounds at the turn of the century—nearly 30 per cent annually—to reach nearly $4.5 billion in 2002. During Premier Zhu Rongji's visit to India in January 2002, it was agreed by both sides to boost it to $10 billion in a few years. For the first time in decades, India and China appear ready to give economics a larger role in driving their relationship forward. Bangalore and Shanghai rather than New Delhi and Beijing are likely to set the pace for future ties between the two nations. Despite its campaign against Chinese dumping in Indian markets, Indian businesses are becoming increasingly aware of the opportunities in the Chinese market. But there is also a concern in China that New Delhi might use security arguments to limit Chinese investment in some sectors and sensitive geographic areas in India.

The expansion of commercial ties and greater flow of people across the borders is likely to end their long-standing ignorance of each other's culture. Despite being two large civilizations with a long history of productive interaction, there has been very little engagement between the two societies in the last five decades. Both China-lovers and China-baiters in India have operated in an intellectual vacuum that had little understanding of Chinese society and its internal dynamics. The same also holds true for China, where India's culture and politics remain mysteries. That is bound to change. The greater self-assurance in India today vis-à-vis China has already begun to put the challenge of China in a more realistic perspective.

During the 1990s, a new pragmatism began to enter the Indian debate on the traditional difficulties such as boundary dispute, Sikkim's relations with China and Tibet. New Delhi believes that it can deal with these issues with patience and persistence and without the excessive political anxiety that coloured its earlier positions. On the boundary dispute, the BJP came to power determined to accelerate the talks with China.[28] Once the nuclear shenanigans with China were over, Jaswant Singh started pressing for an early clarification of the LAC. Both in his visit to China in June 1999 and in a letter he wrote to his counterpart, Tang Jiaxuan, in April 2000, Singh wanted to step up the pace of talks on LAC clarification.[29] The issue was taken up at the highest level by President Narayanan during his visit to China in 2000. In his talks with Jiang, Narayanan insisted that the boundary dispute cannot be left to the next generations but must be resolved in the present. Foreign Minister Tang in his visit to India in July 2000 came back with the promise to accelerate the talks on the LAC, which had proceeded at a glacial pace in the bilateral Expert Group attached to the Joint Working Group.[30]

As a result, the Expert Group began to meet more frequently and started a discussion of the middle sector of their boundary. The exchange of maps on this relatively easy sector was completed in the group's meeting in Delhi in March 2002. This exchange has helped elucidate the two perceptions of the LAC's alignment and bring into relief the differences. The members ran into some problems in dealing with the western sector, where there were strong concerns from Beijing that India's claims on the LAC were far too expansive, but during Chinese Vice Foreign Minister Wang Yi's visit to New Delhi in November 2002, the two sides agreed to move ahead. In dealing with the delineation of the LAC in the western sector, India has had some disadvantages, having lost considerable territory there in the 1962 war, but it is better placed in the eastern sector, where China might have similar problems in coming to terms with the LAC.

More significantly, the intensified effort to clarify the LAC is slowly but surely nudging India and China to resolve the boundary dispute. The exercise on the LAC, without a reference to the boundary question, has been seen in both countries as a practical end in itself that will help preserve peace and tranquillity on the border. Moving forward on the exercise, the two sides have begun to recognize that their perceptions of the LAC can be pretty disparate. The confirmation of the LAC could involve ceding territory the two sides claim to control (not ownership). Thus the attempt to demarcate the LAC should inevitably merge on a discussion of the boundary dispute. It makes sense for both sides to argue that after more than five decades of effort to settle the boundary, they should look beyond a mere confirmation of the LAC. In any case, if territorial adjustments have to be made in relation to the LAC, why not go for a final trade-off of the boundary itself?

The very mention of a final settlement of the boundary question with China sends a shiver down the spine of the Indian political establishment. For many key Indian decision makers, this controversial question is best avoided. Although there is more realism within parts of the system on the nature of an eventual settlement, the question of timing has always been a difficult one, according to a leading China hand in the Indian Foreign Office. He queried,

> When is the best time to do the deal? This is a question we find hard to answer no matter whether you see the India–China relationship in antagonistic terms or in rosier hues as an attempt to create mutually beneficial stakes in the relationship.[31]

Given the searing political impact of the 1962 war and the past untenable public positions that India has taken on the boundary dispute, the political class finds it convenient to postpone rather than confront the contours of a reasonable settlement with China. This dilemma has been accentuated by the unwillingness of the system to prepare the ground at home for a settlement that will have to be 'on the basis of political give-and-take and not based on legal arguments', a former Indian ambassador to China, C.V. Ranganathan, says. He adds that 'in the absence of instructions on the political parameters acceptable to India, so far substantive negotiations for a boundary settlement have not taken place'.[32] Chinese officials too have often wondered aloud if there is political consensus in India to resolve the contentious boundary issue.[33] The difficulties on the Indian side do not take away the fact that China too has been in positions from which it might find hard to resile.

There has been the widespread belief within the Indian political system that no consensus on a settlement can be reached, given the 1962 Parliament resolution seeking the return of all occupied territory by China. Nevertheless, there is also the view that if there is one leader who could gamble on a border settlement with China, it is Vajpayee. Only a strong leader from the Right of the political spectrum, it has often been suggested, is capable of making a deal with China stick. There are few leaders on the horizon who can take such a political risk other than Vajpayee, who has shown that he can break the mould on difficult foreign policy issues. In the first years of his tenure as Prime Minister, he demonstrated his ability to get off the beaten path in relation to both Pakistan and the United States. He might be in a position to do the same by pushing for a final settlement of the boundary dispute with China, despite possible opposition from the ranks of the extremists in his party.

Nevertheless, the early fallout from the nuclear tests on the relations with China might have limited his ability to move forward in this area. His senior aides say that if there is the prospect of a reasonable settlement with China, Vajpayee's government might not be averse to exploring it seriously.[34] It is unlikely that the Congress party will strongly object to a final settlement that would involve departures from the traditional position, if the initiative is taken by the BJP government. After all, it was Rajiv Gandhi who broke the impasse in Sino-Indian relations during his China trip in 1988 and injected the notion that there must be mutual adjustment by both sides, rather than just a return of territory by China. The Left parties will in any case be expected to endorse such a settlement. Avoiding a settlement of the dispute might have suited India earlier, but its interests in the new century demand an intensive effort to resolve the boundary dispute with political imagination.

On Sikkim, throughout the mid-1990s Beijing sent tantalizing signals that it was prepared to recognize the state as part of India. When India integrated Sikkim into the union in 1975, Beijing castigated it. Despite the improvement in bilateral relations since 1988, China has delayed its formal recognition for inexplicable reasons, thus raising some doubts in India about Chinese intentions in Sikkim. Since the mid-1990s, however, China began to signal its readiness to grant an indirect recognition in a border trade agreement between China's Tibet and India's Sikkim. The Indian Foreign Office insists that formal recognition must precede border trade, although there is a sense in India that there is no harm in opening up border trade even without a formal recognition of Sikkim by China. Jaswant Singh has often pointed to his own support to border trade but has referred to objections from 'purists' in the Foreign Office.[35] Sikkim has strongly urged New Delhi to facilitate border trade across the traditional trading routes to Tibet on the argument that it could boost development in the region, and it is hopeful the Central government would eventually change its stand.[36]

When Singh met the Chinese leaders at the end of March 2002, the two sides agreed to discuss Sikkim through a formal mechanism. While this was not stated publicly and no mechanism was announced, official talks between the two took place in 2002. A settlement remained elusive at the end of the year. In return for recognition of Sikkim as part of India, China had apparently been demanding stronger statements from India that Tibet is an integral and inseparable part of China. India has traditionally said Tibet is an autonomous part of China, which Beijing now says is less than satisfactory. China also apparently wants India to drop its alleged objections to its establishment of relations with Bhutan.

The 1990s saw India manage and contain the tensions over Tibet, which had long-soured Sino-Indian relations. Just when the Tibetan cause seemed to acquire greater international legitimacy and the world leaders toasted the Tibetan leader, the Dalai Lama, India seemed to go mute. Vajpayee's meeting with the Dalai Lama in October 1998, a few months after the nuclear tests when Sino-Indian relations were frosty, drew strong condemnation from Beijing. Without apologizing, the Vajpayee government indicated that India's policy on Tibet was unchanged. The government insisted that Vajpayee had received the Dalai Lama in his capacity as a spiritual and religious personage, not as a political leader. The Principal Secretary to the Prime Minister, Brajesh Mishra, also welcomed the prospect of talks between Beijing and the Dalai Lama.[37] The Vajpayee government had no desire to push beyond a point the argument with China on Tibet. Facing its own acute vulnerabilities in Kashmir, Punjab and the North-East, it was unwilling to confront China on the issue. At the same time, India refused to bend by reducing or suspending its support to the Tibetan exiles and the Dalai Lama in India. While India is not willing to give up its leverage over the Tibetan issue, Beijing remains deeply suspicious of India's long-term intentions.

That Tibet and Sikkim remain so central to Sino-Indian relations was reinforced by the inexplicable escape of the seventeenth Karmapa from Tibet to India at the very end of 1999. The trans-Himalayan religious politics of Tibetan Buddhism continue to retain the power to disrupt Sino-Indian relations. The young Ugye Trinley Dorje is widely acknowledged by the Kagyu sect of the Tibetan Buddhism to be the reincarnation of the Karmapa. He has inherited the third most important position in the Tibetan Buddhist hierarchy, and both Beijing and the Dalai Lama have recognized him as the seventeenth Karmapa. China and the Dalai Lama are sharply divided on the identity of the Panchen Lama, the second most important figure in Tibetan Buddhism. After the passing of the Dalai Lama, the Karmapa is likely to emerge as the authentic voice of Tibetan Buddhism in the coming decades.

For nearly a decade, Beijing showered all its attention on the seventeenth Karmapa and hoped to showcase him as the new patriotic Lama of Tibet, but then he miraculously escaped— evading the extraordinary security on the border between Tibet and Nepal. While the world saw the Karmapa's escape an insult to China's policy in Tibet, the security agencies in the Indian establishment wondered if it was a derring-do or a deeper conspiracy by Beijing to foment trouble in Sikkim where the headquarters of the Kagyu exiles is located in the Rumtek monastry. Although China says that the Karmapa has gone to India to collect the sacred black hat so central to the Kagyu sect and hopes to see him return soon, the Karmapa is strongly critical of China, says he has no desire to create trouble in Sikkim and is disappointed at India's insinuation that he could be an agent of Chinese government. His only stated goal is to go to Rumtek, which has been in disarray since the death of the sixteenth Karmapa in 1981. Adding more spice to the story, the regents of the Rumtek monastery have been squabbling among themselves about the right to control the institution and the identity of the real Karmapa.

Despite their wariness, India and China will increasingly be pressed by circumstances on the ground to address their bilateral problems across the Himalayan frontier. Many of the long-standing problems between the two nations are centred around the Himalayas—these include the boundary dispute, misperceptions on Tibet and China's refusal to recognize Sikkim as a part of India. At another level, each side nurses huge political grievances that its right to operate across the Himalayas has been severely curtailed by the other. India is concerned that its traditional cultural and trading links with Tibet have snapped under Chinese control. China, on the other hand, believes that India prevents it from establishing full intercourse with the kingdoms on the southern side of the Himalayas, such as Nepal and Bhutan. Deepening this sense of injury has been the proclaimed loss of territories as well as the notions of buffer states and spheres of influence.

The rivalry of the last four decades has resulted in attaching undue importance to concepts inherited from the imperial age. The ideas on buffer states, spheres of influence and the insulation of national spaces from interaction with one's neighbours have little meaning in the age of globalization. No nation can be kept out of key areas in its own neighbourhood in the name of high principle or a perception of historic injustices. At a time when both India and China are adapting to the logic of trade flows and movements of people across borders, it makes little sense to keep the Himalayas in a state of permanent political tension. The time has come for India and China to begin the transformation of the geopolitics of the Himalayan region towards cooperation.

The easiest place to start would be Sikkim. An unambiguous Chinese recognition that Sikkim is part of India would allow India to reopen the state to trade with China through Tibet. Restoration of trade links would also involve the reopening of the historic silk road that runs between Sikkim and Tibet through the Natu La pass. The establishment of trade offices and the facilitation of travel in larger numbers by tourists, pilgrims and businessmen across the Himalayan divide would follow.

Renewal of trade links across the Himalayas would complement the developmental needs of both Tibet and Sikkim. As part of its strategy of globalizing Tibet, China is seeking to forge economic links between Tibet and its neighbouring regions. It is seeking foreign investment and tourist flows to boost the economic prosperity of Tibet. India now has a good opportunity to restore its historic ties with Tibet, not as a matter of legal right but as a practical outcome of expanding trade and people-to-people contact. On the political questions relating to Tibet, the outlook is promising. Contacts have been re-established in the second half of 2002 between Beijing and the Dalai Lama, the spiritual leader of the Tibetan people exiled in India for more than four decades. China is likely to begin talks with the Dalai Lama's representatives in the near future. India, which has long acknowledged that Tibet is an autonomous part of China, has a strong interest in an early settlement of the issue and the return of Tibetan refugees.

On Bhutan, India should not be seen as obstructing the establishment of diplomatic relations between Thimphu and Beijing. China argues that Bhutan is the only nation in the region with which it has no formal relationship. New Delhi, at the official level, says it is up to Bhutan, which has been generally cautious about expanding its international profile. Over the long run, India cannot stop Bhutan from establishing full-fledged diplomatic ties with China, nor is it worth trying. In 1988 Rajiv Gandhi created a framework for negotiations on the border. In 1993 Narasimha Rao moved the ties forward and got an agreement to maintain peace and tranquillity on the border. A decade later, Vajpayee has an opportunity to identify the elements of a potential settlement of the boundary dispute and transform the Himalayas into a zone of trade and prosperity.

SEVEN

Containing Pakistan

Sisyphus at Agra

July 2001 is likely to go down as the cruellest month Atal Bihari Vajpayee ever endured in his foreign policy endeavour, widely seen as one of the more successful aspects of his prime ministerial tenure. After two days and nights of negotiations at Agra, Vajpayee realized his attempt at finding a breakthrough with Pakistan had collapsed, yet again. His somewhat offensive guest at Agra, the President of Pakistan, General Pervez Musharraf, in his hour-long farewell call, kept pressing a reluctant Vajpayee to sign onto a draft declaration that was negotiated during the summit. If Vajpayee was unable to decide on signing the draft Agra Declaration, Musharraf was telling him that he would like to meet those in Vajpayee's Cabinet who were said to be opposed to it. Vajpayee's famous silences became even longer as the voluble general kept pushing the piece of paper in front of him. Vajpayee had made up his mind. The general had overplayed his hand and undermined the prospects for a broad agreement on initiating a comprehensive dialogue between the two nations.

Extending an invitation to Musharraf was Vajpayee's second gamble in about two years on changing India's relationship with Pakistan. The first was in February 1999, when he hurriedly set up a bus journey to Lahore to meet Prime Minister Nawaz

Sharif. In less than two months, India was at war with Pakistan in the Kargil Heights. Having overcome that bitterness, Vajpayee chose to invite the man who was responsible for Pakistan's aggression across the Line of Control that had held for nearly three decades. Vajpayee's decision to roll the dice again on Pakistan was based on his inner conviction that he could make a difference to relations with India's most exasperating sibling born out of Partition. 'You could choose your friends but not neighbours' was Vajpayee's refrain when he took charge as Prime Minister in March 1998 and sought to convince a doubtful domestic establishment of the importance of engaging Pakistan. But here was Musharraf converting a genuine attempt by Vajpayee to reach out to Pakistan into a terrible political embarrassment.

Vajpayee thought he was being generous in his hospitality and the political substance that he was offering. The swaggering general saw this generosity as weakness, and he was determined to collect as much as he could for the investments his army had made in bleeding India for more than a decade in Jammu and Kashmir. Vajpayee's peace initiative turned to ashes, and the core contradictions of Indo-Pakistani relations stood out red hot in the sweltering Agra of July 2001. The deliberations demonstrated at once the relative ease and elusiveness of defining a viable framework of engagement with Pakistan: an Agra Declaration was all but complete but could not be clinched by the two leaders. The meeting at Agra also highlighted the deep cleavages within the Indian establishment on how to overcome the impasse in bilateral relations with Pakistan. Knowing the sensitivity of the negotiations, Vajpayee took all the members of his Cabinet Committee on Security to Agra. As Musharraf insisted on a formulation that linked progress in bilateral relations to a resolution of the Kashmir dispute, some members of the committee refused to go along. For those who rejected the Agra Declaration, Musharraf's demand was an attempt to smuggle in the very ideology of Pakistan and the divisive two-nation theory. The huge public interest and the media intrusiveness into the summit deliberations showed the extraordinary popular expectations for peace in the subcontinent. Stirred by an intense wave of patriotism just two years earlier during the Kargil War, the Indian public was now hoping for a significant step towards peace at Agra. The proliferation of twenty-four hour news channels at the turn of the century made this the first television summit in India, and the the glare of publicity made negotiations impossible.

Having travelled to Lahore in February 1999, Vajpayee returned with great hopes of a potential breakthrough in the relationship with Pakistan. In his speech at the Governor's House in Lahore on 21 February, Vajpayee outlined his philosophy of live and let live. He proclaimed India's stake in a peaceful and prosperous Pakistan. He visited the Minar-e-Pakistan, the monument in Lahore celebrating the creation of the truculent neighbour. He was the first Indian Prime Minister to do so. The Lahore Declaration, a statement of intent on reworking the relationship, affirmed India's resolve to address the Kashmir issue purposefully. An understanding was also reached to negotiate measures to stabilize nuclear deterrence now in place between the two countries. Finally, Vajpayee recited one of his Hindi poems, 'We will not let war happen now' ('Jang na hone denge').[1] Vajpayee's reference was to the tit-for-tat nuclear tests that took place less than a year before and raised the world fears of a nuclear war between the subcontinental rivals.

The cruel irony, as it turned out, was that even as Vajpayee was reciting his poem against war, the conditions for the first serious military conflict between the two nations since 1971 had already been laid. Nawaz Sharif had already signed on to the plans of Chief of Army Staff Pervez Musharraf to occupy the heights on the Indian side of the Line of Control. Caught napping at the first ever aggression by Pakistan across the Line of Control, Vajpayee threw brave young Indian officers at these heights to vacate the advance in June 1999. The reward for his efforts to build peace with Pakistan at Lahore made Vajpayee a bitter man. Yet on 23 May 2001, nearly two years after discovering the Kargil betrayal, Vajpayee was ready to play Sisyphus all over again.

Overcoming the sense of personal betrayal, Vajpayee reversed India's policy of not engaging Pakistan after Kargil. The Indian invitation to Musharraf in May 2002 broke the nearly two-year political stand-off that followed the war in Kargil. It signalled Vajpayee's determination that a way must and can be found to deal with Pakistan. In his published musings from Kumarakom, a small resort town in Kerala's backwaters where he was spending the New Year holidays in January 2001, Vajpayee reaffirmed his government's commitment to finding a final solution to the conflict in Kashmir by going off the beaten track.[2] He also hinted at flexibility in the rigid posture India had adopted after Kargil in refusing to engage Pakistan until cross-border terrorism came to a halt. As it turned out, the invitation drew approbation from the international community and was also hugely popular in both India and Pakistan. In his letter of invitation, Vajpayee sought to elevate the level of discussion by pointing to the 'common enemy' of poverty, emphasizing that there is no alternative to 'reconciliation' and urging Musharraf to 'walk this high road with us'. He also made a reference to India's willingness to discuss the Kashmir dispute, giving enough hope to Pakistan that India would not avoid the difficult subject.[3]

To demonstrate the seriousness of purpose and probably to introduce a vision for a different future for the subcontinent, the Vajpayee government came up with a series of confidence-building measures on the eve of the summit. These ranged from making life easier for Pakistani fishermen who get caught in Indian waters, to opening up the Line of Control in Jammu and Kashmir to facilitating the movement of Kashmiris across the divide in the disputed state. Other proposals included an offer of fellowships for Pakistani students in Indian technical institutions, the unilateral reduction of tariffs on Pakistani export and the readiness to send the director general of military operations to make the border a peaceful one. Although India made these proposals in good faith, Pakistan was concerned that these might have been aimed at diverting attention from what it saw as the core issue in bilateral relations—the dispute over Jammu and Kashmir.[4]

In the run-up to his visit to India, Musharraf repeatedly insisted that Kashmir would remain the focus of talks with Indian leaders and, to underscore that argument, he would meet the leaders of the Hurriyat Conference, the political umbrella organization of Pakistani-backed Kashmiri militant groups. He did meet the Hurriyat in New Delhi, despite the opposition of his hosts. A disappointed Vajpayee let it pass, but the seeds of a potentially bitter summit were sown. The political devastation would follow, but not before huge expectations for a successful summit deliberations at Agra were raised.

What was to be a get-acquainted meeting between Vajpayee and Musharraf got transformed into a negotiating exercise of considerable scope. On the eve of Musharraf's arrival, senior advisers to the Prime Minister were stating that the summit would be seen as a success if both sides could declare that they had broken the ice and would meet again. That limited outcome was indeed at hand. The discussion between the two sides of a simple factual joint statement transformed into extended negotiations on an ambitious Agra Declaration that would touch upon all the key issues and define a road map to future engagement between the two countries. The Agra talks focussed on a number of contentious questions, including the nature of the negotiating framework, the centrality of the respective Indian and Pakistani concerns on cross-border terrorism and Kashmir, the relationship between these perceived core issues and the overall relationship between the two countries.

Although the two sides could not eventually agree on a final Agra Declaration, considerable political ground was said to be covered in the negotiations. Nonetheless, the initial expectations of a final declaration and the bargaining that went on until the delayed departure of Musharraf created a sense of failure at Agra in the public's mind. Despite the popular perception of a let-down in the aftermath of the summit, the immediate characterization from both sides was positive. At his press conference on 17 July at Agra, External Affairs Minister Jaswant Singh expressed his disappointment at the inability to arrive at an agreed text, but he insisted that 'we will pick up the threads from the visit of the President of Pakistan'.[5] His counterpart Abdul Sattar was upbeat. In his meeting with the press in Islamabad, Sattar declared that Musharraf had returned from Agra 'optimistic about the prospects for better relations between Pakistan and India' and insisted that 'the Agra Summit remained inconclusive but it did not fail.'[6]

The mood in India, however, became dark. The government was blamed for inadequate preparation and for risking a lot on sensitive national security issues relating to Pakistan. The media also focussed on the divisions in the Cabinet, which, according to the Pakistani delegation, was principally responsible for Vajpayee's reluctance to sign the Agra Declaration. The Pakistanis asserted that after many intensive rounds of final consultations, Singh had assured them that the final draft would be acceptable to the Indian side, but he later expressed his regret that the document could not pass muster. Indian officials involved in the negotiations dismissed this Pakistani version of events, and they underlined the fact that no negotiation is complete until both sides give the final seal of approval.

Immediately after the summit, Singh noted three sets of issues on which there were unresolved differences. All were at the centre of Indo-Pakistani relations. Singh identified these as the relationship between Kashmir and the normalization of bilateral relations, the question of cross-border terrorism and the value of past agreements in defining any future course of negotiations. Pakistan had demanded for nearly a decade that progress in the resolution of the Kashmir dispute would have to precede an overall improvement in bilateral relations. India, on the other hand, emphasized movement on all the fronts simultaneously. Pointing to the differences on coming up with a formulation on Kashmir, Singh said, 'India is convinced that narrow, segmented or unifocal approaches will simply not work. Our focus has to remain on the totality of the relationship'.[7] Sattar agreed that the snag in finalizing the declaration related 'to the relationship between settlement of the Kashmir question and progress on normalization' of bilateral relations.[8]

Indian sources questioned Sattar's assessment that progress was made on that issue and that, given a little more time, an acceptable formulation on the linkage between Kashmir and the rest of the agenda could have been worked out. They insisted that any formulation that sought to present the resolution of the Kashmir issue and the normalization of the relationship in a sequential manner was entirely unacceptable. If India had agreed to such a formulation, however neatly finessed by diplomatic language, it would have implied a radical change in the negotiating framework between the two nations. Indian officials add that allowing the Pakistani formulation to go through would have implied the acceptance of the ideology behind the Partition of the subcontinent—the two-nation theory.

A second set of issues that complicated the negotiations at the Agra Summit was the question of Pakistan's support to the proxy war in Kashmir, or what came to be known more popularly as cross-border terrorism. If Kashmir was the core issue for Pakistan, for India it was an immediate cessation of Pakistani support to cross-border terrorism and the discarding of the compulsive hostility against India. Pakistan, however, dismissed Indian charges on its support to militant groups in Kashmir and pointed instead to India's state terrorism and its human rights abuses in the Valley. Pakistan of course had little problem in condemning terrorism in general terms, and such a formulation had indeed been worked out at the Lahore Summit. In that declaration, Vajpayee and Nawaz Sharif asserted that they 'reaffirm their condemnation of terrorism in all its forms and manifestations and their determination to combat this menace' and along with a commitment to 'promote and protect all human rights and fundamental freedoms'.[9]

Pakistan had no intention of giving up the instrument of terrorism that it saw as the only tool with which to press India to negotiate on Kashmir. Sattar pointed out after the Agra Summit: 'If there are any concerns on other side with regard to terrorism across the border, surely this matter can be raised in future meetings. As you know in Jammu and Kashmir, there is no international border but a Line of Control, resulting from the cease-fire of December 1971. No reference has been made to any cross LoC terrorism in the course of the draft of the declaration.'[10] Singh was equally adamant: 'It was made abundantly clear to the Pakistani side during the visit, that the promotion of cross-border terrorism and violence are unacceptable and must cease.'[11]

A third set of issues that bedevilled the drafting exercise at Agra was the importance of past treaties in defining the future. Musharraf and Sattar were strong critics of both the Simla Agreement and the Lahore Declaration. They argued that previous bilateral agreements between India and Pakistan did not place enough emphasis on resolving the Kashmir dispute. Musharraf and Sattar were determined to put their own stamp on future negotiations with India. India went along with the Pakistani proposition that all references to Simla and Lahore be dropped in the Agra Declaration. In return Pakistan was prepared to discard references to the United Nations resolutions on Kashmir, with the notion of a plebiscite in the disputed state built into them. While pragmatists on both sides were ready to live with an absence of references to old markers, purists found it objectionable. On the Indian side, the refusal to mention the Simla Agreement was sacrilegious in the sense that it was tantamount to giving up the principle of bilateralism enshrined in the document. The traditionalist position on Simla had won out within the Indian Cabinet. Jaswant Singh told the press:

We continue to believe that every compact, or agreement, or effort that has preceded the present effort cannot be negated, rescinded, or wished away. That is why we made it clear that . . . the effort at Agra was a continuation not simply of the Lahore process but also as a building upon the foundations that were laid by Simla. It is that central objective which again had some difficulty in being accepted by our distinguished visitors.[12]

The question of the draft declaration at Agra would not go away. Sattar suggested at the end of the summit that it could be the basis for future negotiations: 'The two leaders succeeded in covering a broad area of common ground in the draft Declaration. That will provide a valuable foundation for the two leaders to reach full agreement at their next meeting.'[13] The next day India asserted that the process would have to start all over again. An unfinished deal was no deal in the rules of negotiations among countries, and the draft Agra Declaration could not in any way be given legitimacy for future talks. India insisted that Simla and Lahore remain the bedrock on which future relations be built. As the spokeswoman of the Indian Foreign Office pointed out on 18 July, 'It was disappointing that no closure was reached on the text of an agreement. We will, therefore, have to begin again on the basis of the existing agreements, i.e., the Simla Agreement and the Lahore Declaration, which are cornerstones of India-Pakistan bilateral relations.'[14] It was back to square one and the triumph of the curse on Sisyphus.

Burying the Simla Agreement

The collapse of the Agra Summit and the quick evaporation of the positive sentiments signalled an end to the efforts by India and Pakistan for more than a decade to negotiate and resolve outstanding problems between the two nations. Rajiv Gandhi tried to break the mould with Pakistan in the late 1980s when he engaged General Mohammad Zia ul-Haq and later reached out to Prime Minister Benazir Bhutto. There was some hope that the two young leaders, Gandhi and Bhutto, could help push the bilateral relations in a positive direction. Gandhi was already on his way out, and Bhutto could not resist the temptation of taking advantage of India's troubles in Kashmir.

The eventual kick-start for the negotiations came from the United States, which in the wake of the May 1990 military tensions between India and Pakistan, pressed both sides to begin talks and bring down the temperature on the border. As a result the two sides began talks at the Foreign Secretary level at the end of 1990. The talks lasted until January 1994. They produced two modest military confidence-building agreements as well as a broad-based dialogue. As India reeled under pressure from the heightened insurgent activity in the state of Jammu and Kashmir backed by Pakistan, Bhutto began to set preconditions for a dialogue, in the form of Indian measures to reduce its troop presence in Kashmir and an end to human rights violations in the Valley. In New Delhi the Narasimha Rao government in consultations with the opposition parties, particularly the BJP, closed ranks at home by adopting a unanimous resolution in the Parliament proclaiming Kashmir an integral part of India.[15]

The election of the Nawaz Sharif government in February 1997 began to thaw relations, and at the initiative of Gujral government, the two sides began to engage each other. They broadly agreed upon a framework of negotiations in June 1997. The collapse of the Gujral government at the end of 1997 and the nuclear tests of May 1998 under the first Vajpayee government further delayed mutual engagement. When Nawaz Sharif and Vajpayee met in New York after September 1998, there was an agreement to pursue negotiations on all issues on the basis of the 1997 agreement.[16] After that Vajpayee visited Lahore and following the Kargil War, the Agra Summit was convened.

This engagement since the late 1980s produced an agreement not to attack each other's nuclear facilities (1988), a couple of military confidence-building measures (1991) and an agreement to negotiate more measures to bring more military stability (1999). Twice in this decade the two sides appeared close to an understanding on ending the military stand-off at Siachen (1989 and 1992). There was the Lahore Declaration (1999) and the opening up of a bus service between New Delhi and Lahore the same year, until it was suspended at the end of 2001. A brief backchannel pre-negotiation on Kashmir took place between R.K. Mishra, a close political confidante of Vajpayee, and Niaz Naik, a former Foreign Secretary of Pakistan and envoy to India, in the spring of 1999 (between Lahore and Kargil). The two sides agreed to a tacit ceasefire on the LoC in July 2000 and a more explicit one that endured for a couple of months from December 2000, and the draft Agra Declaration in July 2001. Given the burden of their past and the record of military tensions of winter 1986-87, May 1990 and the Kargil War in 1999, these agreements were not to be dismissed as inconsequential. But the 1990s also demonstrated the fundamental difficulties of sustaining a dialogue amidst unending cross-border terrorism and incrementally building upon previous agreements.

The 1991 CBMs on advance notification of military exercises and non-violation of each other's airspace were not a conscious attempt to chip away at the agreements through technical interpretation of their meaning.[17] There was no political ownership of these agreements, and the overall political atmosphere was never conducive to implementing the CBMs and expanding their scope. India could not muster the necessary political will at home to push ahead with an agreed withdrawal from the Siachen glacier in the late 1980s and early 1990s. Rajiv Gandhi backed off from such an agreement in 1989, and so did Narasimha Rao in 1992. The central question that remained, however, was one of finding a way to deal with the Kashmir problem. Must talks on Kashmir precede those on all other issues, as Pakistan insisted, or should they move along simultaneously, as India wanted? The attempted diplomatic finesse on this core issue at Lahore and Agra did not work.

India in fact agreed to lend attention to the discussion on Kashmir both procedurally and substantively, but its moves were not enough to satisfy Pakistan, which, as Musharraf insisted at Agra, had to focus on Kashmir.

The failure at Agra reflected a deeper flaw in the negotiating process that the two sides tried to structure in the 1990s. Central to that failure was the conscious rejection of the Simla Agreement by Pakistan and its determination to alter the nature of the negotiating framework between the two nations. The argument against Simla might have been put across sharply by Sattar and Musharraf at Agra, but it was a sentiment that was widely shared in the Pakistani establishment. The rejection of Simla started in the late 1980s as Pakistani representatives began to rake up the issue in the United Nations fora. The outbreak of popular uprising against India at the end of 1989 seemed to offer Pakistan a historic opportunity to push India on the issue by all available means and settle the scores for the vivisection of Pakistan in 1971. Pakistan, fresh from a triumph in Afghanistan against the Soviet occupation, found it easy to apply the same model in Kashmir. The strategy of training, arming and sending mujahedin groups across the Durand Line to fight the Soviet troops in Afghanistan while denying any responsibility for their actions succeeded far beyond expectations. Cocky from that victory, Pakistan replicated that strategy across the Line of Control in Kashmir and leveraged it against India.

India's deepening crisis in Kashmir gave Pakistan an unprecedented opportunity to reverse two core assumptions of the Simla Agreement. One was that the disputes between the two sides must be resolved peacefully. The proxy war that Pakistan initiated in Kashmir from the late 1980s undermined the notion of peaceful resolution of bilateral problems. The other principle of Simla was that the disputes must be settled bilaterally. The tensions over Kashmir and the international concerns about their escalation to the nuclear level gave Pakistan an opening to internationalize the dispute.

The thrust of Pakistan's diplomacy from the 1980s was about breaking out of the Simla framework. What transpired at Agra in July 2001 was a nearly successful attempt by Musharraf to bury the Simla Agreement. Although India finally baulked, Pakistan's diplomatic strategy and military actions on the ground had already killed the Simla Agreement. At Agra Musharraf was looking for a diplomatic obituary.

Many reasons are cited in Pakistan for the rejection of the Simla Agreement, but India grew disillusioned with the treaty in the 1990s too. For some in Pakistan, it was a document signed in the aftermath of a humiliating defeat in the December 1971 war. The attempts to break out of the Simla Agreement were also justified in Pakistan by citing the failure of India to negotiate on Kashmir within the framework of the treaty. After all, there were no serious negotiations between the two sides on Kashmir during the 1970s and 1980s. For India, at the official level, the Simla Agreement was the cornerstone of the relationship with Pakistan. Yet for many Indians, Simla was no longer the symbol of the triumph in 1971 against Pakistan but of political failure— the inability to cash in on the victory by getting a final settlement of the Kashmir dispute. For many critics of the Indian foreign policy, particularly from the right wing, the Simla Agreement was a colossal failure, resulting from the naïve assumptions of the Nehruvian foreign policy establishment that let the Pakistani leader Zulfikar Ali Bhutto off the hook in the peace settlement that followed the 1971 war.

The best argument of those in India who defend the treaty is that Bhutto had informally agreed to a final solution based on the Line of Control that emerged after the 1971 war, but he was reluctant to formalize it before consolidating his own position at home. He had promised to return after improving his standing in Pakistan, but he never did.[18] By the turn of the millennium it was quite clear that Pakistan had no desire to comply with the treaty, and India did not have the power to persuade it to do so. For the balance of power between India and Pakistan changed irrevocably by the end of the 1980s.

It was this shift in favour of Pakistan that gave Islamabad the confidence to renege on the core assumptions of the Simla Agreement. The altered balance of power was about Pakistan's acquisition of nuclear weapons. From the late 1970s, India carefully watched Pakistan build its nuclear weapons programme, which came to fruition in the late 1980s. The Pakistani programme indeed stirred up the Indian nuclear debate for the first time since 1964, when China went nuclear. That India, with a much deeper and broader nuclear programme, would follow suit and acquire nuclear weapons to remove the asymmetry with Pakistan and China was inevitable. Once India was convinced that Pakistan had nuclear weapons by 1987, its nuclear decision inevitably followed. Subsequently the debate was about whether India wanted to test nuclear weapons and overtly declare its nuclear status.

India's nuclear debate in the 1980s and 1990s missed the central strategic significance of Pakistan becoming a nuclear weapons state. India's intellectual energies went into making the case for its own nuclear decision and rejecting the international pressures to roll back its nuclear weapons programme. Instead of looking at the long-term consequences of nuclearization of the subcontinent and its implications for the balance of power with Pakistan, the Indian strategic establishment focussed its ire on the Western arguments against non-proliferation in the subcontinent and the resulting strategic instability between the two countries.

India rejected the notion that nuclear weapons could be destabilizing; it saw this as a racist argument from the West that was unwilling to see developing countries acquire nuclear weapons. Equally dominant were the arguments about equity and fairness in structuring a global nuclear order. The mainstream Indian strategic view was that the introduction of nuclear weapons would stabilize the balance between India and Pakistan and prevent a traditional conventional war between the two arch-rivals. The belief was also that the problems of nuclear instability could be resolved through a wide-ranging set of military confidence-building measures, similar to what the Soviet Union and the United States had instituted during the cold war. This was the view that informed the Indian establishment as it went to Lahore less than a year after the nuclear tests, with the sense that overt nuclear deterrence between the two sides had opened an opportunity to settle the Kashmir issue along the lines of territorial status quo. India also believed that a Pakistan secure with its nuclear deterrent might now be prepared to reciprocate and open itself for a comprehensive engagement with India.

The Pakistani perception was radically different. Like India, Pakistan understood that a traditional military conflict with India was no longer possible. Pakistan, however, saw a huge window of opportunity that had opened for a low-intensity conflict with India, particularly in Kashmir, without the fear of a conventional military retaliation from New Delhi. Having neutralized Indian conventional military superiority with the nuclear weapons, Pakistan found the space to pursue a subconventional conflict using terrorists and militants against India. An infrastructure to pursue this war was already available, thanks to Pakistan's decade-long effort to foment insurgency in Afghanistan. For the first time in decades, Pakistan was confident that its Western borders had been secured and was triumphant at its unprecedented influence in the affairs of Afghanistan. Pakistan's assumptions turned out to be essentially right. Unlike before, when India did not think twice about crossing the dividing line in Kashmir to attack the militant camps, it was now restrained from doing so. India had per force to fight the war against terrorism in Kashmir on its own soil, unable to either destroy the militancy at its source or prevent the unending the infiltration of militants by Pakistanis into Kashmir. The option of responding in kind to Pakistan—through sustained support to separatism and terrorism—was never pursued seriously by the Indian political leadership despite the occasional clamour from the security establishment.

Despite the direct correlation between the nuclearization

of the subcontinent and Pakistani proxy war in Kashmir, India failed to absorb its meaning. According to the Subrahmanyam Committee that examined the Kargil debacle, since 1991 the Indian intelligence agencies were pointing out the implications of Pakistan's nuclearization for managing the situation in Kashmir.[19] But this did not affect the debate much.

For Pakistan, the nuclearization of the subcontinent offered the two simultaneous pressure points against India—one was the new freedom to pursue a proxy war in Kashmir and the other was to play upon the international concerns on nuclear proliferation in the subcontinent. In the West, the concerns on the spread of nuclear weapons fused with the fears that Indo-Pakistani tensions in Kashmir would end up in a war that could escalate to the nuclear level. The idea of a nuclear flashpoint in Kashmir animated the policymakers in Washington into intense activism over both preventing nuclear proliferation in the region and promoting a resolution of the Kashmir problem. India found itself in an unenviable position.

The Kargil Watershed
If there were any doubts left about the death of the Simla Agreement, they were destroyed by the Kargil War in the spring and summer of 1999. In the early spring of 1999 in a seemingly brilliant tactical manoeuvre, the Chief of Army Staff, General Musharraf, ordered a seizure of the heights in the Kargil sector across the Line of Control. Musharraf implemented a plan that had existed for a while in the drawers of the Pakistani army headquarters. His predecessors were sceptical of its success. That Pakistan chose to pursue a line of action that was considered unwise for nearly twenty-seven years reflected the new mood in Islamabad. There was a sense in Islamabad that the freedom to pursue unconventional warfare against India could be expanded into a limited conventional war with a specific political objective. Yet Pakistan failed to anticipate accurately the nature of the Indian military response and the kind of international reaction that would isolate Pakistan in its

war with India. The result was a political disaster for Pakistan. A variety of explanations have been offered for Pakistan's misadventure in Kargil. These included its frustrations at India's lack of seriousness in negotiating with Pakistan on Kashmir and the importance of avenging India's occupation of the Siachen glacier, which was seen in Pakistan as a violation of the Simla Agreement. The main thrust of the Kargil initiative has been summed up in a RAND report:

> It must be recognized that Kargil *was*, in some sense, a limited aims war in that at least one of Pakistan's objectives was to secure territory, however marginal. Of course, its other objective, to internationalize the conflict, was just as salient—if not more so—than these meagre territorial ambitions. . . . Pakistan did seem to believe that the international community would intervene in a fashion both timely and consonant with Pakistan's strategic interest once it had secured its operational aims early in the conflict.[20]

The Indian decision to respond with full military force on its own side of the LoC, the relentless pressure from the United States on Pakistan to restore the status quo ante unconditionally and unambiguously, China's reluctance to back Pakistan in any meaningful way and the entreaties from Saudi Arabia to walk back clearly surprised Pakistan's decision makers. Despite the setback it suffered in Kargil, Pakistan refused to acknowledge that Kargil was either a defeat or that Kargil-like operations are unacceptable and dangerous for stability in the subcontinent. Assessing the Pakistani debate on the Kargil experience, the RAND report states that

> Pakistan's lessons learned are more complex. Even as the overall failure of the Kargil operation dominates the consciousness of many Pakistani stakeholders, several important constituencies still tend to rationalize Kargil, even if only as an after-thought, as some sort of a victory—the brilliance of the tactical planning, the effectiveness of operational performance, the conflict as progenitor

of India's political dialogue with the Kashmiris—differ often as a result of where the constituency is located in Pakistan's state-society structure, but the 'residue' of such beliefs implies the possibility that Pakistan might be tempted to carry out Kargil-like operations in the future.[21]

For India, the biggest gain from Kargil was that the international community would not allow any military attempt to alter the territorial status quo in Jammu and Kashmir. When India discovered the Pakistani occupation of the Kargil heights and began to mobilize for its military operations, it had little expectation of international support. When the first indications of American backing to India came, they had to be conveyed through the unusual channels, including the author, to both signal a sceptical security establishment in New Delhi and convince the public of America's changed attitude towards the Kashmir conflict.[22] Through a series of public formulations and direct diplomatic pressure throughout June 1999, the United States compelled Pakistan to cease its aggression unconditionally. The final act of Kargil was conducted in the 4 July 1999 meeting between President Clinton and Prime Minister Nawaz Sharif in which they came up with a statement that announced the Pakistani intent to withdraw and respect the sanctity of the Line of Control.

Indian analysts differ on the impact of America's intervention in bringing the Kargil conflict to quick closure. The predominant view is that stressing America's diplomatic role undermines the fact that the Indian Army was advancing by the end of June and could have soon evicted the aggression on its own. This line of argument underestimates the diplomatic space that American support provided in isolating Pakistan internationally and limiting the costs of the military operations in vacating the aggression. American neutrality in the conflict would have significantly expanded India's political burden.

India could also count on three important long-term strategic gains vis-à-vis Pakistan from the Kargil conflict. First was the success in turning the nuclear flashpoint argument on its head and limiting the benefits that Pakistan accrued from the nuclearization of the subcontinent. Although the Kargil aggression represented a kind of culmination of Pakistan's post-nuclear strategy towards Kashmir, the Subrahmanyam Committee suggests that the nuclear factor did not have a substantive role in how the crisis was managed and resolved:

> Since India did not cross the LoC and reacted strictly within its own territory, the effort to conjure up escalation of a kind that could lead to nuclear war did not succeed. Despite its best efforts Pakistan was unable to link its Kargil caper with a nuclear flashpoint, though some foreign observers believe it was near thing. The international community does not favour alteration of the status quo through nuclear blackmail as this would not be in the interest of the five major nuclear powers.[23]

But a more complex argument could be developed on how the nuclear factor played out. While nuclear blackmail was inherent in Pakistan's Kargil strategy, a surprising development was the Indian willingness to leverage the international fears of a nuclear flashpoint to its own advantage.

India did not cross the Line of Control as a matter of choice in its military operations to vacate the Kargil aggression and won widespread international approbation for the restraint it had demonstrated during the crisis as opposed to Pakistan's nuclear adventurism. But approbation alone, the BJP-led government understood, was not enough in quickly vacating the aggression in Kargil and limiting the costs of the war on the eve of an impending national election. Vajpayee's advisers understood the value of the American position on Kargil but wanted more—direct and unremitting pressure from Washington on Pakistan to withdraw from across the Line of Control. They demonstrated restraint but did not rule out crossing the LoC. Pointing to the domestic pressures to do so and the costs of fighting with one hand tied behind its back,

India kept up the message that its restraint could not be taken for granted. By mobilizing its armed forces into a high state of alert and concentrating its naval power in the Arabian Sea, India signalled that it was fully prepared for a horizontal escalation of the conflict.

It was in the meeting with US National Security Adviser Sandy Berger in Geneva on 16 June 1999 that India's National Security Adviser Brajesh Mishra conveyed an explicit message from Vajpayee that his country's patience was running out and that, unless the aggression was reversed within a few weeks, India's hand might be forced.[24] Mishra apparently handed over what was later described by the American media as an 'alarming letter', which made the Clinton administration conclude that India was about to cross the Line of Control and an escalation was imminent.[25] Coupled with disturbing intelligence inputs from Pakistan that it was getting its nuclear forces ready, the Clinton administration moved quickly to increase the pressure on Pakistan. Washington dispatched the top gun of Central Command, General Anthony Zinni, to convey to the Pakistani leaders, especially Musharraf, that the US wanted an immediate withdrawal from Kargil. After Zinni's talks in Pakistan, India was informed that Islamabad had been delivered a 'blunt, unambiguous and direct' message to the army brass in Pakistan that it must restore the status quo ante on the Line of Control; India also refused to accept Pakistani demands for a linkage with a dialogue on Kashmir.[26]

Second, while the nuclearization of the subcontinent opened new strategic possibilities for Pakistan vis-à-vis India in the late 1980s, the international context appeared to turn in favour of India at the end of the 1990s. Although motivated by the US assessment that it should not reward Pakistan's nuclear adventurism, the definitive American pressure on Pakistan to withdraw from Kargil was taking place in the context of a redrawing of the parameters of the international involvement in the subcontinent. A key factor was the reversal of India's and Pakistan's economic fortunes. Through the 1990s India grew at a steady pace of 6 per cent in a historic break from its traditional rate of 3.5 per cent. In the same period Pakistan shed its traditional high growth path of at least 5 to 5.5 per cent. During the 1990s the Pakistani economy stagnated at the growth rate of about 3 per cent. Coupled with a continuing high growth rate of population (2.4 per cent), Pakistan began to find itself in an increasingly tight economic situation.

For the first time India could bring its attractiveness as an emerging market with a potential for high growth rates to bear upon the relations of the major powers. India's simultaneous improvement of political relations with all the major powers in the 1990s put an end to the cold war context where Pakistan enjoyed a special relationship with the West, China and the Islamic world. While India offered the prospects of a successful economy, Pakistan was increasingly seen as a failing state, one torn apart by sectarian divisions, the rise of extremist Islamic forces and the failure of the political class as a whole. India's successful Kargil diplomacy rested on this fundamental change of international perceptions of India and Pakistan. This allowed India to increase its own weight vis-à-vis Pakistan in the diplomatic calculus of key international constituencies aligned with Islamabad in the cold war.

The third gain for India from the Kargil crisis was somewhat counter-intuitive, and some would question if it is a benefit at all. The much-feared international intervention had indeed taken place in the Kargil crisis, and surprisingly not against India but in its favour. Some would see the intervention of the United States as being purely contingent on the circumstances of the Kargil conflict rather than a fundamental shift in its position. Yet the Kargil crisis appears to have been partly instrumental in moving the United States towards the notion that the Line of Control could be the most reasonable basis for a final settlement of the dispute over Jammu and Kashmir. While the US might not prescribe such a solution formally and would argue that any solution must come out of a negotiating process between India and Pakistan, India after Kargil could be more sanguine in its assessment that the international community would do nothing to facilitate a forcible change in the territorial status quo in Jammu and Kashmir.

The Kargil crisis left India neutralizing, if not reversing, the considerable strategic advantages that Pakistan had accrued from the nuclearization of the subcontinent. Pakistan's effort to alter forcibly the territorial status quo in Jammu and Kashmir was repulsed. While the international community came down heavily on Pakistan to end its aggression in the Kargil sector, there was no real pressure on Pakistan to give up on cross-border terrorism. Pakistan itself might have been surprised by the results of the Kargil adventure, but it did not believe real constraints had been put in place against any use of violence in Kashmir and India. As the RAND report states,

> The Kargil fiasco does not appear to have extinguished Pakistan's belief that violence, especially as represented by low-intensity conflict, remains the best policy for pressuring India on Kashmir and other outstanding disputes.[27]

Expanding on that theme, the report adds,

> Pakistan perceives its diplomatic and military options to be quite limited as far as resolving the issue of Kashmir is concerned. Given these constraints, Pakistan believes that one of its few remaining *successful* strategies is to 'calibrate' the heat of the insurgency in Kashmir and possibly pressure India through expansion of violence in other portions of India's territory.[28]

In its post-Kargil diplomacy, the United States called for restraint on both sides, sought a resumption of the Indo-Pakistani dialogue and promoted a ceasefire on the Line of Control, but it did not explicitly demand that Pakistan put an end to cross-border terrorism. In other words, the instrument of cross-border terrorism remained intact despite the reverses Pakistan had suffered during Kargil. India's attempts to get around the issue when the dialogue resumed at Agra had to confront Pakistan's refusal to give up the one instrument which it found so effective against India. It took the cataclysmic events of 11 September and the dramatic attack on the Indian Parliament on 13 December for India and the world to confront Pakistan on the issue of cross-border terrorism.

India's Coercive Diplomacy

The attack on the Indian Parliament on 13 December forced India to adopt a new strategy towards Pakistan that called for a head-on confrontation with the neighbour's support to cross-border terrorism. After a decade of the proxy war, the attack on the Parliament was the last straw. India delivered a formal demarche to Pakistan on 14 December, demanding a crackdown on the operations of the terrorist organizations on its soil. Implicit was the threat that if Pakistan did not respond, India would be compelled to use force. India was also signalling it might be fully prepared for a Pakistani retaliation, which could lead to escalation and military confrontation.

The terrorist activity against India by groups based in Pakistan and nurtured by the Pakistani military establishment had become increasingly bold. The attack on the Assembly of Jammu and Kashmir in Srinagar on 1 October 2001, on the Parliament on 13 December 2001 and at Kaluchak in Jammu and Kashmir on 4 May 2002 signalled the determination of these groups to wage a full-scale war against India.

India had to act after 13 December, and it did so by launching the biggest military mobilization in its history. Unlike in the 1965 and 1971 wars when it had to keep the border with China reasonably manned, India could put all its available forces at the border and thus lend credibility to its threat to use force against Pakistan. As in the Kargil crisis, India also moved its eastern fleet to the Arabian Sea to join the mobilization of the western fleet against Pakistan. Reinforcing the military threat at the political level, India pulled back its envoy from Pakistan; sought a reduction of staff at the Pakistan High Commission in New Delhi; restricted the movements of those who stayed back; and terminated rail, road and air transportation links with Pakistan.[29] There was also a debate on whether India should scrap the Indus Waters Treaty of 1961 with Pakistan that had survived past conflicts with its neighbour, but the idea was too extreme to be implemented.

In response Musharraf threatened serious repercussions if India were to launch an attack on Pakistan. India was not unaware of the potential nuclear escalation that its troop movements could incite, but there was a growing belief in New Delhi that the time had come to call Pakistan's nuclear bluff. For too long India had restrained itself in responding to Pakistan's cross-border terrorism, in the light of potential nuclear consequences. After the Kargil War, India realized the importance of regaining strategic space between low-intensity conflicts and a full-scale nuclear war. Recognizing that a war could occur despite its restraint, India debated conventional military options of a limited war.[30] Although limited military operations could indeed be undertaken, no planner could promise that they would not escalate to a higher level. In its effort to force a change in Pakistan's behaviour, India was determined to exploit the nuclear dimension to the hilt.

New Delhi understood that the intensification of military tensions between India and Pakistan with the threat of nuclear conflict would inevitably involve the international community, particularly the United States. In the winter of 1986-87, when the Pakistan Army responded aggressively to the Brass Tacks exercises being conducted by the Indian forces, Washington became active diplomatically. It again came into the picture in May 1990, when Indo-Pakistan tensions began to build up over Kashmir. A high-level team of officials came from Washington to pull the two countries apart. Likewise, during the Kargil War the US intervened to force Pakistan to withdraw from across the LoC. Just as it had used the threat of crossing the LoC in the Kargil conflict to make the US put pressure on Pakistan, India after 13 December threatened to launch an all-

out war against Pakistan if it did not stop cross-border terrorism.
As expected, the Anglo-American powers intervened in an intensive diplomatic engagement with New Delhi and Islamabad. Although the US debated the prospect that the Indian threat to go to war could just be a bluff, Washington could not leave India and Pakistan alone. The results of this intervention were out of tune with past patterns of Anglo-American policy in the region. While cautioning India against too aggressive a posture on the border, the US and Great Britain did not oppose the Indian military mobilization itself or its objective of ending cross-border terrorism. The focus of their efforts instead was on pressing Pakistan in an unprecedented manner to end its support to cross-border terrorism, put down the jihadi organizations at home and get Pakistan on a different national course, one that shunned terrorism as an instrument of state policy. Under the combined Anglo-American pressure, Musharraf promised to unveil a new direction for Pakistan on 12 January 2002. As he prepared for the speech, Prime Minister Tony Blair arrived in Islamabad with a blunt message that cross-border terrorism must end, and Secretary of State Colin Powell burnt the telephone lines to get substantive commitments from Musharraf.

Consequently Musharraf did come up with the formulations India was looking for.[31] He insisted that Pakistani soil would not be used to promote terrorism anywhere in the world. Musharraf also declared that he would not allow the fomentation of violence in the name of fighting for the Kashmir cause. India's own response to the speech was positive, but it insisted that there must be evidence of actual cessation of cross-border terrorism before it could resume engagement with Pakistan. India suggested that the evidence would not come until a comprehensive assessment of trends in cross-border violence could be assessed after the winter months, when infiltration has generally been low. It also wanted action by Pakistan on the list of twenty criminals sought by India and believed to be in Pakistan. In his response, Jaswant Singh expressed India's best wishes for the proposed transformation of Pakistan and Musharraf's proclaimed intent to launch an all-out offensive against the forces of jihad in Pakistan.[32]

The crisis, which appeared to ease in the aftermath of Musharraf's speech, resumed with great intensity when another terrorist attack took place on 14 May at Kaluchak, this time against the armed forces and their families. Indian forces moved to high alert and were ready to go to war on a few hours notice. As India prepared, the international community intervened with greater vigour. President Bush announced that he was despatching two high-level envoys, the Deputy Secretary of State Richard Armitage and Defence Secretary Donald Rumsfeld, to the region. Convinced that the probability of a war between India and Pakistan was reasonably high, the US, the UK, Japan and a number of Western governments urged their citizens to leave the region and reduced the size of their missions. Amidst the height of these military tensions, Armitage extracted the commitment from Musharraf that Pakistan would end cross-border infiltration permanently. Armitage conveyed this commitment, which he claimed was for the international community, to the Indian leadership in early June.[33] In response India agreed to pull back some of its naval forces from the Arabian Sea, reduce the alert level of its armed forces, lift the restrictions imposed on Pakistani overflights and name a new envoy to Islamabad. Even as India took the first steps towards a de-escalation of the confrontation with Pakistan, it was unwilling to resume political dialogue with Pakistan until it implemented its promises.[34]

The full implementation of the promise never occurred. Within days of offering to end infiltration on a permanent basis, Musharraf seemed to suggest that India would have to do its part by opening negotiations on Kashmir. The US publicly insisted that Pakistan keep its promise. The Anglo-American powers strongly supported the Indian position that a dialogue would only follow an end to cross-border terrorism and a military de-escalation. As Pakistan wriggled out of its word,

Washington could not threaten Musharraf. Although infiltration was lower in June and July, it continued. The US also pressed Musharraf to desist from disrupting the elections to the assembly in Jammu and Kashmir during August and September, although violence in the Valley did not stop. Concluding that the US was unwilling to hold Musharraf's feet to the fire, India unilaterally announced a redeployment of its troops from the border in October 2002.[35]

India's first serious attempt at forcing Pakistan to end cross-border terrorism ended inconclusively. Its policy of coercive diplomacy was a bold departure from its previous passive posture on cross-border terrorism. India sought to get out of the uncomfortable box it found itself in from the late 1980s, when Pakistan discovered the advantages of a sustained low-intensity conflict. Although it could not claim victory, India made significant political gains from its coercive diplomacy, including the unambiguous international characterization of violence in Kashmir as terrorism, getting the Western powers to hold Pakistan responsible, obtaining specific assurances from Islamabad to stop cross-border terrorism and an American endorsement of the elections in Jammu and Kashmir as free and fair. Yet India's coercive diplomacy could not be presented as concluding on a positive note. Having unilaterally withdrawn its military mobilization, India was in no mood to engage Pakistan in dialogue.

The Logic of Containment
It will be debated for a long time whether India could have better handled its coercive diplomacy in the first half of 2002. Three broad schools of thought emerged on India's conduct. One believed that India's threat to go to a war and its attempt to manipulate the nuclear risk with Pakistan was reckless. The second school argued that India's coercive diplomacy was long overdue but incomplete in its unwillingness to use military force against Pakistan. It believed that New Delhi should have gone to war or at least launched a limited set of strikes across

the Line of Control. Such use of force would have helped India demonstrate that it will not be deterred by the threat of Pakistani nuclear retaliation. India's reluctance to go to war, this school feared, might have reinforced the perceptions across the border that India had no means to punish Pakistan for its transgressions. This school also argued that it was entirely naïve of India to have assumed that the United States would deliver Pakistan when Washington's dependence on Musharraf had become so acute.

It is the third school that best captured the policy debates within the government on coercive diplomacy, its opportunities and limits. The events of 13 December and 14 May made it clear that India could not have let them pass. India understood that its threat to go to war must be a credible one. At the same time, India knew the dangers of the conflict escalating and leading to a nuclear exchange. New Delhi recognized the importance of tight control over its military forces in its coercive diplomacy. Issuing a credible threat of war but avoiding an unnecessary escalation and exploiting the narrow space between the two for diplomacy was at the heart of India's strategy during the military confrontation with Pakistan after 13 December.

India correctly calculated that the international community would put pressure on Pakistan. For the first time since Pakistan launched the low-intensity conflict against India in the mid-1980s, the United States and Great Britain pressed Islamabad and got verbal commitments from Musharraf to cease infiltration, but they could not get him to implement them fully. The third school suggested that India's problem lay in not defining an appropriate exit strategy from its coercive diplomacy. By poorly articulating its demands and leaving no flexibility in its tactics, India might have squandered the opportunity to maintain international pressure on Pakistan for a longer time.

When to engage and when to yield and how to define victory in the coercive diplomacy were difficult questions for the political leadership. Some within the establishment suggested that India had opportunities on 12 January and in early June to proclaim a victory of sorts. It could have offered more than the tepid response that was put on the table and engaged Pakistan in a new political framework while retaining the military pressure on the border. By making far too many demands, it is argued, India wasted critical moments in its coercive diplomacy. For example, the insistence on handing over the twenty criminals was a demand that Pakistan could never fulfil and only shifted the focus from the key issue of cross-border terrorism. It has also been argued that India could have sustained the military mobilization for an extended period of time while offering to begin talks on cooperative steps to end cross-border terrorism. This school suggested that without the threat of war, the US might have little incentive to keep up the pressure on Pakistan. Preserving the threat of war and keeping the international community involved in finding specific ways to address the problem of infiltration would have been more productive than a unilateral withdrawal of troops without a clear sense of achievement.

India had also not fully determined how best to handle the international involvement in the Indo-Pakistani tensions that it had so deliberately mobilized in its coercive diplomacy. The key question should not have been whether the US could deliver Musharraf in toto; exercises of this kind necessarily end in political ambiguity. The trick lay in managing this ambiguity well, taking advantage of the new openings and nudging the overall context in India's favour. This required an understanding of the limits to coercive diplomacy that by necessity involves third parties, the constraints on the third parties and the unintended consequences. In raising the prospect of a nuclear war, India sought to exploit its newly globalized security environment but failed to go the full distance. When proposals from Washington and London came up for joint assessments on the levels of Pakistani infiltration by officials from India, the US and Great Britain or for Anglo-American monitoring of the Line of Control in Kashmir, New Delhi found it difficult to rid itself of its baggage on bilateralism. Involving the Anglo-Americans in the process of controlling infiltration across the Line of Control in the midst of the crisis could have put sustained pressure on Pakistan. Avoiding the impression of third-party meddling in its disputes with Pakistan seemed more important at the political level.

A final problem with India's coercive diplomacy was that the threat of war seemed to undermine India's own economic prospects, in particular those of the globalized software industry. The spectre of a nuclear war in the subcontinent and the travel advisories for Westerners to leave the country brought forth the full implications of manipulating the nuclear risk with a view to end cross-border terrorism.

Despite all its limitations, India's experimentation with coercive diplomacy involved an important shift to the notion of containing Pakistan. Incremental bureaucratic negotiations in the early 1990s and the attempts by Gujral and Vajpayee to secure political deals at the highest levels with Pakistan did not bear fruit. Containment, which is rooted in the history of US-Soviet relations during the cold war, has emerged as India's only option in dealing with Pakistan. Although there was no formal articulation of a strategy of containment, India's policy towards Pakistan acquired all its characteristics.

India's policy of containment is rooted in the assumption that the establishment in Pakistan is committed towards unremitting war of terror against India. It suggests that India must have an effective mix of military and diplomatic options to confront Pakistan. It would call for a full exploitation of Pakistan's contradictions with its neighbours and the international system and stepping up economic, diplomatic, political and military pressures against Pakistan. The objective of a containment policy towards Pakistan is to engineer, through external pressures, an internal transformation of Pakistan that puts an end to the sources of compulsive hostility towards India. Containment, by nature, is a long-term strategy that calls for patience. It also does not rule out negotiations with the adversary. While India did not demonstrate complete clarity in the pursuit of its coercive diplomacy, a number of new ideas were injected into the Indian thinking, including cooperating with the United States to transform the internal dynamics of Pakistan's society.

Finally a containment policy towards Pakistan would be successful only if India maintains its internal coherence and unity. Even as it launched one of its most important strategic manoeuvres against Pakistan since Partition, India found itself hobbled by an internal crisis of great magnitude. The renewed focus on the Ayodhya temple in early 2002 reopened one of the more controversial issues at home. The destruction of the Babri Masjid in Ayodhya by Hindu mobs in December 1992 and the clamour to build a temple for Lord Ram on the same site heightened Hindu–Muslim tensions in the country throughout the 1990s. The communal carnage in Gujarat, starting in February 2002 when riots against Muslims followed the burning in Godhra of a train carrying Hindu pilgrims who were returning from Ayodhya, shook the nation. The apparent complicity of the BJP-led government in the state in fanning the flames of majoritarian extremism threatened the very organizing principles of the Indian state. More fundamentally, it exposed the deepest Indian vulnerability in dealing with Pakistan—the Hindu-Muslim divide in the country. An India that is communally polarized and politically divided will find it difficult to deal with the external security threats from Pakistan.

EIGHT

Rediscovering Lord Curzon

Grasping at Curzon's Legacy

'Curzon was among the greatest of the Indian nationalists,' former Foreign Secretary J.N. Dixit says.[1] Such enthusiasm in the new century for Lord Curzon of Kedleston, former Viceroy of India and British Foreign Secretary may appear intriguing. In the textbooks of Indian history, he is largely remembered as the man who perpetrated the hugely unpopular partition of Bengal in 1905. However, for sections of the Indian foreign policy elite who have long dreamt of a powerful role for India in its surrounding regions, Curzon remains a source of strategic inspiration.

Writing at the peak of British imperial presence in the subcontinent, Curzon emphasized India's centrality in the Indian Ocean littoral, Asia and the world as a whole. In his 1909 essay *The Place of India in the Empire,* Curzon laid out the essence of his understanding of India's pivotal role:

> It is obvious, indeed, that the master of India, must, under modern conditions, be the greatest power in the Asiatic Continent, and therefore, it may be added, in the world. The central position of India, its magnificent resources, its teeming multitude of men, its great trading harbours, its reserve of military strength, supplying an army always in a high state of efficiency and capable of being hurled at a moment's notice upon any point either of Asia or Africa—all these are assets of precious value. On the West, India

must exercise a predominant influence over the destinies of Persia and Afghanistan; on the north, it can veto any rival in Tibet; on the north-east and east it can exert great pressure upon China, and it is one of the guardians of the autonomous existence of Siam. On the high seas it commands the routes to Australia and to the China Seas.[2]

While Pakistan has always accused independent India of nursing hegemonic ambitions over the Indian Ocean region, many in the nation's foreign policy elite bemoan the loss of the geostrategic perspective that had informed the British rulers of India. Jaswant Singh, India's external affairs minister from 1998 to 2002, belongs to the Curzonian school in defining India's role in its neighbourhood.[3] He is sharply critical of the failure of Jawaharlal Nehru in creating a strategic culture suited to its geographic requirements.[4] Singh laments that India lost its extraordinary influence in the regions abutting the subcontinent and criticizes the past governments for having 'accepted the post-Partition limits geography had imposed on policy'.[5] Traditionalists in the Indian foreign policy establishment bristle at Singh's charge, but others point to the realistic limits on what independent India could have done. Strategic analyst K. Subrahmanyam says,

The British strategic tradition could not be passed on to the new Indian republic because, from the time of Waterloo up to until [*sic*] the 1930s, Britain was the sole superpower in the world. It could hold sway over the entire Indian Ocean arc and convert Tibet, Afghanistan, Iran and Thailand as buffers to protect its empire in India . . . Jawaharlal Nehru . . . knew very well that India could never exercise in the rapidly decolonizing world the power the British Empire could as part of the then sole superpower of the world. It does not make sense to expect the Indian elite at the dawn of independence to have any traditional strategic thinking derived from the British imperial perspective.[6]

The Partition of the subcontinent and its geopolitical consequences constituted a key obstacle to India's ability to exercise a powerful influence in the Indian Ocean littoral. The unending conflict with Pakistan hobbled India. The two wings of Pakistan became geographic barriers to retaining the dominance exercised by the British from Calcutta and New Delhi. Unresolved tensions with a rising China to the north and the east also complicated independent India's regional strategy. If geography imposed a number of limits, insular economic policies increasingly disconnected India from the trade flows in the region. India's espousal of Third World politics did win it a measure of goodwill in its neighbourhood, but its drift towards the Soviet Union and an anti-Western political orientation limited India's ability to shape the dynamics of peace and stability in the Indian Ocean region.

Although Curzon postulated a role for India within the matrix of the British imperial interests, his ideas constituted an Indocentric vision of South Asia and the Indian Ocean littoral. While India does not dominate the region as Great Britain did, it is likely to emerge as a regional centre of power as it realizes its huge growth potential. The neo-Curzonians concede that the implementation of a larger strategic vision for India will have to be entirely different from the original vision and take into account the new realities. Central to the vision will have to be finding ways to act in tandem with the now dominant power of the region, the United States. Until the 1990s, India sought to keep the Western powers out of the Indian Ocean region. In the new situation, political cooperation with the United States becomes central to India's attempts to realize its own primacy in the region. Henry Kissinger has often argued that the Indian Ocean region is the natural strategic space for India. He suggests that as India acquires great power status, it can be expected to return to the policies of the British Raj and it will seek an influential, if not dominant role in the Indian Ocean. New Delhi and Washington, according to Kissinger, do not have a direct conflict of interests in the region, and the two should be able to work together to promote such shared interests as energy security, safeguarding the sea lanes, political stability, economic modernization and religious moderation.[7]

In Search of a Forward Policy

The story of Indian foreign policy in the last decade of the twentieth century was in part about laying the foundations for a recovery of India's role in what increasingly came to be called India's extended neighbourhood. A globalizing India and its improving relations with the West created the space for reordering India's relations with neighbouring regions. This period saw the re-establishment of economic ties between India and its extended neighbourhood as well as an expanded political dialogue between New Delhi and key capitals in the Indian Ocean littoral. India's activism in South-East Asia, Afghanistan, Central and East Asia, the Persian Gulf, and parts of Africa became an important feature of India's new foreign policy. With or without a grand strategic conception, India was forced to deal with each of these regions at the end of the cold war. The results have been impressive and have given rise to hopes for a significant increase in Indian influence in the region.

Forward policy, an idea strongly associated with Lord Curzon, has begun to animate Indian diplomatic activism in the neighbourhood. During the nineteenth century in Great Britain, the forward school argued that India's security demanded British control of the maritime routes and key ports en route to India, the creation of territorial buffers to insulate direct contact between other empires and British India, and an active political role for London and Calcutta in managing the affairs of the buffer zones. The forward school dominated British policy for the region and led to a dramatic expansion of British colonial acquisitions and political activity from the Red Sea to Thailand via the Arab Gulf, Persia, the Central Asian Khanates and Tibet. At the same time there were those who saw this as an expensive policy and argued for a more modest approach, consolidation of British India within closed borders and accommodation with the rival European great powers, particularly the Soviet Union, and the dormant Chinese Empire. The closed-border school was denounced by opponents in Great Britain with the phrase *masterly inactivity*.

Although there is some risk in stretching the analogy of the contest between forward and closed-border schools to Indian policy after Independence, one dimension remains relevant to the understanding of India's approach to its neighbouring regions. The tension between playing a larger role in the neighbourhood and defending its own territory has indeed dominated India's security policy since Independence. After decolonization and Partition, India had to retrench on many of its commitments inherited from the British, with the exception of those relating to the kingdoms in the southern Himalayas. Subsequently, New Delhi increasingly moved towards the ideas of a closed-border approach for India's security. Defending the unsettled borders with Pakistan and China and preventing hostile activity by its neighbours took up much of its energy. Partition, the process of decolonization, the revival of national identities and the territorial expansion of China into Tibet made the ideas of ensuring buffers increasingly untenable. But could India have transcended these geographic and political changes, as was implicit in Jaswant Singh's question? Its ability to do so was circumscribed by the economic orientation India adopted. Its focus on socialism at home and its preference for import substitution rather than export promotion began to make it impossible to develop trade links with its neighbouring regions.

At the political level, India's emphasis on Third World solidarity and Asian identity raised its profile in regional affairs, but it also led to the creation of an illusion about the country's leadership role. Although the focus on Third World politics sounded fine in the multilateral settings, it did little to create a basis for peace and stability within the neighbouring regions. The Non-Aligned Movement did not have the power to insulate the regions from the great power rivalries of the cold war. Even India itself had to adapt to the dynamics of the shifting power balances around it. As it turned out, India, increasingly aligned with the Soviet Union, found itself on the losing side of the cold war in the region. In the security arena, the emphasis on non-alignment led to an isolationist policy on the question of defence links with key players in the abutting regions. Nations like Singapore in South-East Asia and the sheikhdoms in the Gulf, which looked to India as provider of security, found India reluctant to undertake that responsibility. India was big with words on global macrosecurity issues, but it had little to offer in terms of security for small nations beyond the subcontinent.

The end of the cold war and the efforts to globalize the economy put India willy-nilly on the path of a new forward policy. India never consciously articulated its approach in terms of theory that demanded activism in the neighbouring regions to enhance its own security. Its regional initiatives were presented in terms of mutual economic benefit and the restoration of historic links, but their strategic significance was unmistakable.

Comprised of six elements, India's new forward policy was simple in its design. First, it sought to revive commercial cooperation wherever possible. As India looked for markets for its goods and investments for domestic growth, it was inevitable that it would concentrate on East Asia during the 1990s. The Gulf became an attractive partner, particularly in relation to energy security. Second, the Indian diplomacy also focussed on building institutional and political links with neighbouring regions.

Third, developing physical connectivity to the neighbouring regions became an important preoccupation for India. Pakistan has been a geographic and political barrier to Pakistan and Afghanistan. Bangladesh is an obstacle to reaching its own territory in the North-East as well as South-East Asia. Overcoming these physical barriers by developing road links to the extended neighbourhood has emerged at the heart of the Indian strategy. Mega-energy projects such as transregional pipelines to connect sources of natural gas in the neighbourhood to the energy-hungry Indian market form the fourth dimension of the country's forward policy. The fact that India was the biggest potential consumer of natural gas resources in the Gulf, Central Asia and South-East Asia gave it extraordinary leverage in shaping the terms of these projects.

The fifth aspect of India's forward policy was the initiation of defence contacts with key nations in the extended neighbourhood as well as the major powers. In the 1990s India began to shed its defence isolationism and step up security engagement in the region. Besides the expanding military cooperation with the United States, it began to increase port calls by its naval ships in the region and take part in frequent naval exercises with nations of South-East Asia and the Gulf. India's peacekeeping operations worldwide also went up significantly in the 1990s. Likewise, India got more directly involved in the civil war in Afghanistan by extending military assistance to the Northern Alliance. It posted military attachés in its missions in Central Asia. Institutionalized defence and strategic dialogue with important nations of the region also became a norm. India's steady advances in the arena of defence diplomacy were by no means spectacular, but they demonstrated a new intent by New Delhi to become an important element in the balance of power in various regions of the Indian Ocean littoral.

Sixth, strategic competition with China and Pakistan emerged as an unstated element of India's forward policy in the neighbouring regions. In East and South-East Asia, India's economic and strategic approaches were animated by an undeclared rivalry with China. India was not going to join a future containment of China, but it was developing its own political equities in the region by promoting trade and defence contacts. Although New Delhi did not have economic resources or political assets comparable to those of Beijing, it was determined to regain its lost standing in the region. India managed to stave off the attempts by Pakistan to gain entry into the political structures associated with Association of South-East Asian Nations (ASEAN) and denied it the membership of Indian Ocean Rim Association for Regional Cooperation

(IORARC), and in Afghanistan and Central Asia the rivalry with Pakistan became a relentless one.

Looking East

One of the most comprehensive and successful examples of India's forward policy has been in relation to South-East Asia. The Look East Policy was unveiled by Narasimha Rao in Singapore in 1994 and paid handsome dividends to India in the following years. It sought to end the political neglect of South-East Asia in the preceding decades and gain from the economic miracle that transformed the region during the late 1970s and 1980s. By the turn of the century its economic, political, strategic and institutional relations with the ASEAN got a big boost.[8] India's Look East Policy was not limited to South-East Asia. It also involved a conscious effort to improve relations with Japan, South Korea and Australia, all of whom, like the ASEAN, became politically distant from India during the cold war.

India's Look East Policy went through two distinct phases. The first focussed on renewing political and commercial contact. Despite widespread doubts in the region about India's economic prospect and its ability to become a consistent partner, India's new engagement with the East turned out to be a productive one thanks to the strong political support from key nations like Singapore. At the institutional level, India's interaction with the ASEAN dramatically expanded with New Delhi becoming a sectoral dialogue partner with the ASEAN in 1992 and a full dialogue partner in 1996. In 1996 India was also invited to join the ASEAN's discussions on regional security in the ASEAN Regional Forum, which had been created in 1994.[9] The ASEAN held a collective summit with India (the ASEAN Plus One Summit) for the first time in November 2002 in Cambodia.[10]

As India launched itself on the course of globalization in 1991, East and South-East Asia began to loom large in its national economic strategy. The first years of the Look East Policy saw a steady expansion of trade and investment links with the region. ASEAN–India trade in 2001-02 was about $7.8 billion, over

three times the 1993-94 trade figure of $2.5 billion. From a
negligible amount in 1991, cumulative approved foreign direct
investment (FDI) (January 1991 to May 2002) from the ASEAN
was over $4 billion in May 2002; this represents a share of 6.1
per cent in the total FDI approved by India in this period. Actual
inflow of FDI from the ASEAN during this period (January
1991 to May 2002) was, however, more modest: $620 million,
representing 3.4 per cent of total FDI flows in to India.[11] The
slow pace of India's economic reforms, however, frustrated
nations like Singapore that were rooting for India. Moreover,
the economic crisis that rocked South-East Asia in the late 1990s
also dampened the prospects for a rapid economic integration
between India and the ASEAN.

Yet Singapore and Thailand kept pressing for free trade
arrangements with India. After considerable hesitation initially,
India began to recognize the importance of free trade
arrangements with the region, and it was decided at the ASEAN
Plus One Summit that India and the grouping as a whole would
explore the creation of a liberal trading order among themselves.
Besides the ASEAN, South Korea and Australia emerged as
important economic partners of India in the 1990s and as the
fifth and eighth largest foreign investors in India at the turn of
the century. The expectations of a dramatic growth in Indo-
Japanese economic relations, however, were not realized,
because Tokyo was beset by its own internal troubles and was
slow in responding to Indian economic reforms.

The second phase in India's Look East Policy had a new
dimension—the development of India's remote North-East.
India's search for a new economic relationship with South-
East Asia was driven by considerations of globalization and the
domestic imperative of developing the North-East by increasing
its connectivity to the outside world. Instead of consciously
trying to isolate the region from external influences as it had
done in the past, New Delhi began to recognize the importance
of opening it up for commercial linkages with South-East Asia.
India has sought to improve the road connections between the

North-East and Myanmar by investing in the transport infrastructure of the neighbour. India and Thailand have planned a trilateral project with Myanmar to link the three nations through a road corridor. By taking advantage of Myanmar as a land bridge to South-East Asia, India hopes to transform the North-East from a security burden into a land of economic opportunity.[12]

The second phase of the Look East Policy also saw the unveiling of the geopolitical dimension. As the region looked around in the post-cold war world, the focus began to shift from the threat posed by the Soviet Union to the consequences of a rising China for a regional balance of power. There was an expectation in South-East Asia that an economically vibrant India could contribute to a stable balance of power in the region. But India's nuclear tests of May 1998 at once magnified its potential standing in East Asia and complicated its immediate relations with the region. The ASEAN was relatively muted in its criticism of the tests, and it resisted pressures in 1998 from the US, China, Japan, Australia and New Zealand to condemn them.[13]

After the nuclear tests, India's relations with Japan and Australia soured, and it took considerable effort to restore normal ties. While Tokyo and Canberra followed Washington's lead in sharply criticizing New Delhi, they found it difficult to grasp the meaning of the immediate attempt by New Delhi and Washington to explore a nuclear reconciliation. Japan and Australia took an activist role in setting the global arms control agenda since the late 1980s, and they were strong supporters of the CTBT. India's rejection of the treaty in 1996 and its nuclear tests deeply offended the political sensibilities of Tokyo and Canberra. New Delhi in turn was angered by the high-handed diplomatic reactions to the tests in the two capitals. Australia sent home Indian officers attending defence courses in the country, and Japan cancelled high-level official visits and appeared to shun political contact. Both took the lead in multilateral meetings in isolating India. Japan went further by trying to befriend Pakistan to prevent it from conducting its own nuclear tests. Moreover, India took strong exception to Japan's efforts to take on an activist role on Kashmir and its unacceptable offers to mediate between the two.

As an Indo-US nuclear reconciliation unfolded and the political ties between New Delhi and Washington moved in a positive direction, it was a matter of time before Tokyo and Canberra climbed down from the high political horse they had mounted after Pokhran-II. Australia was quicker, and Prime Minister John Howard's visit to India in 2000 resulted in an agreement to unfreeze bilateral relations and expand cooperation. The visit to Australia in June 2001 by Jaswant Singh led to an agreement to hold institutionalized strategic dialogue between the two countries, the first round of which took place in August 2001.[14] This provided a forum for the first time in decades for Australia and India to discuss political stability and the balance of power in Asia and to work together for maritime security in the region.[15] India and Australia have finally put behind them the cold war-induced political separation and the differences over the nuclear tests, and they are beginning to rediscover their many common interests. Australia, which launched a political campaign against India and its naval ambitions in the 1980s, was now ready to look at India as a partner in the security politics of the region.

Japan took much longer to re-engage India and was virtually the last major power to reconcile itself to India's emergence as a declared nuclear weapons power. Jaswant Singh's visit to Japan in November 1999 and Prime Minister Yoshiro Mori's visit to India in August 2000 helped normalize the bilateral relations. The period of acrimony after the nuclear tests did serve a purpose, according to a senior Indian diplomat, S. Jaishankar, who served in Tokyo at the difficult juncture. He explained, 'For all its downside, it provided a much needed reality check which, by briefly stripping our ties of false sentiment, allowed for a serious engagement, perhaps for the first time.'[16] After Japan lifted the sanctions it had imposed on India in October

2001, Vajpayee travelled there in December, and the commitment to build a wide-ranging partnership was reiterated.

Stagnant trade and economic relations as well as political wariness, however, seemed to limit the prospects for a deeper relationship. While there was considerable interest in India in expanding the political relationship with Japan, Tokyo seemed hesitant. Even when the Japanese political leadership appeared to show interest in transforming bilateral political relations, the bureaucracy of Tokyo's Foreign Office appeared reluctant to let things move forward. A huge bilateral agenda, ranging from energy security to protection of the sea lanes in the Indian Ocean to maintaining a stable balance of power in Asia, awaits India and Japan.

Despite the slow pace of movement in bilateral relations, it is inevitable that Indo-Japanese strategic cooperation will begin to expand in the first decade of the twenty-first century. As Japan considers its own growing marginalization in Asia amidst the rise of China and confronts a fast-changing security scenario in the region, political cooperation with India is likely to emerge as an important priority for it. A study on the relations between Tokyo and New Delhi in the 1990s argues that

> Japan and India do have interrelated security concerns. Of course, both countries are faced with a more and more confident, but also more and more uncertain, China, a rival for their own influence in Asian affairs and on the global scene. . . . More deeply, Japan and India are faced with the challenge to influence the world order established before the cold war to better accommodate the realities of the early 21st century, including those bearing on their security.[17]

The first hints of a possible movement came from the Japanese foreign minister, Yoriko Kawaguchi. On the eve of her visit to India in January 2003, she talked about injecting some strategic content into the ties with New Delhi.[18] India and Japan began tentative defence contacts in the late 1990s, but they were suspended in the wake of the nuclear tests. In January 2000 George Fernandes undertook the first official visit by an Indian defence minister to Tokyo. Both sides agreed to initiate a regular defence and security dialogue and expand defence personnel exchanges, military education and training. Fernandes, who travelled again to Japan in 2001 and 2002, is believed to have developed an extraordinary personal rapport with Japanese political leaders. His extensive contacts with the socialists in Japan were matched by the political empathy with those in Japan who see China as a long-term threat. Fernandes's own reputation as a China-basher endeared him to the nationalist forces in Japan. Subsequently the Indian Navy and the Japanese Maritime Self-defence Force have begun to exchange ship visits to participate in joint exercises to combat piracy on the high seas.[19]

During her visit to New Delhi, Kawaguchi highlighted the prospect for intensifying military and strategic cooperation between India and Japan. Endorsing the new defence relations between New Delhi and Washington as contributing to Asian stability and noting the advances in Indo-Japanese defence contacts, Kawaguchi said, 'Cooperative maintenance of the security of maritime traffic in the sea-lanes [*sic*] that stretch across the Indian Ocean and the Straits of Malacca are among the security and defence issues which deserve our increased attention. Both countries share common interests and concerns regarding these issues.'[20]

As with Japan, the potential for building strategic cooperation with South Korea remains immense. Unlike Japan, South Korea moved quickly to expand economic cooperation with India in the 1990s and emerged as the fifth largest foreign investor in India. During the cold war, India drew closer to North Korea and dismissed the importance of the South. Recently it has made important adjustments to its policy. Besides an expanding economic relationship, political contacts have increased and led to some interesting agreements in the areas of high technology. India agreed in 1993 to supply heavy water to Seoul's nuclear programme under international safeguards. In 1999, a South Korean satellite was put into orbit by the first commercial launch of the polar satellite launch vehicle.[21] As reports of clandestine nuclear and missile cooperation between Pakistan and North Korea came in, New Delhi and Seoul began to recognize the interconnections between the security environments of the subcontinent and the Korean Peninsula. Sections of the South Korean establishment are keen that defence and strategic cooperation with India must be taken forward.[22]

Playing the Great Game

The humiliating retreat of Soviet troops from Afghanistan in 1988 and the emergence of the Central Asian republics (CARs) from the defunct Soviet Union opened up the north-western neighbourhood of India to extraordinary dynamism in the 1990s. Just as Afghanistan and the Central Asian Khanates were a perennial concern for the defence of British India's north-west frontier and a source of rivalry with Russia in the nineteenth century, so for India they constituted a key foreign policy preoccupation from the last decade of the twentieth century. The region at once became the source of new threats as well as opportunities to expand India's strategic role in the region.

The return of Central Asia to the world from the innards of the Soviet Union generated a political romance in New Delhi about rekindling the historic links between India and the region. The metaphor of the Great Game—invoking the rivalry between imperial Russia and Great Britain in the nineteenth century for influence in the region—became the dominant prism through which the Indian elite viewed Central Asia. The discovery of large quantities of oil and natural gas in the region intensified the competition for influence in the region. Unlike the Great Game of the past in which Calcutta played the key role, New Delhi had to work extremely hard to be counted in the region amidst wider and more complicated rivalries involving the Soviet Union, the United States, China, Pakistan, Iran, Saudi Arabia and Turkey. India's policy towards Afghanistan and Central Asia demonstrated the dichotomy between its aspirations for a larger role in its north-western neighbourhood and the real constraints on it. Nevertheless, there was considerable progress in India's engagement of the region which went through many twists and turns.

India's first challenge was to pick up the pieces from its shattered Afghan policy at the turn of the 1990s. India's refusal to criticize the Soviet military intervention in Afghanistan at the end of 1979 isolated it from much of the international and regional opinion as well as from large sections of the Afghan people. Although it privately urged Moscow to reconsider its military intervention in Afghanistan in the early 1980s, New Delhi was not really prepared to deal with the Soviet withdrawal from Afghanistan in 1988. The capture of Kabul by the Pakistan-backed mujahedin, supported by the United States, the Islamic countries and China, seemed to bring to a close the long-standing special relations India had enjoyed with Afghanistan since Partition.

Pakistan, chafing at the good ties between India and Afghanistan, desperately sought strategic depth in Afghanistan by installing a friendly if not pliable regime there. Pakistan wanted not just military space for itself in its confrontation with India but also to use Afghanistan as a bridge to Central Asia and emerge as a powerful force in the region. The romance in Islamabad about the grand historic opportunity in Afghanistan and Central Asia was far more intensive than that in New Delhi.[23] The triumphalism in Pakistan in 1992 after ousting the Najibullah regime backed by Moscow and New Delhi, however, quickly yielded to concern as the mujahedin squabbled among themselves and pushed Afghanistan into a tragic civil war. As contradictions between Pakistan and the new rulers of Kabul began to unfold, India found its first opportunity to re-establish a positive relationship with the leaders of Kabul. For a moment it appeared that the traditional framework of Afghanistan's problems with neighbouring Pakistan and the natural friendship with once-removed India would begin to re-emerge. Pakistan, however, was determined to prevent a return to the old paradigm in the triangular relationship.

To end the internecine warfare among the mujahedin and bring a measure of control over Afghanistan, Pakistan helped create the Taliban, a new force that came into prominence in 1994. Backed by the Pakistani military support, the Taliban gained substantial control of Afghanistan in 1996 and 1997.[24] As Pakistan gained the upper hand in Kabul, India found itself in a quandary. While the Taliban government departed from the traditional Kabul policy of seeking friendly relations with New Delhi, India began in 1997 a modest level of economic and military assistance to the opponents of the Taliban holed up in the northern parts of Afghanistan. Later India would step up coordination with Iran and Russia to strengthen the Northern Alliance more purposefully.[25]

As it extended support to the Northern Alliance, there was brief debate within the policy circles in New Delhi about the possibility of finding an accommodation with the Taliban. The movement had its strongest support among the Pashtuns, the dominant group in Afghanistan and historically the one segment of the Afghan population with which India had been intimate. Many realists in New Delhi questioned the wisdom of opposing the Pashtuns and handing them over to Pakistan. The Taliban leaders often suggested that they were ready for an engagement with India and that New Delhi should not see them as an extension of Pakistan.[26] But the religious extremism of the Taliban, its support to terrorist groups operating in Kashmir, and the deep links between the Pakistani security establishment and the Taliban leadership proved a deterrent against any attempt to explore a serious rapprochement with the regime in Kabul. The Taliban's role in humiliating India in the hijacking of the Indian Airlines flight IC 814 to Kandahar in December 1999 shattered all illusions.

By early to mid-2001, the Taliban looked ready to oust the Northern Alliance from its strongholds in north-eastern Afghanistan. Many neighbouring countries and major powers, despite their distaste for the Taliban, were beginning to consider the possibility that engaging the Taliban might become inevitable. On the very eve of a huge political triumph for the Taliban, its fate was sealed. The dramatic developments of 11 September brought America to wage war against the Taliban and to oust it from Kandahar in December 2001. The developments of late 2001 dramatically reversed India's and Pakistan's fortunes in Afghanistan. Under pressure from the United States, Pakistan had to end its support for the Taliban and facilitate its demise. The rebel groups earlier supported by India now occupied key positions in the interim government set up in Kabul with the backing of the international community.

For India it was a double victory. The defeat of the Taliban represented a huge gain for India as Afghanistan under the Taliban had become a sanctuary for extremists operating against it. More fundamentally, the ouster of the Taliban allowed India to regain entry into Kabul and expand its political and economic weight in Afghanistan in a radically different international and regional framework. Seizing the opportunity, India quickly moved in to establish diplomatic missions in different parts of Afghanistan. Besides the embassy in Kabul, India reopened its earlier consulates in Kandahar and Jalalabad and set up new ones in Herat and Mazar-e-Sharif. Taking advantage of the significant role the leaders of the Northern Alliance had acquired in Kabul, India created the basis for substantive economic, political and security interaction with Afghanistan and was engaged in building the nation from scratch. While friends from the Northern Alliance were valuable in the new Afghanistan, India still had the task of rebuilding bridges with the Pashtuns who might have the reason to believe they got less than their due in the new arrangements and were alienated from India over the previous two decades.

India's post-Taliban diplomatic activism alarmed Pakistan, and its concerns were conveyed to India by the United States, which worried that the Indo-Pakistani rivalry might have its debilitating effects on Afghanistan.[27] Pakistan also refused to give overland transit facilities for Indian aid and goods to reach Afghanistan. While the US was keen to promote economic cooperation among India, Pakistan and Afghanistan, there was little interest in Islamabad to create the basis for commercial contacts beneficial to all. With geography coming in the way of a larger role for India in Afghanistan, India once again had to find alternative ways of reaching Afghanistan. It tried to break out of this box by developing cooperation with Iran to find another route.

At the beginning of 2003, New Delhi, Teheran and Kabul signed a memorandum of understanding to build a new transport corridor from the Chabahar port in south-eastern Iran to central Afghanistan, where it will connect with the garland road system linking all major Afghan cities. India is expected to build a section of this road in Afghanistan, and Iran will develop the port at Chabahar and facilitate the movement of Indian goods into Afghanistan. Tehran offered substantial cuts in various tariffs in the shipment of goods to Afghanistan. This corridor will allow India to circumvent the Pakistan barrier and provide access to the Afghani and Central Asian markets.[28] It could also be the basis for a free trade agreement with Afghanistan that New Delhi has been negotiating with Kabul since the end of 2002. While the situation in Afghanistan remains fragile and Pakistan is determined not to give up its leverages there, India has gained a new standing in Kabul; consolidating it will be an important task for New Delhi.

In Central Asia too, the gap between India's strategic aspirations in the region and the reality on the ground was substantial. India defined for itself a fourfold objective in Central Asia. First, it wanted to gain a political and economic presence in these countries. Second, it was interested in preserving the moderate religious character of the regimes, most of whom were led by former Soviet communist party bosses. Third, it wanted to gain access to the large hydrocarbon resources in the region. Finally, it had its unstated objective of limiting Pakistani influence in the region. The results of a decade-long intensive engagement with Central Asia present a mixed picture.

India, which was among the few countries Moscow allowed

to interact with the Central Asian leaders before the collapse of the Soviet Union, found itself quite welcome in the region, but its ability to achieve its objectives was constrained by its lack of physical access and economic resources to play the Great Game in Central Asia. India was among the first countries to establish diplomatic relations with the Central Asian republics— Turkmenistan, Uzbekistan, Tajikistan, Kyrgyzstan and Kazakhstan—and its focus was riveted on these countries located to the east of the Caspian. Its engagement of Azerbaijan, Armenia and Georgia in the Caucasus was to come later and remain secondary.

Facing the land barrier in the form of Pakistan and Afghanistan, India sought alternate routes into Central Asia through Iran in the mid-1990s, but the agreements to create rail corridors into the region through Iran did not take hold. India also had difficulty financing commercial cooperation because of its own precarious economic situation in the early 1990s. Although it gave credit lines to the countries of the region in the order of a few million dollars, they were too insignificant to make an impact. Moreover, India did not move quickly to set up banking facilities or get its airlines operating in the region.[29] On the political front, India had little problem in finding common cause with Kazakhstan, Kyrgyzstan, Tajikistan and Uzbekistan in opposing religious extremism and ethnic separatism. They were frightened by the rise of the Taliban in Afghanistan and its effects on their own stability. The Taliban was funding dissident groups in Uzbekistan, Tajikistan and Kyrgyzstan, but the region's ability to deal with internal violence appeared dubious. Although India and the CARs began to develop security cooperation against terrorism in the mid-1990s, it was Moscow, Beijing and Washington that eventually became the players in dealing with these challenges. Russia and China set up the Shanghai Cooperation Organization (SCO) with the neighbouring CARs in 2001. While India was keen to join the SCO, it would not make a formal request sensing opposition from China, for Beijing argued that the organization must deepen its cooperation rather than broaden the membership.[30] Beijing hinted that if India were to become a member, Pakistan should also be allowed to join. Russia and a few Central Asian republics were supportive, but they were not influential enough to get India admitted.

To access the hydrocarbon resources, India had to overcome the Pakistani and Afghani barriers. The US energy company UNOCAL was keen to build a natural gas pipeline from Turkmenistan to Pakistan and India via Afghanistan. Pakistan strongly supported the project, and the two tried to get the Taliban's backing, but its leadership seemed less than enthusiastic, despite the obvious benefits from such a pipeline.[31] Eventually the Taliban's steadily declining political credit with the United States and the continuing political instability in Afghanistan forced UNOCAL to withdraw from the project in the late 1990s. The demise of the Taliban after 11 September revived the interest in pipelines from Turkmenistan running southward to the Indian Ocean and the subcontinent.[32] At the end of 2002, Turkmenistan, Afghanistan and Pakistan signed an agreement to build a natural gas pipeline.[33] Although India was one of the obvious markets for the natural gas resources from Central Asia, it could not join these efforts because of the tense relations with Pakistan and an unwillingness to accept pipelines running through Pakistan. India was nevertheless confident that these projects would not succeed without its participation and was willing to wait until the problems with Pakistan were sorted out. While taking a passive approach to the pipelines, India sought opportunities for investing in the projects to develop hydrocarbon resources in Central Asia. As its economic situation improved in the late 1990s, India was confident about putting large sums of money in the greenfield projects of the region.[34]

The Central Asians deeply distrusted Pakistan's policies of promoting religious extremism, in particular the Taliban, but they found it necessary to engage Pakistan in managing their problems in Afghanistan. The desperate need of the Central Asian nations, many of whom had to cross the territory of at least one or two nations to get access to the world markets, made them look to Pakistan to provide a gateway to the Indian Ocean through Afghanistan. Some, like Turkmenistan, ended up supporting Pakistan's policies in Afghanistan, and others, like Uzbekistan, were often willing to elevate relations with Pakistan above those with India.

While post-Partition geography, lack of resources and rivalry with Pakistan hobbled Indian policy towards Central Asia in the early 1990s, the American war on terrorism following the ouster of the Taliban, and stronger instruments of economic diplomacy created the foundations for a more productive engagement with the region. While criticism at home for not pursuing an effective policy towards Central Asia remains, external observers saw India's moves in the region as reflecting a restoration of the Curzonian vision. One American analyst argued that 'India has rediscovered its prior history, including that of the British Raj, which articulated very clear strategic concepts regarding Central Asia. Historically the Raj kept a close watch for threats emanating from Central Asia and Afghanistan that could threaten British sovereignty in India and the country's integrity, among them Islamic insurgency. Today India has had to return to this process.'[35]

Rethinking the Middle East

As in South-East Asia and in Afghanistan, India woke up to a vastly altered reality in the Middle East, one which demanded significant political adjustments to foreign policy towards a region of vital importance to it. The American war to liberate Kuwait from Iraq in 1991 found India unable to take a clear position, and the gap between its assumptions and the reality was wide. Although Rajiv Gandhi began to bring a fresh approach to the region, it was only after the Gulf war that India undertook changes in its policy towards the Middle East. Driven by the imperatives of the post-cold war world and the requirements of internal economic reform, the Narasimha Rao government began the reorientation of Indian diplomacy towards the region.

The Vajpayee government lent it some robustness, and by the turn of the decade India was wooing the full spectrum of Middle Eastern states on a broad-based agenda.

The first step was to remove the perceptions in the region of total Indian commitment to Saddam Hussein in the Gulf war and its inability to stand up for the sovereignty of Kuwait. Pictures of External Affairs Minister I.K. Gujral embracing and kissing Saddam Hussein in 1990 seemed to freeze the image of India as being unwilling to challenge Iraqi aggression and ready to acquiesce in the subjugation of Kuwait. Gujral has argued that his principal concern was to ensure the safe return of thousands of Indian migrant labour trapped in the region during the 1990-91 Gulf crisis, and cooperation with Saddam Hussein at that time was indeed crucial.[36] Nevertheless, the kingdoms of the Gulf were deeply disappointed with India's support of Saddam Hussein. The Indian political class in turn was shocked at the demonstration of the American power in the Gulf war and concerned at the emergence of an imbalanced international system dominated by one superpower. Although India extended overflight and refuelling facilities to the American military aircraft operating under the UN mandate against Iraq, signs of popular opposition to American bombing forced a withdrawal of Indian cooperation, just a couple of days before the US called an end to military operations. India appeared to have lost its way in the region. The defeat of Iraq also meant the marginalization of the radical forces in the Arab world and creation of political space for negotiations between Israel and Palestine and between the Jewish state and moderate Arab states. As the peace process unfolded in the Middle East, India's own total identification with radical Arab positions on Israel also had to be reconsidered.

The new Indian outreach to the Middle East was marked by five important conceptual shifts in Indian foreign policy. The first was the transition from an ideological approach to a pragmatic one. This verbal self-hypnosis of non-alignment meant that New Delhi had no time for some very important countries in the Middle East. Nothing else can explain India's long neglect of Saudi Arabia and Turkey. It had virtually written off these two nations as either lackeys of the United States or staunch friends of Pakistan until a very serious bid was made in the late 1990s to repair relationships with both. In its ideological approach to the region, India also preferred to deal with secular republics rather than conservative sheikhdoms. This differentiation has largely become irrelevant, as many of the secular republics have degenerated into authoritarian regimes, and some conservative monarchies have kept up with the times by attempting cautious political liberalization. As India's approach to the region changed, its dominant friends in the region began to change too. Among the radical Arab nationalists, Egypt moved closer to the United States, and Syria and Iraq became increasingly isolated in the 1990s. While the importance of Egypt and the Baathist states had declined for India, Turkey, Saudi Arabia, Iran, Oman and other moderate Gulf regimes began to loom larger in its view.

A second important change was the shift from a one-sided position in favour of Arabs in their dispute with Israel to a more balanced stance. As an emerging power, India recognized that it must be able to do business with all sides in a region. After considerable hand wringing, nagging doubts about the political fallout at home and in the Middle East from engaging Israel, and widespread consultations, Narasimha Rao decided to re-establish diplomatic relations with Tel Aviv in January 1992. There was same vocal opposition from those within the Congress party who believed India should do nothing to dilute Indian support to the Palestine cause and Arab nationalism.[37] The decision not to engage Israel during the earlier decades was closely linked to domestic politics. During his visit to Israel in July 2001, Jaswant Singh said that India's policy was tied to the Muslim vote bank politics. In the early years of the Partition, he suggested, '[I]t was felt that injustice must not be done to Muslims . . . . India's Israel policy became captive to domestic policy and therefore an unstated veto.'[38]

Singh's remarks coming amidst an aggressive pursuit of cooperation with Israel by the BJP-led government caused some dismay among Indian traditionalists and the Arab world. But his views were widely shared within the foreign policy establishment, many of whom felt India's national interests were sacrificed to meet domestic political objectives.[39] Given the extraordinary goodwill for Israel in India and the enormous potential for bilateral relations, the ties between the two nations expanded rapidly in the 1990s and included highly sensitive defence and security cooperation. The relationship with Israel became one of the most important ones for India during the 1990s.[40] While there were many gains in the new relationship with Israel, it was not a substitute for engaging the Arab and Muslim world. India had considerable economic and political interests in the Middle East that could not be ignored. As India quickly discovered, it did not have to choose between Arabs and Israelis; it could do business with both.[41]

India's new Middle East policy recognized the shades of grey in the region and acknowledged the pragmatism of the Arabs themselves, who did not really object to India's new relations with Israel despite Pakistan's effort to discredit India in the region. There were some fears in the Arab world about the strategic dimensions of the cooperation between India and Israel in the reported nuclear and defence fields. The expression of Arab concerns, although partly promoted by Pakistan, could be seen as a caution to India not to try to alter the military balance in the Middle East. As the peace process broke down in the late 1990s, the Arab nations showed concern that India's voice had become either too muted or neutral in the Arab-Israeli conflict. As Prime Minister Ariel Sharon launched his aggressive campaign against the Palestinians, India's position was attacked at home for being too balanced; in fact it was a significant retrenchment of traditional support to the Arab cause. Indian support could no longer be taken for granted by the Arabs in its disputes with the US and Israel. This new Indian approach was to develop equities on both sides, and

New Delhi was loath to project itself as a potential interlocutor between Israel and the Arabs. India's diplomatic energies were focussed more on the Gulf than the Arab-Israeli dispute.

A third important transition in India's policy in the Middle East was on the commercial front—from the mercantilism of the past to the quest for deeper economic integration. Earlier its commercial policy towards the region was simple—figuring out the best possible deals on oil purchases and counting the value of remittances from Indian expatriate labour in the Gulf. The lack of adequate energy sources at home had always made the Persian Gulf crucial in India's energy arithmetic. Even with a modest growth of 5 to 6 per cent in the economy, the size and quality of India's dependence on energy imports will continue to rise and make up a substantial portion of its import bill. By the 1990s, however, India was no longer talking just about oil dependence on the Gulf; it began to articulate the concept of energy security.[42] Looking beyond simple buyer–seller relationships, India began to explore more enduring energy links. The new focus on natural gas as a clean energy source, the discovery of large natural gas fields in the Gulf and India's emergence as a major importer of this fuel deepened the concept of energy security. Natural gas requires the creation of fixed assets like pipelines and negotiation of long-term price and supply contracts. Plans for pipelines connecting the Gulf with the subcontinent brought into bold relief the idea that peace and prosperity in the Gulf and the subcontinent are inextricably intertwined.

After a decline in the wake of the Gulf war in 1991, the numbers of Indian migrant labourers in the Gulf swelled to nearly three and a half million by the end of the 1990s. An overwhelming majority of them, nearly 1.5 million, were in Saudi Arabia. If oil purchases and remittances by Indian labour were taken into account, the financial value of India's relationship with the Arab Gulf countries (excluding Iraq) was estimated in 2001 to be around $15 billion.[43] India began to focus on creating formal and institutional structures to develop relations with the Gulf countries that included activation of joint commissions, regular consultations between foreign offices and high-level political exchanges. Basic agreements on investment protection, avoidance of double taxation and exploration of defence contacts began to be put in place.

The Gulf was no longer just a source of oil and a destination for Indian labour; it was also seen as an economic and political partner. While engaging traditional friends like Oman, India was also prepared to take the initiative in transforming the difficult relations with Saudi Arabia, which was long seen as being too supportive of Pakistan. Jaswant Singh's visit to Saudi Arabia in 2001, the first by an Indian foreign minister since Nehru visited in the 1950s, reflected India's determination to build solid cooperative relationships with the region without the past ideological baggage.[44] India's warming relations with the Arab Gulf states were partly overshadowed by the rapid improvement in ties with the Islamic Republic of Iran. Besides energy security, their common opposition to the Taliban and shared interests in Central Asia brought India and Iran together in the mid- to late 1990s. The visits to Iran by Singh in May 2000 and Vajpayee in April 2001 and by the Iranian President, Mohammad Khatami, to India in January 2003 helped consolidate a valuable strategic partnership between the two.

Fourth, New Delhi has found a new common agenda with the key nations of the Middle East on the political front—support for political moderation and opposition to religious extremism. From secular Algeria and Turkey to deeply religious Saudi Arabia and Iran, one single threat looms large in the Islamic world: the rise of new religious fanaticism and extremism that threatens peace in large parts of the Middle East. The rise of the Taliban in the mid-1990s facilitated a new political convergence between India and as diverse a group of Islamic nations as Turkey, Iran and Saudi Arabia. The extremist threats to peace and stability have altered the political discourse in the Islamic world, encouraging regimes of different persuasions—from the conservative to the radical—to recognize the importance of working together to defeat the new messianic forces. The evolution of the political discourse against extremism in the key Islamic nations augurs well for India. Many of them see India as a responsible power that is wedded to regional stability. As India sheds its past ideological inhibitions in dealing with the Middle East, it has become possible to build a solid regional coalition to isolate and contain the forces of terror and destabilization. After the events of 11 September, the prospects for such cooperation between India and the Middle East have significantly improved.

Finally, the biggest transition has been India's handling of the Pakistan factor in dealing with the Middle East. Neutralizing Pakistan and its ability to play the card of Islam in the Middle East has been an important consideration for India since Independence. Emerging from Partition, India found a hostile Pakistan that claimed to be a land for all Muslims. This put India in a rather uncomfortable situation with the Middle East. Pakistan's claim to the state of Jammu and Kashmir, the only Muslim majority state in India after Partition, also introduced Islam as a factor in Indo-Pakistani relations and influenced the international perceptions of the persistent conflict over Kashmir. The fact that India had a large number of Muslims who remained in India after Partition also lent an important dimension to the way India dealt with the Middle East. With the dominant discourse in the Arab and Islamic world in the 1950s being led by nationalists and socialists in the 1950s and the international standing of Nehru, Islam seemed hardly a troubling factor in India's relations with the nations in the Middle East and South-East Asia. The ties between India and these countries were cemented by their shared colonial experience and quest for autonomy in international affairs.

In trying to neutralize Islam in its relations with the Middle East, India stressed the historic links between the subcontinent and the region even before these nations adopted Islam. India was seen in the Islamic world as the legatee of Hindustan, which had deep historic ties to the Middle East. Muslims leaders from the secular Indian elite were natural ambassadors, officially and unofficially, in India's political and cultural interaction with the region. The many centres of Islamic learning in India reinforced the broad engagement between India and the Muslim countries in the Middle East and South-East Asia. That India hosts a large population of Muslims is constantly cited by Indians in countering the Pakistani propaganda on Kashmir as a case study of India's oppression of Muslims. The most dramatic, if unsuccessful, case of India presenting itself as a Muslim nation was at Rabat in 1969 at the first summit of the Islamic nations.

India found itself in a different context in the 1990s. The increased tensions with Pakistan and the unending trouble in Kashmir allowed Pakistan to mobilize the Organization of Islamic Conference (OIC) to pass strictures against India. New Delhi's own commitment to secularism, highly valued in the Islamic world for it ensured the rights of Muslim compatriots in India, was seen as becoming shaky with the demolition of the Babri Masjid in 1992 and the extended rioting in Gujarat that targeted Muslim communities. Nationalist and secular forces in the Middle East were under pressure from the radical political Islam that gained ground in the 1980s and 1990s. In dealing with the new situation, India adopted a number of approaches. One was to reiterate India's own commitment to secularism and to assure the nations of the Middle East that Muslims in India were secure even under BJP rule. Claiming that Islam is 'part and parcel of our national and social life', Vajpayee told Iranian legislators in April 2001 that India's commitment to secularism was deep and enduring.[45]

While the killing of Muslims in Gujarat troubled leaders in the Middle East, they were willing to abide by the hope that the riots were an aberration rather than a new pattern in India.[46] India also attempted to create a mutuality of economic interests that could help avoid an excessive focus on Kashmir and tensions with Pakistan in bilateral relations with key nations in the Middle East. India no longer objects to the deep ties between Pakistan on the one hand and states such as Saudi Arabia and Turkey on the other, but it believes that there is enough political and economic business that it can do with these countries without demanding that they cut their ties with Pakistan. This new self-assurance and pragmatism has brought significant strategic dividends to India in its engagement of the Islamic world. In order to prevent the OIC from becoming a forum for India-bashing by Pakistan, India made a renewed bid to develop quiet contacts with the institution. It also quietly sounded out key OIC states like Saudi Arabia to see whether it could eventually become a member.[47] Support for Indian membership began to grow in the OIC, and in 2002, Qatar, which held the chairmanship, argued that as one of the world's largest Muslim communities, India could not be kept out of the OIC. It proposed that New Delhi be associated with the organization. While the Qatari proposal for Indian membership of the OIC might have been put forward prematurely, it reflected the new advances India was making in the Middle East.[48]

India's Ocean?

The forward policy since the end of the cold war added both exceptional range and depth to relations in India's extended neighbourhood. Trade with neighbouring regions has begun to rise rapidly. Considerations of energy security have helped move India towards long-term strategic relationships with key nations of the Gulf, and India has begun to invest large sums of money in hydrocarbon projects in the littoral. From Sakhalin in the Russian Far East, to Sudan in Africa, through Central Asia and the Gulf, India is making major investments to build oil equities across the region.[49] Politically, India broke out of the isolation that it had found itself at the turn of the 1990s and is intensely engaged with all the regions in the littoral at the dawn of the twenty-first century. The only exception to this new-found dynamism in Indian foreign policy has been Africa.

The emergence of a non-racial South Africa in the early 1990s was a major triumph for India, which had campaigned from the late 1940s against the apartheid regime. India and South

Africa announced their commitment to build a strategic partnership when President Nelson Mandela visited India in 1997. But there were many surprises and disappointments in store for the two nations. Differences over India's nuclear tests, and the attempts by the Western countries to project South Africa as a new and alternative leader to India in the NAM created mutual suspicion. India was also concerned by Mandela's apparent readiness to intervene in the Indo-Pakistani dispute over Kashmir. But by the turn of the new century, sentimentalism was beginning to give way to a more realistic appraisal of bilateral relations and the importance of building a relationship on the basis of common interests.

In the early years of the twenty-first century, India was also discarding sentimentalism in Africa as a whole and finding a way to enhance its standing in the troubled continent. In a speech in mid-2002, Jaswant Singh identified Africa as an important neighbour of India.[50] Physically, Africa forms the western fringe of the Indian Ocean, which connected it to the subcontinent by maritime trade routes through the ages. But after Independence, India saw Africa through the lone prism of Third World solidarity and non-alignment. Africa was seen not as a neighbour but as a rhetorical item on India's exalted global agenda. Africans became fellow travellers in the struggle against imperialism, neo-colonialism and racial discrimination.

In redefining Africa as a neighbour, Singh was emphasizing economic intimacy, and in seeing it as an important part of the Indian Ocean community, he was giving Africa greater weight in India's regional strategic calculus.[51] India recognized that the post-colonial challenge in Africa was no longer fighting the West but working with the advanced nations in contributing to the accelerated development of the continent. India was also keen to join the international initiative led by the Group of Eight (G-8) industrialized nations to facilitate the economic and political modernization of Africa.[52]

A new engagement with Africa completes the new Indian framework for its larger role in the Indian Ocean littoral. This role will no longer be in opposition to the United States but in cooperation with it—a notion that remains to be fully digested by the Indian foreign policy establishment. For decades India insisted that great powers should leave the Indian Ocean. Get rid of the great powers and their rivalries in the region, India suggested, and the newly decolonized nations of the Indian Ocean littoral would create peace and harmony through cooperation. Although the proposal was not initiated by New Delhi, the idea of the Indian Ocean as a Zone of Peace found a particular resonance in India. For the Indian political elite, committed to the values of liberal internationalism, the talk of a power vacuum in the region was crass and reflected the outmoded European thinking about international politics. For many in India, the Zone of Peace was a continuation of the anti-imperialist struggle to rid the Indian Ocean the ruinous great power intervention and rivalry that had gone on for centuries.

Thirty years after the British quit their job as the top cop on the Indian Ocean beat, the idea of the Zone of Peace in the littoral remained elusive as ever. Instead of regional collective security alliances, great power security guarantees and a balance of power politics have dominated the political order in the Indian Ocean. Even more galling for the promoters of a Zone of Peace is that the Indian Ocean had become, for all practical purposes, an American lake.

American interest in the Indian Ocean littoral began with the establishment of a permanent base on the island of Diego Garcia in the 1970s and was followed by the creation of Central Command in Florida in 1983. The Persian Gulf War saw the United States move from an over-the-horizon military presence in the region to the deployment of troops in Saudi Arabia and Kuwait. As part of its expanded permanent naval presence in the Arabian Sea, the United States also created the Fifth Fleet in the mid-1990s, its first new naval command since the end of the Second World War. On the eastern side of the littoral, America's withdrawal from Vietnam was followed by a forced vacation of its largest foreign military bases in the Philippines in the late 1980s. But by the late 1990s, the US was reviving its military alliances with Japan, Australia and South Korea and renegotiating military access arrangements with South-East Asian nations. Although China was not declared a rival, the US appeared to be creating the building blocks of a future containment of China—albeit in the name of security multilateralism. It was establishing military structures to prevent the rise of a competitor or a coalition of rival powers in the region.

After 11 September, the security context of the entire region altered with the prospect of a longer term American military presence in the region. The war against terrorism has seen the Americans gain new military bases in Central Asia and Pakistan. In the eastern Indian Ocean, American special forces joined the war against the Muslim Moro rebels in southern Philippines. This was the first direct participation of American forces in the region since its humiliating retreat from Vietnam in 1975.

As the US has begun to consolidate its new military presence in the region, the traditionally deep suspicion of American intentions has surfaced in the Indian political discourse. While the traditionalists responded with unease, the BJP-led government appeared comfortable with the US military presence and saw 11 September as an opportunity to expand military cooperation with America. The interest was matched by the enthusiasm of the Bush administration, which was ready to intensify security cooperation with India.

The sense of a new convergence of interests with the United States in its war against international terrorism helped India overcome much of the traditional resistance to military cooperation with it. The visit of the US aircraft carrier the *Carl Vinson* to Mumbai in December 2001 seemed to signal an end to India's thirty-year-old bitter memory of Washington's decision to dispatch another aircraft carrier, the USS *Enterprise*, to the Bay of Bengal during the 1971 war with Pakistan.[53] That incident had gone down in the lore of Indian strategic mythology as an enduring symbol of American military hostility to India. Since 11 September, the US also sought Indian naval escort for its vessels moving through the Malacca Straits. After considerable internal debate and consultation with the South-East Asian countries, India agreed. The decision to patrol the Malacca Straits transformed Indian military support to the United States from a passive to an active one, and it could presage Indo-US security cooperation in the preservation of sea lanes and the maintenance of peace and stability in the Indian Ocean littoral.

New Delhi is unlikely to make an attempt to regain the hegemonic role of British India in the Indian Ocean region. Working with Washington towards the common objectives of peace and stability in the Indian Ocean is likely to enhance India's standing, just as China's profile in Asia increased in the 1980s as it collaborated with the United States.

India has a long way to go in structuring intensive security cooperation with the United States. Its reluctance to support unilateral American military action against Saddam Hussein during 2002 and early 2003 shows the old inhibitions remain in place against a complete overhaul of its earlier approaches to the Indian Ocean security. Over the long term, however, increased cooperation with the United States is likely to emerge as fundamental to Indian strategy in the region. India's quest is not for primacy in the region. It wants to ensure for itself a weighty role in the future balance of power arrangements in the Indian Ocean and Asia-Pacific regions.

NINE

Re-forming the Subcontinent

The Ugly Indian?

It took a mere rumour to generate two days and nights of anti-Indian rioting in Kathmandu in January 2001. Kathmandu is one of the friendliest cities in the world, and it has had a very intimate and special relationship with New Delhi, yet the report that Indian film star Hrithik Roshan had said something condescending about the Nepali people inflamed the city. The intensity of the reaction against Indians and the attacks on their properties and schools dismayed New Delhi. There was speculation that pro-Pakistan lobbies in the once tranquil Himalayan kingdom had engineered the riots. Equally disturbing for New Delhi was the fact that the violence hurt Nepal more than India; the incidents scared off Indian tourists, an important source of income for the Nepalese economy, which was depressed since the hijacking of Indian Airlines flight IC 814 from Kathmandu in 1999. Nepal's resentment of India and its self-defeating policy of turning a blind eye to forces hostile to India on its soil seemed irrational to the foreign policy establishment.

Nepal is not the only country in the subcontinent to harbour indignation for India. In most neighbouring countries a simmering anti-Indian feeling animates the establishments and the chattering classes. These resentments are easy targets for forces inimical to India, which have lost no opportunity to exploit them. India in turn is frustrated by the extreme difficulties of dealing with its neighbours.

Indians clearly have a Gringo problem in their neighbourhood. Much like the United States in North and South America, India has found that the dominance of one nation in a region evokes complex reactions. This is generally true of all large nations with small neighbours. China elicits a similar sentiment in Asia. There is a built-in instability arising from the tension within the neighbourhood between economic dependence and cultural similarity and the political anxieties of preserving a separate national identity.

The Indian elite, which fulminates against the unfair policies of the great powers when dealing with New Delhi, finds many of the charges repeated against it by the neighbouring countries. A hegemonic, overbearing attitude, condescension and cultural imperialism are accusations that Indian analysts often hurl against the United States. They come back in more than ample measure to haunt India. India looms large, both physically and psychologically, over its neighbours. The reactions are enduring and pervasive. Flagrantly untrue anti-Indian headlines are commonplace. Accusations against the Indian intelligence agency, Research and Analysis Wing, are similar to the superhuman skills New Delhi used to ascribe to the American CIA. There are frequent references to the corrupting cultural influence of Bollywood, now made ubiquitous in the region by satellite and cable television—the very same arguments India's social conservatives and radicals on the Left employ against Western television channels. India's sense of being a victim of an unjust world order is mirrored in the subcontinent, where its neighbours complain of the inequities about the South Asian regional order.

India has attempted to uphold a regional security order on the premise that the subcontinent must be an exclusive sphere of influence for itself and that it must prevent other powers from intervening in the region. The notion of a Monroe Doctrine, similar to the one that the US proclaimed for the

Western Hemisphere in the nineteenth century, was expounded by none other than Nehru. India's first Prime Minister stressed the importance of keeping foreign powers out of Asia in the context of the attempts by the colonial powers to regain territories after the Second World War. Referring to the fact that America had secured itself from foreign aggression under the Monroe Doctrine, Nehru insisted that foreign armies have no business on the soil of any Asian country.[1]

Although the idea of keeping the great powers out of Asia was beyond India's reach, it was at the heart of New Delhi's policy towards the subcontinent. The special relationships India had inherited from the British with regard to the security of some of the smaller neighbours reinforced the sense of South Asia as India's sphere of influence. During the Indira Gandhi years, India's Monroe Doctrine was buttressed by the principle of bilateralism. Under the so-called Indira Doctrine, New Delhi insisted that problems in the region must be resolved bilaterally and that external powers should have no role in the region. The principle became a matter of faith for Indian foreign policymakers.

But the contradictions between India's global policy and its regional approach were real. At the international level, India rejected the notions of balance of power and exclusive spheres of influence; within the region it clung to them. India was strongly opposed to intervention by major powers in the internal affairs of weaker ones, but within the subcontinent it had to perform the function of a provider of security to smaller nations and their regimes. India was all for multilateralism at the global level, yet in the region it insisted on bilateralism. India was one of the biggest recipients of international assistance, but within the region it doled out substantive sums of aid to Nepal and Bhutan. On trade, India castigated the West for its protectionist policies, yet in the region it had liberal arrangements with Nepal and Bhutan but was closed to others, like Sri Lanka and Bangladesh.

India seemed to move effortlessly between the roles of

protestor at the global level and that of manager of the security
order within the region. Its ambassadors were relentless critics
of the international system in the global fora. Within the region,
its envoys were transformed into proconsuls and viceroys in
neighbouring capitals. These contradictions in Indian policy
became unsustainable by the early 1990s. India's tough stance
of imposing a trade embargo against Nepal and its interventions
in Sri Lanka and the Maldives in the late 1980s contributed to
India's image as a regional hegemon. The neighbours felt a
growing unease at the political attitudes in New Delhi, and the
anti-India forces within the neighbouring countries acquired
even greater strength.

Many unresolved problems between India and its
neighbours—whether it was the demarcation of boundaries or
the sharing of water resources—began to accumulate into major
challenges. The growing internal crises within the neighbouring
countries—the tensions between ruling establishments and
those seeking greater democratization as well as the deepening
of ethnic cleavages—demanded that India pay attention to these
problems and take sides in its neighbours' domestic squabbles.
This inevitably drew accusations of intervention in their internal
affairs and consequent political resentment against New Delhi.

India was miffed by the cussedness of its neighbours; their
constant attempts to mobilize political support from China
and Pakistan and to encourage or ignore activities hostile to
Indian security; and the continuous promotion of anti-India
sentiment within their public opinion. Prickly nationalism and
an exaggerated sense of national sovereignty prevented the
neighbouring states from cooperating with India even when it
served their own interests. Cooperative development of water
resources in Nepal became impossible amidst whipped up fears
that India was grabbing the kingdom's only natural asset.
Similarly Dhaka has gone through a painful domestic debate
on whether it should export natural gas to India. It also refuses
to give India transit facilities to the North-East. Instead of
making money on trade between Indian territories, Dhaka cites

reasons of sovereignty to justify its opposition.

Despite its pre-eminence in the region and the inherited British foreign policy legacy, handling the relations with its neighbours was never easy for New Delhi. It constantly oscillated between generosity and toughness. The deepening crises in India's relations with its smaller neighbours at the turn of the 1990s demanded a new approach from New Delhi.

The Gujral Doctrine

The response to this new challenge from Narasimha Rao was to let tempers cool. After the extraordinary developments during the Rajiv Gandhi years—the trade blockade of Nepal and the disastrous military intervention in Sri Lanka in the late 1980s—Narasimha Rao wisely chose to adopt a hands-off policy. No problems were resolved, but neither were tensions stoked up. That opened the space for the foreign minister of the United Front government and later its Prime Minister, I.K. Gujral, to outline a bolder regional policy.

His willingness to go the extra mile in resolving problems with neighbours and his refusal to insist on reciprocity came to be widely termed the Gujral Doctrine. He first outlined it in a speech at Chatham House in London in September 1996:

> The United Front government's neighbourhood policy now stands on five basic principles: firstly, with neighbours like Nepal, Bangladesh, Bhutan, [the] Maldives and Sri Lanka, India does not ask for reciprocity but gives all it can in good faith and trust. Secondly, no South Asian country will allow its territory to be used against the interest of another country of the region. Thirdly, none will interfere in the internal affairs of another. Fourthly, all South Asian countries must respect each other's territorial integrity and sovereignty. And finally, they will settle all their disputes through peaceful bilateral negotiations. These five principles scrupulously observed, will, I am sure, recast South Asia's regional relationship, including the tormented relationship between India and Pakistan, in a friendly, cooperative mould.[2]

This new attitude made a huge impression on the region and the world in general as a welcome departure from the muscular ways India had adopted in the earlier decades. The readiness to give up reciprocity and the idea of being generous to its neighbours also invited criticism from voices within the foreign policy establishment and from those outside who saw it as too idealistic. The critics argued that the Gujral Doctrine put far too much faith in the goodwill of neighbours who were increasingly seen as unreliable partners. Although Gujral got many bouquets and brickbats for his attempt to change the dynamics of India's regional policy, the attempts were rooted in a rethinking that had begun across the political spectrum. During the 1996 and 1998 elections, all political parties, including the BJP, endorsed the importance of regional cooperation in the subcontinent through the South Asian Association of Regional Cooperation (SAARC). The Gujral Doctrine, although identified with one individual, was the product of a slow but sure change in the world view of the Indian foreign policy establishment that began to address these important compulsions.

Three major factors may have helped push India into developing the new policy toward its neighbours. First, the economic imperative. As India and its neighbours launched themselves on the path of economic reform and globalization, the importance of regional economic cooperation became obvious to most of them. Barring Pakistan, the others were keen on proceeding towards a regional free market in the subcontinent. For many of them, economic openness towards each other, in particular to India, became important. Faced with the emergence of other regional economic blocs, India was now far more conscious of the urgency of improving trade flows within the region.

Second, there was a growing recognition in India that New Delhi's aspirations for a global political role would remain unrealized so long as it was mired in intractable regional conflicts. For India to break free, it needed a framework for positive cooperation with the smaller neighbours. Breaking out of this regional quagmire called for a patient, sensitive and sophisticated policy of engaging its neighbours, removing obstacles to cooperation and gaining trust incrementally. Strict reciprocity could not be the basis on which an effective neighbourhood policy could be built.

Third, despite the tough rhetoric of the Indira Doctrine of the 1970s and 1980s and the Indian call for non-intervention by the great powers, there has been a steady growth of the political profile of both China and the United States in the neighbourhood. Pakistan, too, has used New Delhi's problems with its smaller neighbours to expand its anti-India activities. Changing this negative dynamic called for an initiative based not on absolute symmetry but on facilitating the development of common interests with each neighbour. The case for greater generosity to the smaller neighbours and giving more for less— the essence of the Gujral Doctrine—could then be explained on the basis of India's self-interest and considerations of realpolitik. This policy has meshed with the state interests of many of its neighbours. India's emphasis on symmetry and reciprocity in its approach to resolving bilateral conflicts tended to limit the political space within the neighbouring countries to pursue mutually beneficial bilateral cooperation with India. The Gujral Doctrine was an attempt to get round this real constraint.

New Delhi was conscious, however, of the fact that ultimately relations between states cannot be built on unilateral concessions. The Gujral Doctrine did not mean that India would pay endlessly for cooperative relations with its smaller neighbours. The hope behind the Gujral Doctrine was that non-reciprocity and asymmetry from the Indian side would allow the smaller countries to look positively at the enormous potential of bilateral political and economic cooperation with India.

Gujral's success in removing obstacles on the Indian side for renewing the Ganges Waters Treaty with Bangladesh in 1996, his willingness to address the economic and political grievances of Nepal and his strong support of the SAARC process began to alter the grim mood in the subcontinent. But the management of difficult security problems remained. Contrary to the criticism that Gujral ignored India's security compulsions in promoting a generous policy towards its neighbours, he insisted that they should not allow activities hostile to India in their territories. It was not easy for India to persuade its neighbours to abide by this principle. During the 1990s, Pakistan used Nepal and Bangladesh to foment terrorism in India. Gujral diagnosed the problem rightly, but he did not have the extended tenure to force the Indian bureaucratic system to be genuinely cooperative on the ground or get its neighbours see the value of this policy. Another missing link in the Gujral Doctrine was the reluctance to pursue aggressively free trade in the region.

The BJP-led government that followed the United Front did not explicitly reject the Gujral Doctrine. Jaswant Singh often said that the BJP government would go beyond words and produce more substantive results on the ground. But the BJP-led government was unable to sustain a serious diplomatic focus on the subcontinent. Its preoccupations with managing the fallout from Pokhran-II and handling the ups and downs in the relations with Pakistan meant there was little energy left to deal with the complex problems with other neighbours in the subcontinent. Only major crises in relations with Nepal, Sri Lanka and Bangladesh would force it to pay attention to these countries.

As India struggled in the 1990s to cope with the challenge of terrorism, the inability or unwillingness of some of its neighbours to confront the sources and support structures for terrorism in their territories angered India. The hijacking of Indian Airlines flight IC 814 brought into focus the extensive activities of Pakistani intelligence agencies in Nepal and the willingness of Kathmandu to tolerate them despite the long-term threat to its own security. In Bhutan different Indian insurgent groups had taken shelter, and Thimphu had found it difficult to confront them. In Bangladesh, the elections at the end of 2001 saw the return to power of Khalida Zia in alliance with Islamic groups and heightened terrorist activity from Bangla soil. When India's efforts to urge these nations to demonstrate sensitivity to India's security concerns, New Delhi went public with its blunt assessment:

> Virtually all our neighbours, by choice or default, by acts of commission or omission, compulsions of geography and the terrain, have been or are involved in receiving, sheltering, overlooking or tolerating terrorist activities from their soil directed against India.

> We have very friendly relations with Nepal, but the open border with that country gives opportunities for foreign agencies to push in terrorists. Bangladesh has long been used as a sanctuary for insurgent groups engaged in violence against India, especially in the North-East.

> Bangladesh effectively refuses to recognise that this problem exists, as some lobbies in that country want to use it as a pressure point against India. We have excellent relations with Bhutan, but Bhutanese soil is currently being used by three Indian insurgent groups for launching terrorist attacks against India.[3]

Nearly five years into the rule by the BJP-led government, it was becoming clear that even if India tended to ignore its neighbours, the problems arising from them would not leave it alone. While the demands for a tough approach were intensifying, there was also recognition that India must find a way out of the renewed tensions with its neighbours. Yashwant Sinha, Jaswant Singh's successor as external affairs minister in July 2002, sought to put his own stamp on the policy by reiterating India's commitment to the Gujral Doctrine.[4] Sinha traced its origins back to the period when Vajpayee was the foreign minister of India from 1977 to 1979. At that time Vajpayee had worked to promote a good neighbourhood policy, one opposed to the tough approach practised by Indira Gandhi.

Regretting SAARC's failure to achieve progress on regional economic cooperation, Sinha declared India had the political will to enter immediately into a free trade agreement in South Asia. To step up the pace of negotiations on such an arrangement, he proposed a change in the format of trade talks in the region. Instead of exchanging small positive lists of tradable items, he suggested that South Asian nations offer small negative lists of items on which there would be no preferential trade. Sinha also called for a harmonization of tariffs to prevent the misuse of tariff differentials by unscrupulous traders and an agreement to facilitate the free flow of capital and services across the borders in the subcontinent. Looking to the future, Sinha called, probably for the first time by a senior Indian minister, for a political union of the subcontinent:

> We will be interested in negotiating a new agreement which will create a South Asian Union [SAU] and in course of time, . . . [it] will not merely be an economic entity. It will acquire a political dimension in the same manner which the European Union has come to acquire a political and strategic dimension. That is the direction in which I suggest we move. I am not suggesting an end to SAARC but an upgradation of SAARC into a South Asian Union.[5]

Privately Sinha was stating that India was prepared to move unilaterally on the economic front to promote economic integration. While India was ready to move quickly on economic cooperation, Sinha insisted that respect for each other's security concerns remain key to broad progress on regionalism in the subcontinent. Pointing to the security dimensions of the Gujral Doctrine, Sinha said, '[I]f those security concerns become overpowering, then many other areas of cooperation are lost sight of temporarily or in the long run'.[6] While insisting on the importance of security considerations, Sinha was also reflecting on India's new determination to take advantage of economic globalization to transform the nature of regional cooperation in the subcontinent.

Ending the Economic Partition

One of the unintended consequences of globalization, which enveloped the subcontinent in the 1990s, was the prospect of ending its economic partition of 1947. The break-up of British India into India and Pakistan and the creation of Bangladesh in 1971 carved the region into separate economic entities. By the 1960s most of India's neighbours followed its lead on a development model that focussed on import substitution, high tariff walls and self-reliance. The Congress party in India, the Sri Lanka Freedom Party, the People's Party of Pakistan, the Awami League in Bangladesh and the Nepali Congress all owed intellectual allegiance to one kind of socialist populism or another.

The closed nature of South Asian economies deepened the impact of Partition and choked off the natural commercial links that had existed in the subcontinent. The enduring hostility between India and Pakistan prevented the deepening of trade links, with Islamabad consciously avoiding economic cooperation with India. Likewise, Bangladesh, except in the immediate years after its liberation, was not enthusiastic about economic cooperation with India. Road, rail and riverine links that united British India were subject to severe economic and political barriers after Partition. Natural ports were cut off from their hinterlands—as Chittagong was from India's North-East and Kolkata from the western part of East Pakistan, now Bangladesh. Twin commercial cities like Mumbai and Karachi have become distant neighbours. Thanks to the new borders and the official perception of them as barriers to be defended, border trade has never been encouraged by the South Asian states.

This ossified system of regional economic separation got its first challenge from the process of globalization. The pressure from the International Monetary Fund and the World Bank as well the dynamics of the GATT and the WTO demanded that the region adopt policies aimed at export promotion, remove barriers to imports and integrate with the global economy. As the nations of the subcontinent opened themselves to the world, the illogic of remaining closed to each other began to dawn on the political elites of the region. While economic reforms moved forward in the 1990s, it was soon apparent that India would be the natural engine of growth in the region. As a CIA report points out, the economies of the smaller nations will inevitably be integrated into India's in the first decades of the twenty-first century.[7] The political classes in the region could either recognize the inevitable and facilitate globalization or remain resistant and delay it. The message on the necessity of regional economic integration has begun to sink in, if somewhat unevenly, within the region.

While Pakistan has been determined to resist the implications of globalization for regional economic cooperation, the smaller countries in the region have begun to recognize that their economic future is tied to that of the Indian market. Sri Lanka pushed for a bilateral free trade treaty with India that was signed in 2000. Colombo has been the most articulate in suggesting that the logic of globalization demands integration with the Indian economy. Bangladesh is less enthusiastic about a free trade arrangement with India, but it has demanded duty-free access to its goods. Nepal wants to bolster its preferential access to the Indian market.

While the smaller nations of the subcontinent have recognized the need for economic integration, the biggest beneficiary of the process of expanded regional trade, India, has been reluctant to lead the charge for unifying the South Asian market. From the mid-1990s, thanks to the opening up of the markets in the region, India's exports have flooded Bangladesh and Sri Lanka.[8] Its neighbours have become markets for Indian exports, but their exports to India have barely risen and have facilitated huge trade surpluses in India's favour. Although this imbalance has incited protests from its neighbours, the Indian establishment has been unwilling to consider the demands to open up its market.

Sections of India's Foreign Office have begun to see the political benefits from globalization and regional economic integration. These include the opportunity to use the natural geographic contours of in the subcontinent to unite the region economically. India's long border with Pakistan cannot remain bereft of commerce forever. Nepal, sandwiched between India and China, will have to continue to rely on the Indian economy. Bangladesh, but for a small border with Myanmar, is surrounded by India. Sri Lanka, which tried to seek membership in the ASEAN in the late 1970s, has come to recognize the value of meshing with the booming economy of south India. The inevitable economic integration of the region has the potential to alter fundamentally the international relations of the subcontinent. Expanded commerce between India and its neighbours could offer a different template for the resolution of the political problems facing the region.

India, slowly but surely, has begun to internalize the geopolitical consequences of economic integration of the region. As it arms itself with a new economic vision for the subcontinent, it has a variety of instruments at its disposal. SAARC is one of them. When it was first mooted in the early 1980s, India was cool to the idea, concerned that the forum was designed to isolate it politically in the region. But at the turn of the 1990s India began to emphasize the importance of economic cooperation within the association.

In this respect, Pakistan has been the slowest camel that has set the pace for the caravan. It has been more interested in bringing its bilateral dispute with India over Kashmir into SAARC's ambit than in trade liberalization. Even when it agreed at the political level to accelerate economic integration, it has used bureaucratic devices to slow down the process. Pakistan insists that there can be no economic progress unless political issues are resolved. This approach is the exact opposite of what the other regional organizations have successfully adopted—

expand economic cooperation despite political differences. Pakistan's refusal to benefit from regional cooperation has beggared itself, and India has to find ways to prevent Pakistan from holding back the rest of the region.

As a result, the construction of a two-speed SAARC has become an important option for India. Such a commitment would unveil a simple principle: India is prepared to advance economic integration in the region—with Pakistan if possible, and without it if necessary. SAARC's charter permits subregional cooperation that involves two or more countries. There are serious possibilities for rapid movement on economic integration among India, Bangladesh, Nepal and Bhutan on the one hand and India, Sri Lanka and the Maldives on the other. Pakistan can join this process whenever it is prepared to put commerce above politics.

Despite some political concern in Pakistan that subregional cooperation could cut it out of new processes in the subcontinent, Nepal, Bangladesh and Sri Lanka have begun to express interest. India has engaged in some formal discussions, but not surprisingly this governmental track has made little progress. There is growing interest in the Indian private sector and the Asian Development Bank (ADB) to promote economic integration in the eastern part of the subcontinent. The concept of a South Asian Growth Quadrangle (SAGQ) involving Nepal, Bhutan, Bangladesh and India's eastern and north-eastern regions has taken root.[9] Citing its successful experience in funding such transregional projects in the Greater Mekong subregion involving China and South-East Asia, the ADB has offered to fund similar projects with the participation of the private sector.

The ADB's vision is indeed striking:

Out of an estimated 900 million people living below the poverty line in Asia, some 500 million live in the SAGQ countries; especially Bangladesh, the eastern states of India including Bihar and eastern Uttar Pradesh, and Nepal. This region is home to the largest and deepest concentration of the world's poor. . . . [T]his challenge can also be transformed into an opportunity. . . . The natural endowments of the region, the hydropower potential in Nepal and Bhutan, the coal resources of West Bengal and Bihar, and the hydrocarbon reserves in Bangladesh, Assam and Tripura also make this region one of the world's great storehouses of potentially cheap energy. Additionally, there are large non-energy mineral deposits, forest resources, livestock and marine resources in the region, and a useful network of port cities in Chittagong, Mongla, Calcutta, and Haldia. How many regions can we think of in the world, which have this remarkable combination of endowments? Since the early 1990s, the countries of the subregion have also been implementing broad ranging market-oriented reforms. These have created a sound environment for accelerated investment over a broad front. Thus, all the essential ingredients are available here and now to transform one of the poorest subregions in the world into a leading subregion of dynamic economic growth. I should add that, geopolitically, the subregion is of great strategic significance as the gateway linking the whole of South Asia to Southeast Asia and East Asia in a vast Asian economic community. It is this long-term vision of transformation of the subregion, and its potential role in integration across Asian subregions, which underlies ADB's strong commitment to this area.[10]

This expansive vision of an emerging East in the subcontinent has found a resonance among sections of the intelligentsia and industry, but the Indian government has remained less than enthusiastic. The Foreign Office in particular has been hesitant about accepting an expanded role of the ADB in promoting projects with India's smaller neighbours, particularly Bhutan and Nepal. These concerns are rooted in old-fashioned thinking about resisting the influence of the multilateral lending institutions, preserving India's primacy in the shaping of the economic developments in its neighbourhood and retaining the traditional leverages from economic aid to its smaller neighbours. While Pakistan has blocked economic integration on the SAARC front, India seemed to squander the opportunities for subregional economic cooperation. While China has gladly allowed international capital and the financial institutions to promote economic integration between its border regions and the neighbouring countries, India is holding itself back.

If SAARC fails to take off either as a collective or in the subregions, India will have to explore the options of transregional cooperation that could involve South-East Asia and China. Here again reservations from the foreign policy establishment have held up proposals from Beijing for regional cooperation involving eastern India, Bangladesh, Myanmar and the south-western part of China. Sections of the Indian establishment are not ready to let China gain access to the sensitive North-East. Although India has been positive at the political level to create free trade arrangements with South-East Asia that could involve some of its smaller neighbours, the slow pace of Indian reforms has held back the prospect of economic regionalism. With opposition to freer trade diminishing at the turn of the century, India has began to explore such arrangements with Singapore, Thailand and the ASEAN as a whole and a range of other countries and regional groupings.[11] Free trade treaties with other nations in the extended neighbourhood could create a framework in which to integrate the subcontinent. Trade as an instrument of neighbourhood strategy has finally begun to take shape in New Delhi.

Large transborder projects have brought new opportunities to reconnect the region with India. The United States set up the South Asia Energy Initiative in the late 1990s to promote regional energy projects and transborder exchanges of natural gas and electric power. American companies are keen to build hydroelectric plants in Nepal and export electricity to India. They are also interested in exporting natural gas from Bangladesh and Myanmar to India. They see the prospects for a grid of pipelines linking Myanmar, Bangladesh, India's North-

East and the mainland. Consequently, the Clinton and Bush administrations have been pressing reluctant governments of Bangladesh to take an early decision on exporting gas to India. In the early twenty-first century, the global pressures on the region to integrate will be relentless. India is well positioned to take advantage of these trends. For some among the Indian neighbours, this could raise the spectre of an Indian hegemony deepened through economic integration. An alternative view holds that, under globalization and regionalization, the natural economic unity of many South Asian subregions could be restored.[12] As Nepal and north India, the two Punjabs across the dividing line between India and Pakistan, the two Bengals, Sri Lanka and south India engage in expansive commercial interaction, the fears of Indian hegemony among India's neighbours might gradually ease.

Beyond the Monroe Doctrine

If the logic of global capitalism worldwide at the end of the twentieth century has created new opportunities for an economic restructuring of the subcontinent, the security issues of the region have also become globalized from the 1980s. Weighed down by the perception that the subcontinent is its exclusive sphere of influence and the sense that bilateralism must remain the dominant method of resolving regional disputes, India has found it difficult to make the necessary adjustments to its policy. If it can discard the old mindset, it might find that the changed international context offers many opportunities to enhance its leading role in the region. Indian primacy in the subcontinent can no longer be exercised in the old forms, nor should New Delhi want to underwrite the security of the region unilaterally. An India that seeks to modernize its bilateral relations in the region and works with the international community to resolve regional conflicts will at once improve its regional standing in the neighbourhood and liberate itself to play a larger role in the world.

India must rethink its British legacy. Maintaining buffer

states and preventing the intrusion of other major powers into the subcontinent were illusions that were shattered quickly after the British left the region independent and divided. China's entry into Tibet in 1950 ended the status of the plateau as a buffer between the two giants of Asia. China never accepted the notion that South Asia is an exclusive sphere of influence for India. Through the decades it kept chipping away at Indian preponderance in the region. Besides the strategic relationship with Pakistan, China began to cultivate the other neighbours of India and raise its profile in the region.

The smaller nations of the subcontinent, initially suspicious of China's intentions, quickly recognized the value of playing the China card against India. As occasional tension and continuous difficulties between India and its neighbours began to manifest themselves, China could gain a lot of goodwill in the region through small gestures—a supply of a little aid and small quantities of arms and a pat on the back for resisting Indian hegemonism. By the end of the 1980s, China's influence had steadily expanded in the subcontinent, and it began to make significant advances in Myanmar, long seen as another buffer between India and China. While the United States and the Soviet Union kept an eye on India's neighbourhood in the cold war, their focus was riveted on Pakistan.

Pakistan never accepted the Indian claims for the strategic legacy of the British Raj, nor did it pay obeisance to India's wishes that great powers should be kept out of the subcontinent. Its alliances with China and Washington were aimed at limiting Indian influence in the region. Over the years, Pakistan began to position itself as the principal force opposing Indian primacy in the region, and it created leverages against India in its neighbourhood. Even India's closest friends did not mind seeing a Pakistan that kept India off balance.

The Soviet intervention in Afghanistan at the end of 1979 removed the last buffer British India maintained. The confrontation between Washington and Moscow in the cold war began the internationalization of South Asian security in its truest sense. The US-led coalition against the Soviet Union in Afghanistan included not only Pakistan as a frontline state but also China, Saudi Arabia and radical Islamic groups from all over the Arab world. While the American strategy to trap the Soviet bear in Afghanistan and bleed it to death was successful, its consequences to the region and world have been dramatized by the events of 11 September.

The end of the cold war brought to the fore concerns on democracy and human rights and the internal dynamics of the South Asian nations increasingly came under global scrutiny in the 1990s. Whether it was the human rights situation in Kashmir, the state of Nepalese refugees in Bhutan or the ethnic conflict in Sri Lanka, they were all of concern to the international community.

In addition, the internationalism of the Taliban and the other extremist Islamic groups showcased the globalization of the politics on the Right. Pakistan and Afghanistan became the new sanctuaries of international Islamic extremism. The ability of the Hindu fundamentalists to mobilize support from among the non-resident Indians in the United States also demonstrated the power of the diaspora in shaping India's domestic politics. The Liberation Tigers of Tamil Eelam's (LTTE's) connections in South-East Asia and in Great Britain and the United States through expatriate populations was another example. The networks financing terrorists became international too. In many cases narco-trafficking greased the operations of terrorists, who began to link up with the underworld. After the Soviet withdrawal from Afghanistan, the high politics of the international system seemed to vacate the subcontinent, but global politics of entirely another kind began to envelop the region.

But 11 September brought high politics back to the subcontinent, ironically to defeat the new forces of extremism and terrorism. The United States emerged as India's newest neighbour in more than one sense. Its military presence was here for the long haul. Washington also seemed more interested than ever before in addressing regional security problems. India was happy to see the US oust the Taliban from Afghanistan. It also consciously mobilized American pressure on Pakistan to give up its support to terrorism after the attack on the Parliament on 13 December 2001. Yet there was deep discomfort among the traditionalists of the foreign policy establishment at the implications of a long-term American role in South Asian conflicts.

The American interest in promoting a peace process in Sri Lanka dates back to the late 1990s, when it blessed the Norwegian initiative to encourage Colombo and the LTTE to come to the negotiating table. After 11 September, the US more directly threatened the LTTE that it would become a target of its ongoing war on terrorism if it undermined the present peace process in Sri Lanka.[13] As Nepal struggled to cope with the Maoist insurgency at the turn of the century, Washington offered military assistance to Nepal. President Bush's decision to receive the Prime Minister of Nepal, Sher Bahadur Deuba,[14] and the Sri Lankan Prime Minister, Ranil Wickremesinghe,[15] at the White House reflected the growing American interest in the subcontinent. In his speech marking six months since 11 September, Bush spoke of a comprehensive and unremitting war against terror across the world, including the prospects of a 'peaceful world beyond the war on terror'.[16] He asserted that

> when the terrorists are disrupted and scattered and discredited, many old conflicts will appear in a new light—without constant fear and cycle of bitterness that terrorists spread with their violence. We will see then that the old and serious disputes can be settled within the bounds of reason, and goodwill and mutual security.[17]

Bush was referring to both the dispute between Arabs and Israelis and that between India and Pakistan over Kashmir. His statement also seemed to apply to the Nepalese government's battle against the Maoist groups and the enduring civil war between Colombo and the Tamil separatists.

The globalization of South Asian security is real, and India has to look beyond the Monroe Doctrine to develop an effective strategy for the region. Anxieties about the intrusion of the world into the subcontinent are unlikely to change the reality on the ground. Any new approach by India to the region involves six important components. First, India must move quickly to rework the treaty relationships with Nepal and Bhutan. The old agreements based on the notion of protectorates cannot be sustained in the twenty-first century. The inevitable review and revision of these treaties will be painful and messy, but India has no alternative.

The 1950 bilateral Treaty of Peace and Friendship with Nepal has long outlived its utility, and Nepal sees it as the symbol of an unequal relationship.[18] The provisions of the treaty that are favourable to New Delhi have long ceased to be operational, but it abides by those aspects of the treaty that benefit Nepal, Nonetheless, New Delhi has found it difficult to discard the instrument.[19]

Under the 1949 treaty with India, Bhutan 'agreed to be guided by the advice of the Government of India in regard to its external relations',[20] but it has not always been easy for India to insist that Bhutan do so. Despite its consistent support to India in various international organizations, Bhutan has often sought to assert its independent positions. India's opposition to Bhutan establishing diplomatic relations with China has been a matter of discordance among New Delhi, Thimphu and Beijing.

Second, India must shed its obsession with Pakistan and devote more political and diplomatic energies towards tending its relationships with other neighbours. Crisis-driven engagement with them in the 1990s has inevitably failed to develop a long-term strategy and a pattern of consistent engagement focussed on problem solving. India's preoccupation with the great powers and Pakistan has bred political resentment among its smaller neighbours, and New Delhi needs to develop institutional mechanisms for sustained interaction with them.

Third, New Delhi needs a massive revamping of its economic strategy towards its neighbours. It needs to take full advantage of natural geographic conditions and the pressures of economic globalization to quicken the pace of the inevitable reintegration of the South Asian market. It cannot allow political pinpricks from its neighbours to hinder its pursuit of freer regional trade through unilateral action where necessary. Separating the agenda on trade and commerce from the political problems of the relationship is critical for India to pursue its own interests and build new constituencies among the neighbours that benefit from expanded trade.

Fourth, despite the bitterness from some of India's past involvement in the civil wars in its neighbourhood, New Delhi must take an active interest in resolving the regional conflicts. Avoiding them, for the fear of domestic political consequences or other considerations, will not provide an escape for India from the spillover of these conflicts. The disastrous intervention in Sri Lanka in the late 1980s, the LTTE's involvement in the assassination of Rajiv Gandhi and the conviction that it is impossible to do business with the organization have led to India staying aloof from the conflict in Sri Lanka during the 1990s. India must find a way to shape the political outcomes of the conflicts next door.

Fifth, India must avoid the temptation to act unilaterally in its neighbourhood. Its intervention inevitably complicates the situation and makes it the target of political manipulation. Despite reservations in sections of the security establishment, India recognizes the difficulties in trying to exclude all great powers from the region, and it has begun to focus on working with friendly powers to promote principled and reasonable solutions to regional conflicts. The emphasis has begun to shift to outcomes from format.

In Sri Lanka, India let the Norwegian mediation unfold after considerable initial scepticism and concern.[21] India's objectives and those of the international community coincided in pursuing a solution that emphasized the territorial unity of Sri Lanka and meeting the aspirations of the Tamil minority. In Nepal, too, despite many reservations, India chose to go along with the Anglo-American initiative in mid-2002 to develop a coordinated international approach in assisting the Nepalese government to deal with the Maoist insurgency.[22] There were differences between India and the Anglo-Americans on the best possible tactics in Nepal as well as on defining an approach to the altering relationship between the monarchy and the political parties in the Himalayan kingdom. Effective coordination with the international community in handling civil wars in the region might need increased trust between India and the West. In 2002 New Delhi and Washington agreed to institute a dialogue on regional issues in the subcontinent.

Finally, the increased activism of the United States, Europe and Japan in resolving the regional conflicts in South Asia has begun to raise eyebrows in China.[23] Although Washington constantly consulted Beijing on Indo-Pakistani tensions in the 1990s and invited Chinese representation at the London conference on Nepal in 2002, China remains wary of the changing situation in the subcontinent. During the cold war, India had to cope with the impact of the US-Soviet rivalry in its neighbourhood. In the future it will have to insulate the region from potential tensions between Washington and Beijing. Unlike the Soviet Union, China is a neighbour of the subcontinent and has far greater leverages for intervention here. Reinforcing its own primacy in the region through cooperation with the United States while limiting the damage in relations with China will demand great diplomatic skills on India's part.

TEN

Diplomacy for the Second Republic

The Porcupine Becomes a Tiger

If a single image captured India's national strategic style it was that of a porcupine—vegetarian, slow-footed and prickly. The famous defensiveness of the porcupine became the hallmark of India's approach to the world. India was a reactive power; when the world impinged on it, India put up its sharp quills to ward off the threats. The quills symbolized the principles of fairness, justice and equality as defence against what India saw as unacceptable demands from the international system. India, it was widely believed at home and abroad, would not seek opportunities or be opportunistic in pursuit of its national interests. Since the successive governments argued their positions in terms of fundamental principles, there was very little to do in terms of reaching out to the others or exploring trade-offs. With the economy focussed on self-reliance and fetching barely 0.1 per cent of world trade in the 1980s, there was no commercial engagement with the world either. The excessive emphasis on normative principles that guided India's foreign policy and the insular economic philosophy severely limited India's manoeuvrability in the international system.

This clearly was not the way India started out. At the dawn of Independence, Nehru gave India a very dynamic and creative foreign policy. With very little national power in hand, he made India a diplomatic force to reckon with in a world that was drifting into a cold war. The exuberance of Nehruvian diplomacy reached its peak in the mid-1950s and began to dwindle by the end of the decade when trouble with China began. If the war with China shattered Nehru, it also exposed the fragility of the balance between idealism and realism that he had so carefully crafted for Indian diplomacy. While raising high moral principles as India's standard in world affairs, he was extremely conscious of preserving and pursuing India's interests in a pragmatic manner. But this balance, already under strain in Nehru's later years, began to elude his successors. Much like domestic policy where Nehru's flirtation with socialism became entrenched with left-wing economic populism, his emphasis on non-alignment abroad was reduced to a mantra bereft of any flexibility. Consequently the legacy of a man who was deeply imbued with Western Enlightenment values became incorrigibly anti-West.

When foreign policy and diplomacy are filtered down to a few popular slogans, they help build consensus across a wide spectrum, but they also begin to lose their agility. As India ran into that problem by the early 1980s, Indira and Rajiv Gandhi both attempted to lessen the ideological accents that had begun to distort Indian diplomacy. Rajiv Gandhi, in particular, tried to loosen the diplomatic straitjacket that was choking India's external options. By reaching out to the West and trying to change the internal economic orientation, he prepared the ground for a fundamental re-evaluation of foreign policy. By the end of the cold war and the collapse of the old economic order in India, the traditional methods of engaging the world were no longer tenable. India had to find new ways for doing business with the world.

In the 1990s India initiated a root-and-branch overhaul of its economy to facilitate globalization, and the imperatives of Indian foreign policy dramatically changed. India's estrangement from the West in the earlier decades was rooted in a world view that insisted on limiting economic interaction with the West and saw non-alignment as a continuation of the anticolonial struggle. The deep ideological hostility to the West that came to dominate the post-Nehruvian outlook could not but be undercut by the logic of economic reforms in the 1990s. The biggest change in the Indian foreign policy in the 1990s has been the shedding of the dirigisme anti-Western orientation that was popular among the generations of the Indian elite after Independence. Equally significant was the recognition that India can move out of the backwaters of the Third World to the centre stage of world affairs. Rather than be a permanent protestor in the international system, India would now strive to get a seat at the top table, if not formally as a permanent member of the United Nations Security Council, then as an emerging economic giant and a great power of substance in Asia and the Indian Ocean region.

The 1990s also saw significant changes in the style of Indian diplomacy. A smug India that was confident in its conceptual premises until the end of the cold war had little reason to reach out to others or take the trouble of handling difficult relations with key international players. The fixity of the international context during the cold war, India's attachment to the Soviet Union and its belief in Third Worldism left little scope for diplomatic innovations on the foreign policy front after 1971, when India emerged triumphant in the vivisection of Pakistan. The outreach of Indian foreign policy in the 1990s demanded that Indian diplomats get off their high horse, seek investments, negotiate market access, trade favours and leverage purchasing power on large contracts. If the economic reforms demanded a selling of India, the pressures on India's nuclear and Kashmir policies forced an activist approach to limit the damage, win new friends and influence opinion. No longer able to hector the world, Indian diplomats had to appeal to key elements in various parts of the world. India's national requirements in the 1990s required a very different mentality from the Indian diplomatic missions, and the Indian Foreign Service officers rose to the new tasks with some aplomb.

As he was demitting office in July 2002 after nearly four

eventful years as external affairs minister, Jaswant Singh summed up his own experience in an emotional farewell to his colleagues. He said diplomacy was 'not about launching crusades' a feature that came to define India's approach to world affairs since the late 1960s.[1] Singh suggested that it was about building relationships, both personal and political. Without directly referring to the transition that had occurred in Indian foreign policy, Singh was summing up his own contribution to changing Indian diplomacy from its old, radical, left-wing ideological orientation to a more pragmatic and interest-driven foreign policy. He asserted that India was no longer a reactive power. The country was now determined to 'influence events' abroad rather than be 'pushed by them'.[2] From preparing for and conducting nuclear tests to forcing the international system to deal with the sources of terrorism in Pakistan, India had initiated a self-confident, outward-looking and pro-active diplomacy during the 1990s. India's coercive diplomacy against Pakistan after 13 December 2001 involved a high-stakes manipulation of the nuclear risk and a self-confidence to mobilize the United States and the international system in India's favour. In combining the threat of the use of force and sophisticated diplomacy, the porcupine had become a tiger.

Are the Changes Sustainable?

My assessment of India's engagement with the world since the early 1990s posits a fundamental change of course and a reconstitution of its core premises. Whether it was the de-emphasis of non-alignment or the new embrace of the US, or the attempts to rethink regionalism in the subcontinent and its environs, a radically different foreign policy orientation emerged by the turn of the millennium.

But is the new Indian foreign policy sustainable? Or does it merely reflect a transient phenomenon associated with the individuals who ran Indian diplomacy or at best institutionally with the BJP-led government? Is there a broad consensus within the Indian political establishment on the new direction of Indian foreign policy? These are questions widely asked by those who welcome the changes in India's world view as well as those who condemn them.

Undoubtedly individuals like Jaswant Singh and Brajesh Mishra, the principal foreign policy aides to Vajpayee, left a strong imprint on India's post-Pokhran diplomacy. Yashwant Sinha has underlined the importance of an activist economic diplomacy, particularly towards the neighbours. A lot of credit goes to Vajpayee, who allowed his diplomats to break the mould on many key issues. While there was some autonomy to foreign policy making, all its key and controversial decisions (except that on nuclear testing) were subject to tortuous consensus building, both within the BJP and the broader coalition led by it. While individuals making India's foreign policy mattered, they did not have a free run.

A more interesting argument would be to attribute the changes in Indian diplomacy to the ideology of the BJP. Critics on the Left insist that the BJP has robbed Indian foreign policy of its progressive, anti-imperialist content and given it the colours of Hindutva.[3] To be sure, the BJP-led coalition installed in March 1998 was the first Indian dispensation without its roots in the mainstream national movement led by the Indian National Congress. All the previous non-Congress governments were led by political formations that at one time or another were part of the Congress culture. The Jan Sangh, the BJP's predecessor, was part of the Janata government, and Vajpayee was its foreign minister from 1977 to 1979, but he did not have the dominant say in its political orientation. During the cold war, the Rashtriya Swayamsevak Sangh (RSS) and its political wings were critical of the Nehruvian foreign policy, questioning its dalliance with communist China and the Soviet Union, opposing non-alignment and demanding a more militaristic approach to Pakistan and China. It could be argued that the BJP was less inhibited by the ideological inheritance of the Indian foreign policy and therefore far more open to reorienting it than any other formation in the Indian political class.

Yet this argument does not square with the reality that during the 1990s the RSS was vehemently opposed to the attempts in New Delhi to deepen India's globalization and improve relations with the West. The right-wing populism of the RSS had virtually adopted the slogans of the Left on both internal and external policies. The idea of swadeshi, which the RSS championed, was no different from the idea of economic self-reliance that was so central to the Left's world view. The distrust of the West was equally shared by the Left and Right extremes in the Indian political establishment. Vajpayee's characterization of the United States as India's natural ally shocked the RSS as much as it did the Left and the traditionalists of the Indian foreign policy establishment. The RSS view of Pakistan also did not square with the policies of Vajpayee's government, which devoted considerable energies towards restructuring relations with Pakistan after the nuclear tests. While the RSS supported the nuclear tests, it was not enamoured with Vajpayee's attempts at Lahore and Agra to befriend Pakistan. His special effort to improve relations with the Islamic world also did not fit into the RSS world view.

The foreign policy of the Vajpayee years cannot be seen as an extension of the RSS understanding of international affairs; instead it must be viewed as a more purposeful implementation of the ideas that were initiated by Rajiv Gandhi and promoted by Narasimha Rao's government. The traditional framework of Indian foreign policy was beginning to limit India's external options by the early 1980s. The challenge of an inadequate relationship with the West was recognized by Rajiv Gandhi and addressed by him during the 1980s. The improved Indo-US relations at the turn of the millennium must be traced back to the Cancun Summit in 1981 between Indira Gandhi and Ronald Reagan and Rajiv Gandhi's special effort to develop personal relations with Presidents Ronald Reagan and George W. Bush. On nuclear policy too, Indira Gandhi toyed with the idea of resuming nuclear tests in 1984, and Rajiv Gandhi ordered the weaponization of the Indian option in 1989. Narasimha Rao gave the green signal to full-scale testing in the early 1990s but withdrew at the last minute in December 1995. While the BJP made bold in testing nuclear weapons in May 1998, the policy was rooted in the initiatives of previous governments. Similarly, in reworking relations with the other great powers and regional actors, the first initiatives came from Rajiv Gandhi and Narasimha Rao's Congress governments. Likewise, the controversial decision to upgrade diplomatic relations with Israel came from Narasimha Rao. Gujral gave the neighbourhood policy new direction, which was sustained in large measure by Vajpayee.

The reorientation of Indian foreign policy during the 1990s was a response to the structural changes in the international system and within the nation. The end of the cold war and the economic imperatives of globalization demanded a recasting of India's external relations. Either of these was potent enough to force major changes in the way India dealt with the world. Together they drove India into a policy framework that was radically different. Although the Indian leadership did not consciously articulate a new foreign policy framework, incremental changes throughout the 1990s accumulated to produce a new approach to the world by the end of the decade. In responding to the external environment as well as the demands of the new economic strategy at home, there was continuous tension between new ideas and old mindsets in the making of the new foreign policy.

Not all the tensions in the Indian foreign policy debate had been clinched even as India moved in a new direction. For example, despite the steadily expanding cooperation with the United States, there are sections of the political class that remain distrustful of American intentions. The centre of gravity of Indian foreign policy, however, shifted from idealism to realism in the 1990s. The new foreign policy orientation of India in the 1990s must be seen as part of the changing perceptions of the Indian nation about itself and the world. India's new foreign policy is a reflection of the reality that a Second Republic was in the making in New Delhi. The idea that a Second Republic was in the making during the 1990s has been articulated by senior journalist Dileep Padgaonkar:

> For as long as one can remember . . . [India] has been cynical about the present, concerned about the future and confused about what to embrace or reject from the past. The subtlest minds reflecting on its state a hundred odd years ago had no doubt that *tamas*, the 'dark and heavy demon of inertia' (as Sri Aurobindo called it), had paralysed its reflexes. . . . Now, however, the mood is distinctly buoyant. India still faces awesome problems. But today you detect a burgeoning confidence that they can be managed, that they will not be allowed to stifle its spirit. You can see a new vigour in the air, a willingness to take on challenges and, no less significant, a yearning to celebrate the creative genius of India.[4]

The BJP has been accused of shattering the national consensus on a wide range of foreign policy issues. The assumption that there was a near national consensus on foreign policy since Independence also deserves some scrutiny. Many of India's initiatives—from non-alignment to the support extended to Soviet intervention in Afghanistan—were all controversial when first mooted by the governments in New Delhi. Nehru had to face serious opposition from his own party in his attempts to befriend communist China and the Soviet Union in the 1950s, and Indira Gandhi's peace settlement with Pakistan in 1972 was controversial too. The Left was unwilling to back non-alignment well into the 1960s, having denounced it initially as a sell-out to imperialists. The question of how to handle the neighbours has always elicited divergent responses from various sections of the establishment.

While the notion of complete consensus is a political myth, the BJP stands vulnerable to the accusation that it did not do enough to take the rest of the country along in making radical departures in foreign policy in the late 1980s. Unlike Narasimha Rao's government, which took pains to consult with the rest of the political class, the BJP has been far less communicative. Neither in the wake of the nuclear tests when India faced international isolation nor during the many ups and down with Pakistan did the Vajpayee government make a special effort to explain the issues involved to the Opposition parties and the public.

While Vajpayee might have failed in creating a consensus around the new foreign policy, it is extremely unlikely that India's new diplomatic direction will be reversed in the coming years. India's economic reforms have continued through the 1990s under a series of governments that represented every possible shade of political views in the country. Similarly, the essence of the new foreign policy would stay intact. There could be subtle change of emphases here and there, and the style of individual premiers and foreign ministers could vary. Just as India cannot go back to the old economic polices, it cannot return to the earlier stress on non-alignment and an anti-Western orientation. There will be segments on the Left and the Right looking for variations on the old themes, but the main line of the new Indian foreign policy will remain focussed more on enhancing its standing in the world in cooperation with the United States rather on renewing anti-Western crusades. India has crossed the Rubicon.

Whither Indian Exceptionalism?
The critics of the new foreign policy have accused India of giving up its unique moral standing and political exceptionalism in the world. In becoming less ideological and intensifying the quest for the traditional attributes of national strength, India has become a normal power that is no longer focussed on transforming the world. Instead of the traditional emphasis on Third World solidarity and improving the lot of the weak in the world, Indian leaders increasingly talked of the nation becoming a developed country by 2020. Self-advancement rather than slogans about uplifting the entire Third World have become the dominant concern in India's new foreign policy.

In setting out to expand national power and bring better life to its teeming millions, modesty and pragmatism have emerged as the principal features of India's changed grand strategy. By the early 1990s, India recognized that the challenge for the nation lies in setting an ambitious agenda at home and a modest foreign policy that serves the interests of the nation's rapid economic progress. India has come to see that the temptations to dabble in extravagant power plays on the world scene and trying to run a Third World trade union are distractions from the pursuit of national strength. It has also begun to understand that enhanced economic and technological capabilities will eventually provide it with geopolitical options that it could carefully explore in the future.

A modest foreign policy is not necessarily a dull or less challenging enterprise, for there is so much that India needs to do to complete its territorial consolidation, settle its unresolved disputes with Pakistan and China, promote regional economic integration and expand areas of cooperation with the great powers. Ending the bitter legacy of Partition, finding a reasonable settlement of the Kashmir dispute and normalizing relations with Pakistan remain at the top of India's foreign policy agenda. The series of Indo-Pakistani crises since the overt nuclearization of the subcontinent in the 1990s might have opened the door for a final settlement with Pakistan, and the external conditions have never been so conducive. The very attempt to move towards the goal could transform the context of India–Pakistan relations. The same approach to problem solving could create the diplomatic space to resolve the long-standing boundary dispute with China. Only when India has settled boundaries with its neighbours can those borders be overcome. Borders in the subcontinent need not necessarily remain political barriers. They need to be transformed into zones of economic cooperation among regions that once were part of the same cultural and political space. India's route to great power status on the world stage and an indispensable role in maintaining peace and stability in the Indian Ocean region will depend on its ability to alter the dynamics of its own neighbourhood. India cannot hope to transcend the region by ignoring the challenges in its neighbourhood.

The modest nature of the new foreign policy does not mean India has to abandon its global activism. In making an effective contribution to multilateralism, India has to go beyond the traditional presumptions of a North–South divide. Building issue-based coalitions and approaching problems in a functional rather than an ideological manner has become far more important to India's approach to global issues from trade to management of environment. The voice of an economically strong India will be heard with more respect than that which pretends to lead a non-existent Third World trade union. On a full range of international issues, India can bridge contending views and facilitate reasonable compromises on global problems.

Finally, a modest foreign policy need not rob India of a sense of exceptionalism. For many in India and abroad, an anti-Western orientation has come to signify the essence of Indian specificity in world affairs. There is no reason, however, to define India's singularity in terms of a permanent opposition to the West. The end of the historic rivalries within the Euro-Atlantic world and the emergence of a post-colonial and self-assured India have led to a situation in which opposition to the West is no longer the central characteristic of New Delhi's foreign policy. In the new world, particularly the one that is emerging from the ashes of the bombing of the World Trade Centre, India's role will increasingly be seen through a new prism. That India remains the single most important adherent of the Enlightenment in the non-Western world has begun to acquire an unprecedented importance in international politics. In a world where the ideas of individual freedom, democracy and rational inquiry are being challenged by both post-modernists and the pre-modernists wearing the garb of religion, India, warts and all, is the living demonstration that Enlightenment values are universal.

At the very moment when India's commitment to the

Enlightenment project has become relevant to world politics and a source of its potential greatness on the world scene, the nation's ability to hold on to the values of the Enlightenment has come under serious scrutiny. The unprecedented riots in Gujarat in the first part of 2002 that targeted Muslims, the connivance of state authorities with Hindu extremists and the victory of the BJP in the state assembly elections riding a popular wave of hatred at the end of the year have led to deep pessimism about the future of democracy, the rule of law and the sustainability of secularism and religious harmony in India. The tragedy in Gujarat has unfolded amidst the growing strength of anti-modern and anti-Western ideas propagated by the Hindutva ideology. The rise of xenophobia, religious intolerance and opposition to cultural diversity has not gone unchallenged, however. India is plunged into a powerful contest between two groups: one seeks to keep it a closed majoritarian society, and the other wants it to maintain the tradition of openness to other cultures and to continue a self-confident modernization through cooperation with the West.

The essence of this struggle for the soul of India was summed up at the end of 2002 by strongly expressed views from two of its most influential men within the same week. One was from K.S. Sudharshan, the head of the RSS, who attacked globalization, accused the 'sons of Macaulay' for their obsession with the English language and demanded that India be rid of all foreign investment.[5] The other was from N.R. Narayana Murthy, the man who launched the most well-known Indian brand abroad, Infosys. At the turn of the century Murthy emerged as the undisputed symbol of the Indian software industry and of the nation's ability to gain through globalization. Murthy demanded that even as India holds on to its great traditions, it should understand its weaknesses and adopt relevant Western values.[6] The proposition that India could learn from the West had long gone out of fashion on the Left and Right of the Indian spectrum, but Murthy made an unabashed case for modernization and taken the best from the West, such as freedom of enterprise, thought and action; secularism; respect for public good; integrity; accountability; respect for merit; and dignity of labour.

Summing up the debate, one Indian analyst comments that the values propagated by Murthy are those

> that unite societies, not divide them. . . . Sudarshan on the other hand pursues a politics of negativism and an economics of defeatism. . . . [H]is desire to hark back to a dead past and imagine external enemies betrays a lack of confidence. Confidence of the kind Murthy has come to symbolize. . . . Murthy is the triumphant icon of our times. Sudarshan a tragic anachronism.'[7]

The ideas of Murthy might have won the debate in the English language newspapers, but the battle with those who want India to march into the past remains to be fought in the political arena. The political outcome from this war of ideas will shape India's standing in the world and the kind of role it will play in international relations.

If the Second Republic abandons its commitment to secularism, the rule of law and the impulse for rapid modernization under the influence of the Hindutva brigade, India could reopen the wounds of Partition, incite a prolonged conflict between Hindus and Muslims and slow down India's economic progress. Such an India would count little in world affairs. An India that stays true to the values of the Enlightenment, deepens its democracy, pursues economic modernization and remains open to the external world will inevitably become a power of great consequence in the coming decades. It will be the model for the political transformation of the volatile Indian Ocean region and a force for peace and progress in Asia and the world.

Notes

The archives of the *Washington File* are available online <http://usinfo.state.gov/products/washfile/>.

Introduction

1 External Affairs Minister Jaswant Singh's interview with Chidanand Rajghatta published in *Times of India* (New Delhi) 15 September 2001. Asked whether India was prepared to lend military support to the American plans for a war on the Taliban, Singh said, 'This is a highly sensitive area. So you will understand if I don't go into details. The prime minister's letter to President Bush is explicit enough when he talks of cooperation in investigations and every other sense. Don't ask me about details.' Pressed further with the inference that India will provide military support, Singh confirmed, 'Yes. The tragedy has imparted to what was already a solid foundation, real operational content of cooperating with each other [India and the United States].'

2 Based on private conversations with informed Indian and American sources.

3 There are few other examples of such dramatic shifts. Communist China's rift with the Soviet Union in the late 1950s and early 1960s transformed Beijing from an ideological ally in the early 1950s with Moscow to a de facto partner of the United States against the Soviet Union by the late 1970s.

4   Two exceptions were the articulation of the so-called Gujral Doctrine by External Affairs Minister Inder Kumar Gujral at Chatham House, London, 23 September 1996 and the speech at the Asia Society in New York on 28 September 1998 by Prime Minister Atal Bihari Vajpayee, in which he proclaimed India and the US 'natural allies'.

Chapter One: The Nuclear Leap Forward

1   Narasimha Rao's speech is reproduced as Appendix 2 in J.N. Dixit, *My South Block Years: Memoirs of a Foreign Secretary* (New Delhi: UBSPD, 1996), 459.

2   In what was a capstone of India's disarmament activism since the 1950s, Rajiv Gandhi called for a global abolition of nuclear weapons by 2010 in his address to the UN on 9 June 1988. He presented before the international community an action plan for comprehensive nuclear disarmament in three stages. In an important move, he suggested that India would be prepared to give up its option to make nuclear weapons if the nuclear weapons powers agreed to give up their atomic arsenals by 2010. This would be the last time that India linked its imperative to acquire nuclear weapons with the broader objective of elimination of nuclear weapons. For a text of the speech, see Ministry of External Affairs, *India and Disarmament : An Anthology of Selected Writings and Speeches* (New Delhi: Ministry of External Affairs, 1988), 280-94. For the text of Rajiv Gandhi's Action Plan and associated documents, see Ministry of External Affairs, *Disarmament: India's Initiatives* (New Delhi: Ministry of External Affairs, 1988), 44-77.

3   The details of the Bush–Narasimha Rao meeting are in Dixit's *My South Block Years*, 75-76. At the meeting in Waldorf-Astoria, Dixit says, the Indian flag was hoisted upside down, but India found it prudent not to raise the issue and complicate the meeting.

4   For a discussion of the Indo-US diplomacy around December 1995 when India seemed set to test nuclear weapons, see George Perkovich, *India's Nuclear Bomb: The Impact on Global Proliferation*

(New Delhi: Oxford University Press, 1999), 353-77.

5   Based on discussions with key Indian officials in 1995 and 1996.

6   There are many insights into the early years of the Indian nuclear programme in Perkovich, *India's Nuclear Bomb.*

7   For an account of India's atomic diplomacy in the first decades, see *India's Nuclear Option* (New York: Praeger Publishers, 1976). For an excellent collection of documents, see J.P. Jain, *Nuclear India*, 2 vols. (New Delhi: Radiant, 1974).

8   See K. Subrahmanyam, "Indian Nuclear Policy—1964-98: A Personal Recollection," Jasjit Singh, ed., *Nuclear India* (New Delhi: Knowledge World, 1998), 44-46.

9   For a strong critique from the traditional perspective that supported keeping the option but was opposed to exercising it, see N. Ram, *Riding the Nuclear Tiger* (New Delhi: Left Word Books, 1999).

10 See Nirmala George's interview with the Chairman of the Atomic Energy Commission, Dr R. Chidambaram, "No More N-Tests Needed: AEC," *Indian Express* (New Delhi), 4 February 1999.

11 The statement by Jaswant Singh on 2 May 2001 is available at <http://www.meadev.nic.in/news/official/20010502/official.htm>.

12 India's Draft Nuclear Doctrine prepared by the National Security Advisory Board was released by the government of India on 17 August 1999. Text can be found in various places including at the web site of the Indian embassy in Washington, D.C. <http://www.indianembassy.org/policy/CTBT/nuclear_ doctrine_aug_17_1999.html>.

13 For the joint statement issued after the first round of talks on CBMs in New Delhi, see Ministry of External Affairs, *India–Pakistan Relations: Documents* (New Delhi: Ministry of External Affairs, 2001), 53-54.

14 For the texts of the various joint statements including the Lahore Declaration issued by India and Pakistan from the late 1990s until the Agra Summit in July 2001, see Ministry of External Affairs, *India–Pakistan Relations*, 25-28.

15 The Indian statement on 2 May 2001 is available online <http://www.meadev.nic.in/news/official/20010502/official.htm>.

16   See the text of the joint statement of the US–India Defence Policy Group, *Washington File*, 5 December 2001.

17   Ibid.

18   For a more detailed discussion, see chapters four and seven.

19   Kanti Bajpai makes a valuable categorization of the main trends in India's thinking on foreign policy and identifies three main schools: Nehruvians, neo-liberals and hyperrealists. See Kanti Bajpai, "India's Strategic Culture" (paper presented at South Asia in 2020: Future Strategic Balances and Alliances, a conference organized by the Asia/Pacific Research Center, Stanford University, Stanford, Calif., 4-5 January 2001), n.p.

Chapter Two: Beyond Non-alignment

1   Speaking on India's emerging foreign policy, Nehru articulated India's policy of non-alignment:

> We propose, as far as possible, to keep away from the power politics of groups, aligned against one another, which have led in the past to world wars and which may again lead to disasters on an even vaster scale. . . . The world, in spite of its rivalries and hatreds and inner conflicts, moves inevitably towards closer cooperation and the building up of a world commonwealth. It is for this One World that free India will work, a world in which there is the free cooperation of free peoples, and no class or group exploits another.

On India's approach towards the US and Soviet Union that were drifting towards a cold war, Nehru said:

> We send our greetings to the people of the United States of America to whom destiny has given a major role in international affairs. We trust that this tremendous responsibility will be utilized for the furtherance of peace and human freedom everywhere. To that other great nation of the modern world, the Soviet Union, which also carries a vast responsibility for shaping world events, we send greetings. They are our neighbours in Asia and inevitably we shall have to

undertake many common tasks and have much to do with each other.
Jawaharlal Nehru, *Speeches*, vol. 1 (September 1946-May 1949) (New Delhi: Publications Division, Government of India, June 1967), 2-3.

2   For an assessment of the origins and evolution of the G-15, see Kripa Sridharan, "G-15 and South-South Cooperation: Promise and Performance," *Third World Quarterly* (London) 19, no. 3 (1998): 357-73.

3   For a scathing critique of the Congress party's foreign policy under Narasimha Rao, see the publication on foreign policy issued by the Communist Party of India (Marxist) (CPI [M]) in the 1996 elections. It accused the party of yielding to American pressures and characterized the BJP as a 'pro-imperialist force'. CPI(M), *Record of Compromising India's Security* (New Delhi: CPI-[M], 1996).

4   See the foreign policy section of BJP's manifesto in 1996, *For a Strong and Prosperous India: Election Manifesto 1996* (New Delhi: Bharatiya Janata Party, 1996), 31-33.

5   See Indian National Congress, *Election Manifesto: General Elections Lok Sabha 1998* (New Delhi: Indian National Congress, 1998), 54-55.

6   Ibid., 54-55.

7   Brajesh Mishra, "Rising World Players in Asia: Implications for Regional and Global Security," (presentation at 36th Munich Conference on Security Policy, Munich, Germany, 4-5 February 2000), 3.

8   For a discussion of the typology of Indian views on international order, see Kanti Bajpai, "Indian Conceptions of Order and Justice in International Relations: Nehruvian, Gandhian, Hindutva and Neo-liberal," in Andrew Hurrell and Rosemary Foot, eds., *Order and Justice in International System,* (Oxford: Oxford University Press, forthcoming).

9   Bajpai, "Indian Conceptions of Order," n.p.

10   "India, USA and the World: Let Us Work Together to Solve the Political-Economic Y2K Problem," Prime Minister Atal Bihari

Notes

Vajpayee's speech at the Asia Society, New York, 28 September 1998 in Ministry of External Affairs, *Foreign Relations of India: Select Statements, May 1998-March 2000* (New Delhi: Ministry of External Affairs, 2000), 57-69.

11 This phrase was popularized by Dennis Kux in *India and the United States: Estranged Democracies 1941-91* (Washington, D.C.: National Defense University Press, 1992).

12 For an analysis of the attempts by Indira Gandhi and Rajiv Gandhi to explore an improvement in relations with the United States during the 1980s, see Satu P. Limaye, *U.S.-Indian Relations: The Pursuit of Accommodation* (Boulder, Colo.: Westview, 1993).

13 There has been considerable speculation on who drafted the Asia Society speech. Indications are that Alok Prasad, the unflappable Joint Secretary (Americas) in the Ministry of External Affairs, and Sudheendra Kulkarni, Vajpayee's speech-writer, shaped the formulations.

14 At a luncheon in Prime Minister Vajpayee's honour during his visit to the US on 15 September 2000, US Vice President Al Gore declared,

> Our two nations share a special bond. As the world's oldest democracy and the world's largest democracy, we are, in your words, 'natural allies'. Our cultures and customs differ, but we share a strong commitment to democracy and equality for all. We are proof that diversity is strength, [*sic*] and that freedom is power.

See Ministry of External Affairs, *Prime Minister Atal Bihari Vajpayee at the United Nations and in USA* (New Delhi: Ministry of External Affairs, 2000), 86.

15 For a flavour of the discussion between India and France on the subject, see *India and France in a Multipolar World, Proceedings of a Seminar in New Delhi 16-17 February 2000* (New Delhi: Manohar and Centre de Sciences Humaines, 2001).

16 The idea of a world led by a few major powers can be traced to Jawaharlal Nehru who visualized in 1946 that China, India and a potential European federation as the great powers of the future:

> Forgetting present problems then for awhile and looking ahead,

India emerges as a strong united state, a federation of free units, intimately connected with her neighbours and playing an important part in world affairs. She is one of the very few countries which have [*sic*] the resources and capacity to stand on their own feet. Today probably the only such countries are the United States and the Soviet Union—China and India are potentially capable of joining that group—no other country, taken singly, apart from these four actually are potentially in such a position. It is possible of course that larger federations or groups of nations may emerge in Europe or elsewhere and form huge multinational states. . . . Whatever happens, it will be well for the world if India can make her influence felt. For that influence will always be in favour of peace and against aggression.

Discovery of India (Bombay: Asia Publishing House, 1961), 535.

17 India was rather hesitant initially to endorse the concept, but a joint press statement issued at the end of Primakov's visit on 22 December 1998 obliquely backed the idea: 'Both sides expressed the view that the development of active and constructive bilateral relations between India, Russia, and other major countries of the Asia and Pacific region would contribute to stability and security.' For a text of the statement, see the web site of the Indian embassy in Washington, D.C. < http://www.indianembassy.org/inews/January99/main.htm >. For a report on the discussions between Primakov and the Indian leadership, see Jyoti Malhotra, "Sign NPT, Says Friend Primakov," *Indian Express* (New Delhi), 22 December 1998.

18 For a report on the meeting, the first of its kind, see Amit Baruah, "Sinha Meets Russian, Chinese Counterparts," *Hindu* (New Delhi) 15 September 2002. For the papers from the officially sanctioned discussions among the academics of the three nations on the triangular cooperation in Moscow during 5-6 September 2001 in Moscow, see *China Report* (New Delhi) 38, no. 1 (January-March 2002): 25-210.

Chapter Three: Returning to the West

1   Sunil Khilnani captures the essence of the Indian experiment in
    democracy:
    [T]he period of Indian history since 1947 might be seen as the
    adventure of a political idea: democracy. From this perspective,
    the history of independent India appears as the third moment
    in the great democratic experiment launched at the end of
    eighteenth century by the American and French revolutions.
    Each is an historic instance of the project to resuscitate and
    embody the ancient ideal of democracy under vastly different
    conditions. . . . Each of these experiments released immense
    energies; each raised towering expectations; and each has
    suffered disappointments. The Indian experiment is in its early
    stages; and its outcome may well turn out to be the most
    significant of them all, partly because of its sheer human scale,
    and partly because of its location, a substantial bridgehead of
    effervescent liberty on the Asian continent.
    The Idea of India (London: Hamish Hamilton, 1997), 4.
2   Tom Friedman describes India's tendency in this way: 'The more
    time you spend in India the more you realize that this teeming,
    multiethnic, multireligious, multilingual country is one of the
    world's great wonders—a miracle with message. And the message
    is that democracy matters.'
    "Where Freedom Reigns," *New York Times*, 14 August 2002.
3   The first meeting of the Community of Democracies Initiative
    was held in Warsaw in May 2000. The second was in Seoul in
    2002. For documents from the conferences see the Council for
    Community of Democracies' web site <http://www.ccd21.org/
    documents.htm>.
4   In his address to the Indian Parliament on 22 March 2000, Clinton
    talked about the lessons India teaches to the world:
    The first is about democracy. There are still those who deny
    that democracy is a universal aspiration; who say it works only
    for people of a certain culture, or a certain degree of economic
    development. India has been proving them wrong for 52 years

now. . . . A second lesson India teaches is about diversity. . . . Under trying circumstances, you have shown the world how to live with difference. You have shown that tolerance and mutual respect are in many ways the keys to our common survival. That is something the whole world needs to learn. Ministry of External Affairs, *Visit of the US President to India, March 19-25, 2000* (New Delhi: Ministry of External Affairs, 2000), 64-65.

5   A translated text of the statement broadcast is available on the BBC's web site <http://news.bbc.co.uk/l/hi/world/south_asia/1585636.stm>.

6   Bernard Lewis, "The Roots of Muslim Rage," *Atlantic Monthly* 266, no. 3 (September 1990): 47ff. This article is also available online <http://www.theatlantic.com/issues/90sep/rage.htm>.

7   Ibid.

8   Kishore Mahbubani, "The United States: 'Go East, Young Man'," *Washington Quarterly* 17, no. 2 (spring 1994): 5-23. See also Fareed Zakaria, "Culture is Destiny: A Conversation with Lee Kuan Yew," *Foreign Affairs* 73, no. 2 (March/April 1994): 109-26. For a critique of Asian values see, Kim Dae-jung, "Is Culture Destiny?: The Myth of Asia's Anti-Democratic Values," *Foreign Affairs* 73, no. 6 (November/December 1994): 189-94, and Amartya Sen, "Democracy as a Universal Value," *Journal of Democracy* 10, no. 3 (July 1999): 3-17.

9   President George W. Bush, *State of the Union Address*, 29 January 2002. The text is available on the White House's web site <http://www.whitehouse.gov/news/releases/2002/01/print/20020129-11.html>.

10 Ibid.

11 Ibid.

12 Ibid.

13 Ibid.

14 Ibid.

15 Ibid.

16 Ibid.

17 Robert Kagan, "Power and Weakness," *Policy Review*, no. 113

(June/July 2002): n.p.; this article is available online <http://
www.policyreview. org/JUN02/kagan.html>.

18   Ibid.

19   Robert Cooper, "Why We Still Need Empires," *Observer* (London)
     7 April 2002.

20   Quoted in Kagan, 'Power and Weakness,' n.p.

21   The Bush administration's strategy talked about the challenges
     from non-democratic China:

> The United States relationship with China is an important
> part of our strategy to promote a stable, peaceful, and prosperous
> Asia–Pacific region. We welcome the emergence of a strong,
> peaceful, and prosperous China. The democratic development
> of China is crucial to that future. Yet, a quarter century after
> beginning the process of shedding the worst features of the
> Communist legacy, China's leaders have not yet made the next
> series of fundamental choices about the character of their state.
> In pursuing advanced military capabilities that can threaten its
> neighbors in the Asia-Pacific region, China is following an
> outdated path that, in the end, will hamper its own pursuit of
> national greatness. In time, China will find that social and
> political freedom is the only source of that greatness.

     In contrast, its focus on India was more positive:

> The United States has undertaken a transformation in its
> bilateral relationship with India based on a conviction that
> U.S. interests require a strong relationship with India. We are
> the two largest democracies, committed to political freedom
> protected by representative government. India is moving
> toward greater economic freedom as well. We have a common
> interest in the free flow of commerce, including through the
> vital sea lanes of the Indian Ocean. Finally, we share an interest
> in fighting terrorism and in creating a strategically stable Asia.

     See the White House, *The National Security Strategy of the United
     States of America* (Washington, D.C.: White House, 2002), section
     VIII < http://www.whitehouse.gov/nsc/nssall.html>.

Chapter Four: The US: A Natural Ally?

1   See C. Raja Mohan, "India, U.S. Should Look Ahead: Jaswant," *Hindu* (New Delhi), 18 March 2000. In a statement the General Secretary of the Communist Party India (Marxist), Harkishan Singh Surjeet, said the formulations of Jaswant Singh on Indo-US relations showed the 'pro-imperialist' stance of the BJP and a lack of knowledge of the role played by India in the past against imperialist designs of the US. Asking the people to stand firmly by the policy of non-alignment that had helped Third World countries preserve their independence, Surjeet warned that the pro-US tilt of the BJP would only jeopardize the country's independence. See "Don't Forget NAM, Surjeet Tells Jaswant," *Hindu* (New Delhi), 19 March 2000.

2   When India began its reforms in 1991, Indo-US trade stood at $5.2 billion. A decade later in 2001 they had more than doubled to $13.1 billion. These figures are for merchandise trade and do not include fast rising software and related exports. (These numbers were provided by the US Embassy in New Delhi in October 2002 and based on US International Trade Commission data.) Expressing anguish at the low level of Indo-US economic relations in comparison to those between US and China, Ambassador Blackwill expressed concern that the low level of economic relations might undermine the emerging prospects for broader partnership between the two nations. He called American investments and trade flows with India are 'flat as a chapati' [*sic*]. See Robert D. Blackwill, "US–India Economic Relations," (speech delivered at the American Chamber of Commerce in India, New Delhi, 28 January 2002) <http://usembassy.state.gov/posts/in1/wwwh12.html#book3>, and "US–India Economic Relations—The Missing Piece," (speech delivered at the Federation of Indian Chambers of Commerce and Industry, New Delhi, 29 October 2002) <http://usembassy.state.gov/posts/in1/wwwh1029amb.html>.

3   Ministry of External Affairs, "Remarks by President Clinton at a Banquet Hosted by President K.R. Narayanan at Rashtrapati

Bhawan on March 21, 2000," *Visit of the U.S. President to India March 19-25, 2000* (New Delhi: Ministry of External Affairs, 2000), 56.

4   For an incisive analysis of the growing influence of the Indian-American community on the US Congress, see Robert M. Hathaway, "Unfinished Passage: India, Indian Americans, and the U.S. Congress," *Washington Quarterly* 24, no. 2, (spring 2001): 21-34.

5   See C. Raja Mohan's interview with Jaswant Singh: " Jaswant Singh for Consensus on CTBT," *Hindu* (New Delhi), 29 November 1999. For the text of the interview, see "India's Not to Engage in a N-Arms Race: Jaswant," *Hindu* (New Delhi), 29 November 1999.

6   See C. Raja Mohan's interview with Strobe Talbott: "Early Solutions to Nuclear Issues Will Help," *Hindu* (New Delhi), 14 January 2000. For the full text of the interview, see "We Are for a Qualitatively Better Relationship with India," *Hindu* (New Delhi), 14 January 2000.

7   The interviews of Jaswant Singh and Strobe Talbott with C. Raja Mohan were a carefully orchestrated effort by New Delhi and Washington to put out public signals of an accommodation on the CTBT and the lifting of sanctions. The Indian government attempted to rally the opinion of the political class to accept a possible signature on the CTBT without its ratification, but the effort did not succeed.

8   For the Clinton speech to the joint session of the Parliament, see "Remarks by President Clinton," *Visit of the US President to India*, 63-76.

9   Mohan, "Early Solutions."

10   The Principal Secretary to the Prime Minister, Brajesh Mishra, in a background briefing to Indian reporters in early June 1999 at the height of the Kargil crisis, talked about the 'paradigm shift' in Indo-US relations. He based his comment on the emerging signals of unprecedented American support to India during the Kargil War.

11   For a substantive account from the American perspective of the

end game in Kargil, see Bruce Riedel, "American Diplomacy and the 1999 Kargil Summit at Blair House," *Policy Paper Series 2002* (Philadelphia, Pa.: Center for the Advanced Study of India, University of Pennsylvania, 2002).

12 Teresita C. Schaffer and Howard B. Schaffer, "India and U.S.: Finding Common Interests," *Hindu* (New Delhi), 10 August 1999.

13 For text of the statement, see *Washington File*, 6 July 1999. The 4 July statement said, among other things, that Clinton and Nawaz Sharif 'agreed that it was vital for the peace of South Asia that the Line of Control in Kashmir be respected by both parties, in accordance with their 1972 Simla Accord.' The brief statement added,

> It was agreed between the President and the Prime Minister that concrete steps will be taken for the restoration of the line of control [*sic*] in accordance with the Simla Agreement. The President urged an immediate cessation of the hostilities once these steps are taken. The Prime Minister and President agreed that the bilateral dialogue begun in Lahore in February provides the best forum for resolving all issues dividing India and Pakistan, including Kashmir. The President said he would take a personal interest in encouraging an expeditious resumption and intensification of those bilateral efforts, once the sanctity of the Line of Control has been fully restored.

14 Schaffer and Schaffer, "India and U.S."

15 For text of the prepared remarks by Secretary of State Madeleine Albright at the Asia Society in Washington on 14 March 2000, see *Washington File*, 16 March 2000.

16 Ibid.

17 In his televised address to the people of Pakistan during his brief stay there on 25 March 2000 Clinton added the following:

> I believe it is also in Pakistan's interest to reduce tensions with India. When I was in New Delhi, I urged India to seize the opportunity for dialogue. Pakistan also must help create conditions that will allow dialogue to succeed. For India and Pakistan this must be a time of restraint, for respect for the line

of control, and renewed lines of communication.

I have listened carefully to General Musharraf and others. I understand your concerns about Kashmir. I share your convictions that human rights of all its people must be respected. But a stark truth must also be faced. There is no military solution to Kashmir. International sympathy, support and intervention cannot be won by provoking a bigger, bloodier conflict. On the contrary; [*sic*] sympathy and support will be lost. And no matter how great the grievance, it is wrong to support attacks against civilians across the line of control.

In the meantime, I ask again: Will endless, costly struggle build good schools for your children? Will it make your cities safer? Will it bring clean water and better health care? Will it narrow the gaps between those who have and those who have nothing? Will it hasten the day when Pakistan's energy and wealth are invested in building its future? The answer to all these questions is plainly no.

The American people don't want to see tensions rise and suffering increase. We want to be a force for peace. But we cannot force peace. We can't impose it. We cannot and will not mediate or resolve the dispute in Kashmir. Only you and India can do that, through dialogue.

For the full text of the speech, see *Washington File*, 25 March 2000.

18   See Clinton's interview with Peter Jennings, ABC World News, 21 March 2000, reproduced in "Remarks by President Clinton," *Visit of the U.S. President to India*, 40.

19   National Security Adviser Brajesh Mishra spoke about India's coercive diplomacy after 13 December and its consequences in an interview on the BBC:

We are happy with what Washington and London have done but not happy with the results which have come because we were promised much more. We were told that General Musharraf will have to carry out his promises. Because these promises are to the US and UK.

For a transcript of the interview, see "Talking with Brajesh Mishra," *Indian Express* (New Delhi), 29 November 2002.

20 In response to a question on Kashmir elections, Powell said, 'I think we'll have to wait and see how the election goes, whether it truly is free and fair and whether there is broad participation. There are some groups now who say they won't participate so I don't know that this election will be definitive in that light, but I think it's one step forward in a process of determining the will of the Kashmiri people.' *Washington File*, 29 July 2002.

21 A senior administration official briefing the press in New York after the talks between President Bush and with General Musharraf on September 2002 summed up the discussions on Kashmir, 'The President, as I said, pushed the Pakistanis hard on the question of infiltration across the Line of Control, but he also noted that this is basically the precursor, the ending of infiltration is the precursor of setting the environment where you can make progress on the underlying issue.' *Washington File*, 13 September 2002.

22 For an assessment of Blackwill's visit to Srinagar at the end of 2002, see Shujaat Bukhari, "US Envoy Takes a Different Track," *Hindu* (New Delhi), 8 December 2002.

23 In response to a direct question from the *Newsweek* correspondent Lally Weymouth on American role in Kashmir, Vajpayee said, 'That of a facilitator'. Asked if it went against the traditional Indian rejection of third party role in Kashmir, Vajpayee added, 'No, that's why I said a facilitator, not a mediator.' For a text of the interview, see the web site of the Ministry of External Affairs <http://meadev.nic.in/govt/pm-newsweek-july2002.htm>.

24 See Condoleezza Rice, "Promoting the National Interest," *Foreign Affairs* 79, no.1, (January/February 2000): 56.

25 See the White House, *The National Security Strategy of the United States of America* (Washington, D.C.: White House, September 2002), Section VIII <http://www.whitehouse.gov/nsc/nssall.html>.

26 Robert D. Blackwill, "The Quality and Durability of the US–India Relationship" (speech delivered at the Indian Chamber of Commerce, Kolkata, 27 November 2002) <http://usembassy.state.gov/posts/in1/wwwh1127amb.html>.

27   Colin Powell, "America Must Be Involved in the World," (opening statement of the Secretary Of State Designate at the US Senate Foreign Relations Committee, 17 January 2001), *Washington File*, 18 January 2001.

28   See the joint statement of the Third US–India Defence Policy Group, New Delhi, 3-4 December 2001, *Washington File*, 5 December 2001.

Chapter Five: Reviving the Russian Connection

1   Based on conversations with sources familiar with the meeting. Brajesh Mishra met Yevgeni Primakov on 10 June 1998 in Moscow. Even before the meeting, the hints from Moscow after India's nuclear tests were disconcerting to New Delhi.

2   Narasimha Rao was explaining the coup against Gorbachev but had no words to condemn it. See "Gorbachev Ouster a Warning: PM," *Times of India* (New Delhi), 20 August 1991.

3   "LS Hails Failure of Soviet Coup," *Times of India* (New Delhi), 23 August 1991.

4   J.N. Dixit, *Across Borders: 50 Years of India's Foreign Policy* (New Delhi: Picus Books, 1998), 368.

5   Ibid., 368.

6   Ibid., 369.

7   See the text of the Treaty of Friendship and Cooperation between the Republic of India and the Russian Federation of 28 January 1993. Mimeo provided by the Ministry of External Affairs.

8   Following the cancellation of parts of the deal, an Indian reporter based in Moscow at that time wrote, 'Over the next few months, India's Russian policy was conducted away from the glare of newshounds and press publicity.' Nandan Unnikrishnan, "Indo-Russian Relations," *World Focus* (New Delhi) 16, no. 4 (1995): 22. There has been unconfirmed speculation that, despite the cancellation of the contract, Russia quietly transferred the technology of cryogenic engines to India.

9   Extending full support to India in its war against terrorism, Putin

said in his address to the Indian Parliament on 4 October:

I would like to share with you ... the information that we have which is absolutely true and verified, according to which, the same individuals, the same terrorist organizations, extremist organizations are organizing and, very often, the same individuals participate in organizing, in conducting and igniting terrorist acts from the Philippines to Kosovo including Kashmir, Afghanistan and Russia's Northern Caucasus.

Ministry of External Affairs, *Visit of the President of the Russian Federation to India, October 2-5, 2000* (New Delhi: Ministry of External Affairs, 2000), 48.

10   For the text of the Delhi Declaration issued by Putin and Vajpayee on 4 December 2002, see "No Double Standards in Fighting Terrorism," *Hindu* (New Delhi), 5 December 2002.

11   See Putin's interview on the eve of his visit, Raj Chengappa, "It Would Be Too Narrow to Call This Just a New Deal," *India Today* (New Delhi) (9 October 2000): 43.

12   For Putin's remarks at the press conference with Vajpayee in New Delhi on 4 December 2002, see Jyoti Malhotra, "Putin Lends His Shoulder: Calls for Nuclear Cooperation with India, Frowns at Pak Weapons," *Indian Express* (New Delhi), 5 December 2002.

13   Amit Baruah, "Concerns over Terrorists Acquiring Pak. Nuclear Arms Remain: Putin," *Hindu* (New Delhi), 1 December 2002.

14   Besides cooperation in civilian nuclear energy, there are indications that Russia might be assisting India in building a nuclear-powered submarine under the programme called an advanced technology vessel. India leased a nuclear submarine in 1988 and returned it after the lease expired in 1991. For cooperation on civilian nuclear energy, see R. Adam Moody, "The Indian-Russian Light Water Reactor Deal," *The Nonproliferation Review* (Monterey, Calif.) 5, no. 1 (fall 1997): 112-22. For non-weapon military nuclear cooperation between India and Russia, see "Indian Nuclear Submarine Fleet Development Programme: Russian Participation," *Arms Control Letters*, 15 March 1999; this article is available online <http://www.nyu.edu/globalbeat/southasia/PIR031599.html>.

15   Jyoti Malhotra, "Icing on *Gorshkov* Cake for India: A Nuclear Submarine," *Indian Express* (New Delhi), 1 December 2002.

16   Ministry of External Affairs, "Declaration on Strategic Partnership between the Republic of India and the Russian Federation, October 4, 2000," *Visit of the President of the Russian Federation*, 84.

17   "Declaration on Strategic Partnership" *Visit of the President of the Russian Federation*, 88.

18   Chengappa, "It Would Be Too Narrow," 46.

19   In what was widely seen a diplomatic rope trick, Jaswant Singh managed to pacify Russian concerns, expressed strongly by Foreign Minister Igor Ivanov about Indian support to the Bush initiative on missile defence. See C. Raja Mohan, "Indian Support for NMD Not at Russia's Cost," *Hindu* (New Delhi), 5 May 2001.

20   For a useful review of Russo-Pakistani relations in the 1990s, see Devendra Kaushik, "Islamabad–Moscow–New Delhi," *World Focus* (New Delhi) 22, nos. 10, 11 and 12 (October, November and December 2001): 58-60.

21   Ministry of External Affairs, "Address by President Vladimir Putin to the Members of the Parliament," *Visit of the President of Russian Federation*, 47-48.

22   For reports on the disconcerting Russian-Pakistani diplomatic pas de deux in Almaty, see "Serious and Positive Signals from Musharraf: Putin," *Hindu* (New Delhi), 5 June 2002; Atul Aneja, "Putin Has Invited Us: Musharraf," *Hindu* (New Delhi), 5 June 2002; Vladimir Radyuhin, "India Grateful to Russia for Support," *Hindu* (New Delhi), 6 June 2002.

23   While there has been some concern in New Delhi on the nature of the Russian formulations, there is continuing confidence in South Block that Russia can be persuaded not to take a hostile position vis-à-vis India on Kashmir and the Indo-Pakistani dialogue. Based on conversations with senior Ministry of External Affairs officials in December 2002.

24   The Russian energy giant, Gazprom, has taken strong interest in building a gas pipeline from Turkmenistan to Pakistan via

Afghanistan and is also seeking to revive energy cooperation between Moscow and Islamabad. For a discussion of the issues, see M.K. Bhadrakumar, "Significant Shifts in Afghanistan," *Hindu* (New Delhi), 28 October 2002; Ron Callari and Tariq Saeedi, "Trans-Afghan Pipeline, A Pipedream Forging Reality," *Central Asia-Caucasus Analyst* (19 June 2002) and available online <http://www.cacianalyst.org/2002-06-19/20020619_TRANS-AFGHAN_PIPELINE.htm>); Aftab Kazi and Tariq Saeedi, "India and the Politics of the Trans-Afghan Pipeline," *Central Asia-Caucasus Analyst* (28 August 2002) and available online <http://www.cacianalyst.org/2002-08-28/20020828_INDIA_AFGHAN_GAS_PIPELINE.htm>.

25 Malhotra, "Putin Lends His Shoulder."
26 "India's Largest FDI Foray—ONGC Invests \$2 Bn in Russian Oilfield," *Indian Express* (New Delhi) 11 February 2001.
27 Nandan Unnikrishnan, "Need to Rekindle the Romance," *Financial Express* (New Delhi), 9 December 2002.

Chapter Six: Emulating China

1 For the text of Jiang Zemin's interview with the Agence France Press in June 1998, see Foreign Broadcast Information Service, Washington, D.C., FBIS-CHI-98-154, 4 June 1998.
2 Citing an Indian proverb, Pramod Mahajan, a political aide to Vajpayee, called the Chinese reaction to the tests akin to the thief scolding the policeman.
3 The Agreement on the Maintenance of Peace and Tranquillity along the Line of Actual Control in the India–China Border Areas was signed in Beijing on 7 September 1993 during the visit of Prime Minister P.V. Narasimha Rao to China; for text of the agreement see the Stimson Center's web site <http://www.stimson.org/?sn=sa20020114287>. The Agreement between the Government of the Republic of India and the Government of the People's Republic of China on Confidence-Building Measures in the Military Field along the Line of Actual

Control in the India–China Border Areas was signed in New Delhi on 29 November 1996 during the visit of President Jiang Zemin to India; the text of the agreement is also available online <http://www.stimson.org/?sn=sa20020114290>.

4   The Line of Actual Control (LAC) refers to the current positions of the two armed forces on the disputed boundary between India and China. Unlike the Line of Control (LoC) between India and Pakistan in Jammu and Kashmir that was delineated by mutual agreement in 1972, the LAC remains to be clarified and confirmed by the two sides. The boundary negotiations between the two countries shifted their focus in the 1990s from the dispute itself to the delineation of the LAC. Both sides agree that this process is without prejudice to the actual claims the two sides have on the territories of the other.

5   For a discussion of the Sino-Indian military and political tensions over the Sumdurong Chu Valley on the Thagla Ridge on the eastern borders between the two countries, see V. Natarajan, "The Sumdorong Chu Incident," *Bharat Rakshak Monitor*, no. 3 (2000); this article is also available online <http://www.bharat-rakshak.com/MONITOR/ISSUE3-3/natarajan.html>.

6   For an assessment of Jiang's visit to India and his speech in Pakistan, see C. Raja Mohan, "India, China Power Equations Changing," *Hindu* (New Delhi), 2 December 1996, and C. Raja Mohan, "A Positive Phase in China's South Asia Policy," *Hindu* (New Delhi), 5 December 1996.

7   For the text, see "Speech by President Jiang Zemin of the People's Republic of China at Islamabad, Pakistan, 2 December 1996," *Strategic Digest* (New Delhi) 27, no. 1 (January 1997): 17-20.

8   Although a series of statements critical of China came from George Fernandes in the weeks before the nuclear tests of May 1998, it does not appear that there was any coordinated effort to create a China rationale for the nuclearization of India. It is not even clear if Fernandes was informed about the nuclear decision. He has a long history of antipathy towards China, but the essence of his statements was not very different from what the Indian defence ministry had been saying about China for years. His

style of articulation and frequency in the early weeks of the Vajpayee government, however, created the problem with the Chinese.

9   For a summary of Chinese reactions, see Ming Zhang, *China's Changing Nuclear Posture: Reactions to the South Asian Nuclear Tests* (Washington, D.C.: Carnegie Endowment for International Peace, 1999), 25-32.

10   Atal Bihari Vajpayee, "Nuclear Anxiety: India's Letter to Clinton on Nuclear Testing," *New York Times*, 13 May 1998.

11   Briefing in New Delhi after the talks, the Ministry of External Affairs spokesman asserted, 'We did convey our concerns that China's assistance to Pakistan's nuclear and missile programme had an adverse impact on regional stability to which we have been obliged to respond in a responsible and restrained manner.' See "Summary of the Press Briefing by the Official Spokesman of the MEA, 8 March 2000," available at <http://www.meadev.nic.in/news/20000308.htm>.

12   Zhou Gang's interview with K.K. Katyal and C. Raja Mohan, "India Must Undo the Knot: China," *Hindu* (New Delhi), 10 July 1998.

13   Author's personal notes from Jaswant Singh's briefing in Manila in July 1998.

14   For a detailed discussion of the theme, see Quangsheng Zhao, *Interpreting Chinese Foreign Policy: The Micro-Macro Linkage Approach* (Oxford: Oxford University Press, 1996), 53-54.

15   Quoted in Zhao, ibid., 54.

16   Venu Rajamony, "India–China–U.S. Triangle: A Soft Balance of Power System in the Making," (Washington, D.C.: Center for Strategic and International Studies, March 2002): n.p.

17   Ibid., n.p.

18   Ibid., n.p.

19   John W. Garver argues the point extensively in *Protracted Contest: Sino-Indian Rivary in the Twentieth Century* (New Delhi: Oxford University Press, 2001), 29-31.

20   For a summary of the so-called Kunming Initiative launched by China in 1999, see Embassy of India, *Kunming Initiative: An*

Introduction (Beijing: Embassy of India, 2000). For a broader discussion, see Muchkund Dubey and Nancy Jetly, eds., *South Asia and Its Neighbours* (New Delhi: Friedrich Ebert Stiftung, 1999).

21   For a brief discussion of Jaswant Singh's diplomacy with Myanmar and Thailand that was shaped by a sense of competition with Beijing, see a series of three articles by C. Raja Mohan in the *Hindu* (New Delhi): "The Great Game in the East," (5 April 2002), "East by North East," (6 April 2002) and "China's Back Door" (7 April 2002). See also Tony Allison, "Myanmar Shows India the Road to South-East Asia," *Asiatimes Online*, 21 February 2001 <http://www.atimes.com/reports/CB21Ai01.html>.

22   See an official note by the Ministry of External Affairs, "Ganga–Mekong Swarnabhoomi Project" online at <http://www.meadev.nic.in/foreign/ganga-mekong.htm>, and the briefing by the spokesman of the Ministry of External Affairs on 7 August 2000.

23   For an assessment, see V. Jayanth, "The Mekong–Ganga Initiative", *Hindu* (New Delhi), 28 November 2000.

24   See Foreign Minister Tang Jiaxuan's interview with C. Raja Mohan, "China Ready to Increase Pace of Talks on LAC," *Hindu* (New Delhi), 22 July 2000; for the full text see "We Want Peace and Stability in South Asia: Tang Jiaxuan," *Hindu* (New Delhi), 22 July 2000.

25   For a discussion of Chinese position during Kargil, see Swaran Singh, "The Kargil Conflict: Why and How of China's Neutrality," *Strategic Analysis* (New Delhi) 23, no. 7 (1999): 1083-94.

26   The two sides established representative offices in both countries in 1994. The first Indian representative was Vinod Khanna, who retired from the foreign service to take up the posting.

27   Bilateral trade reached $1.2 billion in 1997 and fell in the late 1990s to below $1 billion before returning to about $1.1 billion in 2001. The two sides also established direct air links at the end of 2001 at around the same time as such links were set up between India and China. For a brief summary of bilateral relations, see

"Foreign Relations: South Asia," *Taiwan 2002* at <http://www.roc-taiwan.org/taiwan/5-gp/yearbook/chpt09-3.htm#11>.

28 See for example the party's formulation on China in its manifesto for its 1996 general elections:

> Our relations with the People's Republic of China offer an opportunity to now put them on a footing of friendship and cooperation. For this we need to resolve the border question in a fair and equitable manner. It cannot, however, be ignored that the People's Republic of China continues to support Pakistan militarily and otherwise.

Bharatiya Janata Party, *For a Strong and Prosperous India: Election Manifesto 1996* (New Delhi: BJP, 1996), 32.

29 Author's notes on Jaswant Singh's briefing to reporters after his talks with Chinese leaders in Beijing in March 2002. See also C. Raja Mohan, "India, China to Quicken the Pace of LAC Negotiation," *Hindu* (New Delhi), 30 March 2002.

30 Tang Jiaxuan's press conference in New Delhi; see C. Raja Mohan, "Sino-Indian JWG to Meet Often," *Hindu* (New Delhi), 23 July 2000.

31 Private conversation with the author in November 2002.

32 C.V. Ranganathan, "Sino-Indian Relations in the New Millennium," *China Report* (New Delhi) 37, no. 2 (2001): 132.

33 For Wang Yi's remarks in Beijing see, C. Raja Mohan, "China for Consensus on Settling Boundary Row," *Hindu* (New Delhi), 13 September 2001.

34 Private conversations with senior officials in December 2002.

35 Personal notes from conversations with Jaswant Singh in November 2001 and April 2002.

36 Conversations with the Sikkim chief minister and government officials in February and October 2002. See also C. Raja Mohan, "Sikkim: A Gateway to China," *Hindu* (New Delhi), 14 October 2002. In another interview, the chief minister of Sikkim, Pawan Kumar Chamling, spoke on the prospects for reviving Indo-Tibetan trade via Sikkim:

> We would like trade to take place. The issue is being examined by the Centre and so far we have not received any negative

response. I believe that such trade to Tibet would be in the interest of the state. It would enhance tourism and boost the service sector. The Centre has to take the decision.

See Jyoti Malhtora, "Talking with Pawan Chamling," *Indian Express* (New Delhi), 11 November 2002.

37   "India Welcomes China, Dalai Lama Talks," *Hindu* (New Delhi) 29 October 1998.

Chapter Seven: Containing Pakistan

1   For the Hindi text of the poem, see Vajpayee's speech at the civic reception in Lahore, 21 February 1999 in Ministry of External Affairs, *India–Pakistan Relations: Documents* (New Delhi: Ministry of External Affairs, 2001), 18-19.

2   See Atal Bihari Vajpayee, "My Musings from Kumarakom-1: Time to Resolve Problems from the Past," *Hindu* (New Delhi), 2 January 2001. Vajpayee said:

   The Kashmir problem is an unfortunate inheritance from the tragic partition of India in 1947. India never accepted the pernicious two-nation theory that brought about the partition. However, the mindset that created Pakistan continues to operate in that country . . . .

   India is willing and ready to seek a lasting solution to the Kashmir problem. Towards this end, we are prepared to recommence talks with Pakistan at any level, including the highest level, provided Islamabad gives sufficient proof of its preparedness to create a conducive atmosphere for a meaningful dialogue . . . .

   In our search for a lasting solution to the Kashmir problem, both in its external and internal dimensions, we shall not traverse solely on the beaten track of the past. Rather, we shall be bold and innovative designers of a future architecture of peace and prosperity for the entire South Asian region.

3   For the text of Vajpayee's invitation, see Ministry of External Affairs, *India–Pakistan Summit* (New Delhi: Ministry of External

Affairs, 2001), 1-2. Vajpayee said, 'Our common enemy is poverty. For the welfare of our peoples, there is no other recourse but a pursuit of the path of reconciliation, of engaging in productive dialogue and by building trust and confidence. I invite you to walk this high road with us.'

4   These proposed confidence-building measures were publicized by the Foreign Office in three press releases issued on 4, 6 and 9 July, 2001. For texts, see *India–Pakistan Summit*, 7-12.

5   See the transcript of Jaswant Singh's press conference at Agra on 17 July 2001, see *India–Pakistan Summit*, 107.

6   Sattar's press conference at Islamabad, 17 July 2001. The opening statement by Sattar is available on the Pakistani Ministry of Foreign Affairs' web site <http://www.forisb.org/FM01-09.html>. For a report on the press conference, see B. Muralidhar Reddy, "Summit Inconclusive, Not a Failure," *Hindu* (New Delhi), 18 July 2001.

7   Jaswant Singh's press conference at Agra, on 17 July 2001. See *India–Pakistan Summit*, 106-07.

8   Sattar's press conference in Islamabad.

9   For a text of the Lahore Declaration 21 February 1999, see *India–Pakistan Relations: Documents*, 7-12.

10 Sattar's press conference at Islamabad. See Reddy, "Summit Inconclusive, Not a Failure."

11 Opening statement of Jaswant Singh at 17 July press conference. *India–Pakistan Summit*, 107.

12 Ibid., 110

13 Sattar's press conference in Islamabad.

14 See the summary of the briefing by the spokesperson of the Foreign Office on 18 July 2001 in *India–Pakistan Summit*, 141-42.

15 The resolution passed in the Lok Sabha on 22 February 1994 'firmly declares' on 'behalf of the people of India' that
    a) The State of Jammu and Kashmir has been, is and shall be an integral part of India and any attempts to separate it from the rest of the country will be resisted by all necessary means;
    b) India has the will and capacity to firmly counter all designs

against its unity, sovereignty and territorial integrity;
And demands that
c) Pakistan must vacate the areas of the Indian State of Jammu and Kashmir, which they have occupied through aggression; And resolves that
d) all attempts to interfere in the internal affairs of India will be met resolutely.
For a text of the resolution, see *India–Pakistan Relations: Documents,* 69-70.

16   The eight subjects that were agreed for negotiations were peace and security including confidence-building measures, Jammu and Kashmir, Siachen, the Wullar Barrage/Tulbul Navigation project, Sir Creek, terrorism and drug trafficking, economic and commercial cooperation and promotion of friendly exchanges in various fields. For the texts of joint statements on the dialogue issued by Vajpayee and Sharif on 23 September 1998 in New York, see *India–Pakistan Relations: Documents,* 47-51.

17   For a discussion of confidence-building measures in the Indo-Pakistani context, see Michael Krepon and Amit Sevak, eds., *Crisis Prevention, Confidence Building and Reconciliation in South Asia* (New York: St. Martin's Press, 1995); Sumit Ganguly and Ted Greenwood, eds., *Mending Fences: Confidence and Security-building Measures in South Asia* (Boulder, Colo.: Westview Press, 1996).

18   For a wide-ranging discussion of the Simla Agreement, see P.R. Chari and Pervaiz Iqbal Cheema, *The Simla Agreement 1972: Its Wasted Promise,* (New Delhi: Manohar, 2001).

19   The Kargil Review Committee, *From Surprise to Reckoning: The Kargil Review Committee Report, December 15, 1999* (New Delhi: Sage, 2000), 197-99.

20   Ashley J. Tellis, C. Christine Fair, Jamison Jo Medby, *Limited Conflicts under the Nuclear Umbrella: Indian and Pakistani Lessons from the Kargil Crisis* (Santa Monica, Calif.: RAND Corporation, 2001), 80.

21   Ibid., 81.

22   In a series of telephone calls in early June 1999, a senior official of the State Department called the author to convey the message

that the Clinton administration was opposed to the Kargil aggression and was privately urging Nawaz Sharif to withdraw from across the Line of Control. It was also suggested that the US would go public in due course. When this message was conveyed to the Foreign Office, there was utter disbelief in some quarters, but the veracity of message was checked by direct conversations between the officials on both sides. Jaswant Singh suggested to the author that the conversation with the US officials through informal channels must be maintained.

23 *From Surprise to Reckoning*, 242.

24 Private conversation with senior Indian officials in December 2002.

25 Ramesh Chandran, "Clinton Warned India Might Be Forced to Attack: Post," *Times of India* (New Delhi), 28 June, 1999; see also N.C. Menon, "How Clinton Averted Indo-Pak War," *Hindustan Times* (New Delhi), 27 July, 1999.

26 C. Raja Mohan, "Pak Must Pull Out Troops," *Hindu* (New Delhi), 28 June 1999.

27 Tellis, Fair and Medby, *Limited Conflicts*, x.

28 Ibid., 7.

29 These measures were announced by India in two stages on 21 and 27 December 2001. See the briefing by the Ministry of External Affairs spokesman on 21 December on the web site of the Ministry of External Affairs <http://meadev.nic.in/news/20011221.htm> and the announcement by Jaswant Singh on 27 December <http://meadev.nic.in/speeches/eam-stmt-27dec.htm>.

30 See C. Raja Mohan, "Fernandes Unveils 'Limited War' Doctrine," *Hindu* (New Delhi), 25 January 2000.

31 On Kashmir and terrorism, Musharraf said:
    Kashmir runs in our blood. No Pakistani can afford to sever links with Kashmir. The entire Pakistan and the world knows this. We will continue to extend our moral, political and diplomatic support to Kashmiris. We will never budge an inch from our principled stand on Kashmir. The Kashmir problem needs to be resolved by dialogue and peaceful means in

accordance with the wishes of the Kashmiri people and the United Nations resolutions. We have to find the solution of this dispute. No organization will be allowed to indulge in terrorism in the name of Kashmir. We condemn the terrorist acts of September 11, October 1 and December 13. Anyone found involved in any terrorist act would be dealt with sternly . . . .

I would also like to address the international community, particularly the United States[,] on this occasion. As I said before on a number of occasions, Pakistan rejects and condemns terrorism in all its forms and manifestation.

Pakistan will not allow its territory to be used for any terrorist activity anywhere in the world. Now you [the US] must play an active role in solving the Kashmir dispute for the sake of lasting peace and harmony in the region.

For a full text of the English translation of Musharraf's speech, see the Pakistani Ministry of Foreign Affairs's web site <http://www.forisb.org/CE-019.html>.

32 Singh stated:

The Government of India has noted that the major portion of the address of the President of Pakistan yesterday related to reforms to modernize Pakistan. We wish the people of Pakistan well in this endeavour. To the extent that these reforms have a direct nexus to external developments, we welcome them.

We welcome the now declared commitment of the Government of Pakistan not to support or permit any more the use of its territory for terrorism anywhere in the world, including in the Indian State of Jammu and Kashmir. This commitment must extend to the use of all territories under Pakistan's control today. We would assess the effectiveness of this commitment only by the concrete action taken. Consequently, we expect Pakistan to cooperate with India in stopping all infiltration across the International border and the Line of Control . . . .

The Government of India remains committed to the bilateral dialogue process with Pakistan in accordance with the letter and spirit of the Shimla [*sic*] Agreement and the Lahore Declaration. Should the Government of Pakistan operationalize its intention and move purposefully towards eradicating cross-border terrorism, the Government of India will respond fully, and would be prepared to resume the composite dialogue process. We reiterate our conviction that all issues between India and Pakistan can only be addressed bilaterally. There is no scope for any third party involvement. The prepared statement by Jaswant Singh at a press conference in New Delhi 13 January 2002 is available online <http://meadev.nic.in/speeches/stmt-eam-13jan.htm>.

33 For a summary of Armitage's diplomacy, see his interviews to various US media outlets: "Armitage Assesses Reduction of Tensions in South Asia," *Washington File,* 12 June 2002.

34 See briefing by the Ministry of External Affairs spokesperson on 10 June 2002 <http://meadev.nic.in/news/20020610.htm>; see also C. Raja Mohan, "India Allows Pak Overflights," *Hindu* (New Delhi), 11 June 2002.

35 Sandip Dikshit, "Government Orders Withdrawal of Troops from IB," *Hindu* (New Delhi), 17 October 2002; Jyoti Malhotra, "Pak Lowers the Heat Too, but No Signs of a Thaw: Coercive Diplomacy in Phase 2" *Indian Express* (New Delhi), 18 October 2002.

Chapter Eight: Rediscovering Lord Curzon

1 Private conversation with J.N. Dixit on 26 January 2002.

2 Lord Curzon of Kedleston, *The Place of India in the Empire* (London: John Murray, 1909), 12.

3 See C. Raja Mohan, "Jaswant and Lord Curzon's Legacy," *Hindu* (New Delhi), 28 January 2002.

4 Jaswant Singh, *Defending India* (New York: St. Martin's, 1999), 1-61.

5 Author's conversation with Jaswant Singh on 30 November 2001.

6 K. Subrahmanyam, "Introduction," in Singh, *Defending India,* xv.

7 For a summary of Kissinger's views expressed in a visit to New

Delhi in November 1995, see C. Raja Mohan, "Kissinger and the Asian Balance," *Hindu* (New Delhi), 8 November 1995.

8   Frédéric Grare and Amitabh Mattoo, eds., *India and ASEAN: The Politics of India's Look East Policy* (New Delhi: Manohar, 2001); Kripa Sridharan, *The ASEAN Region in India's Foreign Policy* (Aldershot, UK: Dartmouth Publishing Co., 1996); Sandy Gordon and Stephen Henningham, eds., *India Looks East: An Emerging Power and Its Asia-Pacific Neighbours* (Canberra: Strategic and Defence Studies Centre, Australian National University, 1995).

9   Ministry of External Affairs, "ASEAN–India Relations" (a background note updated September 2002, mimeographed), 4. See also Ministry of External Affairs, "India and the ARF" (a background note updated July 2000, mimeographed), 3.

10   The focus of the summit was on expanding cooperation between India and ASEAN in the fields of terrorism, regional peace and stability and developing freer trading arrangements. See *Joint Statement of the First ASEAN–India Summit, Pnom Penh, Kingdom of Cambodia, 5 November 2002* (New Delhi: Ministry of External Affairs, 5 November 2002).

11   "ASEAN–India Relations," 5.

12   For a discussion of the opportunities for the North-East through integration, see B.G. Verghese, "The North-East and Its Neighbourhood: Remembering the Future," Twentieth C.D. Deshmukh Memorial Lecture, New Delhi, 14 January 2003.

13   For reporting on the ASEAN Regional Forum (ARF) meeting at Manila in July 1998 see, Jyoti Malhotra, "ASEAN Resists West's Pressure on N-Rap," *Indian Express* (New Delhi), 27 July 1998; Jyoti Malhotra, "Tough Guy India Has Its Way at ARF Meet," *Indian Express* (New Delhi), 28 July 1998.

14   Ministry of External Affairs, "India–Australia Relations," (a background note updated January 2002), available online at <http://meadev.nic.in/foreign/australia.htm>.

15   See Jenelle Bonnor, "Australia–India Security Relations: Common Interests or Common Disinterest?" *Working Paper no. 67* (Canberra: Australian Defence Studies Centre, April 2001);

Ravi Tomar, "Australia–India Relations: Strategic Convergence?," *Research Note 5 2001-02* (Canberra: Department of Parliamentary Library, 2001) available online at <http://www.aph.gov.au/library/pubs/rn/2001-02/02rn05.htm>.

16 S. Jaishankar, "India–Japan Relations after Pokharan II," *Seminar* (New Delhi), no. 487 (March 2000): 42.

17 Isabelle Cordonnier, *Japan and India: Are There Inter-related Security Concerns?*," JIIA Fellowship Occasional Paper (Tokyo: Japan Institute of International Affairs, 1999), 14.

18 P.S. Suryanarayana, "India a Strategic Partner: Japan," *Hindu* (New Delhi), 2 January 2003; For a text of Kawaguchi's interview, see "Terrorism Can't Be Justified Whatever the Motive" ' *Hindu* (New Delhi), 2 January 2003.

19 Ministry of External Affairs, "India–Japan Relations," (a background note updated November 2001), available online at <http://meadev.nic.in/foreign/indo-japan.htm>.

20 Yoriko Kawaguchi, 'Towards a Brighter Future: Advancing Our Global Partnership" (address to the Federation of Indian Chambers of Commerce and Industry, New Delhi, India, 8 January 2003), 3-4.

21 Ministry of External Affairs, "India–RoK Relations," (a background note updated March 2002), available online at <http://meadev.nic.in/foreign/korea.htm>.

22 Il-Young Kim and Lakhvinder Singh, "Asian Security and Korea–India Strategic Cooperation," *The Korean Journal of Defense Analysis* (Seoul) 14, no. 1 (spring 2002): 175-96.

23 For a discussion of the ambitions of the Pakistani establishment in Central Asia and Afghanistan, see Yossef Bodansky, *Islamabad's Road Warriors* (Houston: Freeman Center for Strategic Studies, January 1998).

24 For a discussion of the rise of the Taliban and Pakistan's role in it, see Ahmad Rashid, *Taliban: Islam, Oil and the Great Game in Central Asia* (London: I.B. Taurus, 2000); see also Peter Marsden, *The Taliban: War, Religion and the New Order in Afghanistan* (Karachi: Oxford University Press, 1999).

25 The tentative assistance began under the stewardship of I.K.

Gujral in 1997 acquired significant proportions in 2001 that included setting up various facilities for military use by the Northern Alliance in Tajikistan. There was media speculation about an Indian military base at Farkhor in Tajikistan. Both India and Tajikistan denied the existence of any Indian bases in the Central Asian republic. See Rahul Bedi, "India and Central Asia," *Frontline* (Chennai) 19, no.19, (14-27 September 2002): 60-61.

26　For the interview with Abdul Salam Zaeef, the Taliban ambassador to Pakistan, see C. Raja Mohan, "Taliban Wants to Engage India," *Hindu* (New Delhi), 13 February 2001.

27　Jyoti Malhotra, "US to India: Lay Off Afghanistan, Please," *Indian Express* (New Delhi), 8 December 2002.

28　Indrani Bagchi, "Indian Foray in Kabul, Tehran," *Economic Times* (New Delhi), 7 January 2003; Aslam Khan, "India Trying to Isolate Pakistan in the Region," *News* (Islamabad), 8 January 2003.

29　J.N. Dixit says India failed to follow up on the initiatives it took in the early 1990s to strengthen relations with the Central Asian republics. See J.N. Dixit, *Across Borders*, 368.

30　Amit Baruah, "India Lobbying for Entry into Shanghai Group," *Hindu* (New Delhi), 10 August 2002.

31　Rashid, *Taliban*.

32　Neela Banerjee and Sabrina Tavernise, "As War Shifts Alliances, Oil Deals Follow," *New York Times*, 15 December 2001.

33　"Jamali, Niyazov, Karzai Sign Gas Pipeline Accord," *Dawn* (Karachi), 28 December 2002.

34　India is said to be interested in picking up stake in one of the oil fields in Kazakhstan.

35　Stephen Blank, "India and Central Asia: The Return of Strategy," *Central Asia–Caucasus Analyst* (11 September 2002) < http://www.cacianalyst.org/2002-09-11/20020911_INDIA_CENTRAL_ ASIA.htm>.

36　Private conversation with I.K. Gujral on 29 November 2002.

37　For an account of the internal debate in the Narasimha Rao government on Israel prior to recognition, see J.N. Dixit, *My South Block Years: Memoirs of a Foreign Secretary* (New Delhi:

UBSPD, 1996), 309-15.

38 Singh's remarks quoted in Jyoti Malhotra, "Arab Diplomats Sore with Jaswant, Advani," *Indian Express* (New Delhi), 17 July 2000.

39 '[T]here is an element of truth in what Jaswant Singh said. It is the leadership of some of our political parties which is inclined to use such an argument on the Muslim vote bank for their own purposes.' J.N. Dixit, "Out of the Closet," *Hindustan Times* (New Delhi) 8 July 2002.

40 For a comprehensive survey of India's relations with Israel, see P.R. Kumaraswamy, *India–Israel Relations: Humble Beginnings, Bright Future* (Washington, D.C.: American Jewish Committee, 2002).

41 Willard Smith and Teresita C. Schaffer, "India Plays Both Sides in the Middle East," *CSIS South Asia Monitor* (Washington, D.C.) (1 December 2000), available online at <http://csis.org/saprog/sam28.html>.

42 For a discussion, see Girijesh Pant, "India Energy Security: The Gulf Factor," *GSP Occasional Paper Series, 2002/2* (New Delhi: Gulf Studies Programme: Centre for West Asian and African Studies, Jawaharlal Nehru University, 2002)

43 Jaswant Singh, "India and Saudi Arabia: Partnership for Security, Stability and Development," (Address to Council of Saudi Chambers of Commerce and Industry, Riyadh, 21 January 2001), 6.

44 C. Raja Mohan, "Jaswant Visit Exceeded Expectations," *Hindu* (New Delhi), 23 January 2001.

45 "Prime Minister's Address to the Majlis of the Islamic Republic of Iran, Teheran, 11 April 2001," in Ministry of External Affairs, *Visit of Prime Minister Atal Bihari Vajpayee to the Islamic Republic of Iran, 10-13 April 2001* (New Delhi: Ministry of External Affairs, 2001), 22.

46 C. Raja Mohan, "Gujarat and the Islamic World," *Hindu* (New Delhi), 25 April 2002.

47 Conversation with a senior Indian diplomat in the Middle East on 23 April 2002.

48 Saeed Naqvi, "Sinha Must Look at West Asia," *Indian Express* (New Delhi), 5 July 2002.

49 C. Raja Mohan, "From Sakhalin to Sudan: India's Energy

Diplomacy," *Hindu* (New Delhi), 24 June 2002.

50 Jaswant Singh's remarks (delivered at the inauguration of the Africa Centre, Indian Council on World Affairs, New Delhi, 13 June 2002), available online at <http://meadev.nic.in/speeches/eam-add-icwa.htm>.

51 C. Raja Mohan, "India Rediscovers Africa," *Hindu* (New Delhi), 27 June 2002.

52 India expressed its strong interest and participated with some vigour in the unfolding international initiative on New Economic Partnership for African Development (NEPAD) launched in 2002. See Digvijay Singh, "India and NEPAD: Furthering India–Africa Economic Cooperation," speech delivered at a conference on India and NEPAD, New Delhi, 26 July 2002), available online at <http://meadev.nic.in/news/official/20020726/official1.htm>.

53 C. Raja Mohan, "India, U.S. Bury Ghosts of 1971," *Hindu* (New Delhi), 7 December 2001.

Chapter Nine: Re-forming the Subcontinent

1 Jawaharlal Nehru, "'A Monroe Doctrine for Asia', speech at a Public Meeting to Celebrate the Liberty Week, New Delhi, 9 August 1947," in *Selected Works of Jawaharlal Nehru, Second Series* (New Delhi: Publications Division, 1985), 133-35.

2 I.K. Gujral, *A Foreign Policy for India* (New Delhi: Ministry of External Affairs, 1998), 74-75.

3 Speech by Foreign Secretary Kanwal Sibal at the French Institute of International Relations, Paris, 17 December 2002. Excerpts published as "All Our Neighbours Have Been or Are Involved in Tolerating Terrorist Activities against India," *Indian Express* (New Delhi), 3 January 2003.

4 Yashwant Sinha's remarks at a seminar of South Asian Cooperation organized by the South Asia Centre for Policy Studies in New Delhi on 10 January 2003 are available at <http://meadev.nic.in/speeches/eam-10jan.htm>.

5   Ibid.

6   Ibid.

7   In an assessment of likely global trends, the CIA stated the following on South Asia:

The widening strategic and economic gaps between the two principal powers, India and Pakistan—and the dynamic interplay between their mutual hostility and the instability in Central Asia—will define the South Asia region in 2015. India will be the unrivalled regional power with a large military—including naval and nuclear capabilities—and a dynamic and growing economy. The widening India-Pakistan gap—destabilizing in its own right—will be accompanied by deep political, economic, and social disparities within both states. Pakistan will be more fractious, isolated, and dependent on international financial assistance. Other South Asian states—Bangladesh, Sri Lanka, and Nepal—will be drawn closer to and more dependent on India and its economy. Afghanistan will likely remain weak and a destabilizing force in the region and the world. Wary of China, India will look increasingly to the West, but its need for oil and desire to balance Arab ties to Pakistan will lead to strengthened ties to Persian Gulf states as well.

US Central Intelligence Agency, *Global Trends 2015* (Washington, D.C.: CIA, 2000). This is available online <http://www.cia.gov/ cia/publications/globaltrends2015/index.html#link13b>.

8   India's trade figures with its smaller neighbours began to rise significantly in the second half of the 1990s. The following are figures on India's exports to Bangladesh and Sri Lanka (in millions of Indian rupees)

	Bangladesh	*Sri Lanka*
1996-1997	29,120	16,947
2000-2001	42,770	28,964

Meanwhile, despite some rise, India's imports remained far below the export figures. Trade balances in favour of India during 2000-

2001 (in millions of Indian rupees): Bangladesh (39,190) and Sri Lanka (26,846). Information received by the author from the Ministry of External Affairs, 16 December 2002.

9   Muchkund Dubey, Lok Raj Baral, and Rehman Sobhan, eds., *South Asian Growth Quadrangle: Framework for Multilateral Cooperation* (New Delhi: Macmillan, 1999). See also Federation of Indian Chambers of Commerce and Industry, *South Asian Growth Quadrangle: Opportunities for Economic Partnership* (New Delhi: FICCI, 2001).

10   Speech by a senior official of the ADB, Yoshihiro Iwasaki at the First Private Sector Forum on South Asian Sub-regional Economic Cooperation, Kolkata, 28-29 November 2000 <http://www.adb.org/Documents/Speeches/2000/sp2000003.asp>.

11   Indrani Bagchi, "Economic Diplomacy Blooms in FTA Season," *Economic Times* (New Delhi), 11 January 2003.

12   Kanak Mani Dixit has offered an alternative vision of cooperation amidst regions of the subcontinent:

In SAARC, the member governments have created an unwieldy structure that is cramped by the insular requirements of the political, bureaucratic and military establishments of each country. This regionalism of SAARC can remain the turf of governments, but the people must at least *think* of South Asia differently. They (we) must consider South Asia as comprising not the seven members but the more than a dozen regions which would have constituted themselves into nation-states had colonialism not intervened. These are units defined by geography, economy and language, and translate loosely into, for example, the states of India that have been demarcated linguistically, or the provinces of Pakistan.

SAARC, as a non-symbiotic coming together, can only be a stepping stone into this other kind of conception, which emphasizes the 'neighbourhood' rather than 'region' of South Asia. And, as long as we define it correctly now, over time this neighbourhood will be one where adjacent areas interact, where local languages get priority, where borders are porous if not open, and where capital cities and their establishments would

be less important.
See Kanak Mani Dixit, "Beautiful Neighbourhood," *Himal*
(Kathmandu) 15, no.1 (January 2002): 30.

13 American pressure on the LTTE to abandon terrorism and settle
for a solution within the framework of a united Sri Lanka has
been an important factor in the rapid movement of the peace
process in 2002. Speaking at the Sri Lanka Donors Conference
in Oslo on 25 November, the US Deputy Secretary of State
Richard Armitage said:

> Of course, peace also requires the full and frank participation
> of the LTTE. And let me leave no doubt: my nation stands firm
> in the resolve that the tactics of terror can never achieve
> legitimate aspirations. So the United States is greatly encouraged
> that the LTTE has made a commitment to the political solution;
> it has agreed to settle this conflict through peaceful means. We
> urge the LTTE to go one step further and add to this
> commitment a public renunciation of terrorism and of
> violence—to make it clear to the people of Sri Lanka and indeed
> to the international community—that the LTTE has abandoned
> its armed struggle for a separate state; and instead accepts the
> sovereignty of a Sri Lankan government that respects and
> protects the rights of all its people.

See *Washington File*, 26 November 2002.

14 During his visit to Nepal in January 2002, Powell, one of the first
high-ranking American visitors to Nepal in decades, extended
strong support to Nepal's war against Maoist terrorism:

> Nepal has come a long way in only half a century and especially
> since democratization in 1990's . . . Nepal's progress reminds
> us that openness and democracy offer the best future for the
> people of Nepal . . . .
>
> Unfortunately, Nepal is no stranger to violence as we have
> been tragically reminded by the recent attacks of Maoists on
> Nepal's people, police and military. There is no room for the
> use of violence to create political change in a democracy.

Powell said he recognized the Nepalese government's right to
protect its citizens and institutions from terrorist attacks, but he

added that he hoped the current state of emergency will be of limited duration and encouraged the elected government to focus on protecting human rights.

For a transcript of Powell's press conference in Nepal on 18 January 2002, see "Powell Pledges Support for Nepal," *Washington File*, 19 January 2002.

A similar message was put out when President Bush received Nepalese Prime Minister Sher Bahadur Deuba at the White House on 7 May 2002. They also apparently discussed the idea of a British-led international initiative on coordinating military and economic assistance to Nepal. Author's conversations with Delhi-based senior Nepali diplomats in mid-2002. See also Chidanand Rajghatta, "Nepal Has Its Day at the White House," *Times of India* (New Delhi), 9 May 2002, and C. Raja Mohan, "India to Join British Initiative on Nepal," *Hindu* (New Delhi), 13 June 2002.

15 Bush received Prime Minister Ranil Wickremesinghe on 24 July 2002 at the White House <http://usinfo.state.gov/regional/nea/sasia/afghan/text/0724wthsrpt.htm>.

16 President Bush's Remarks at a White House ceremony to honour victims of September 11 terrorist attacks, 11 March 2002. *Washington File*, 12 March 2002.

Talking about the conflicts in the subcontinent, a senior US official emphasized the new commitment of the US to help resolve them:

It is our intention that the United States does what it can to move toward resolution of each one (of the conflicts) .... Not as a meddler nor as a mediator, but somebody whose good offices can help bring people to the table to deal with the differences. We hope we will be able to play this role in the region.

Christina Rocca, "U.S. Hopes to Assist South Asian Nations Resolve Their Differences" (speech presented at the United States Institute of Peace, Washington, D.C., 5 September 2002), US Embassy, New Delhi, official text, 5; and *Washington File*, 10 September 2002.

17 Bush's remarks on 11 March 2000; see *Washington File*, 12 March 2002.

18 The Treaty of Peace and Friendship was signed by India and Nepal on 31 July 1950 amidst the Chinese occupation of Tibet. Its core concerned the preservation of a buffer with China in Nepal. Under the treaty, India recognized the sovereignty and territorial integrity of Nepal, which in return agreed to abide by eternal friendship with India. The treaty and its associated documents declared that they would not tolerate aggression against the parties and committed both to devise effective countermeasures in the event of an aggression.

India also believes that the treaty, in its spirit, allows Nepal to import arms only with India's consent. India offered many other concessions to Nepal, such as non-discriminatory treat of Nepali citizens in India without securing similar benefits to India. It also offered generous economic aid from India—all this in return for Nepal's commitment to respect India's security concerns.

19 During his visit to India in July and August 2000, when Prime Minister G.P. Koirala broached the subject of revision of the treaty, Vajpayee insisted that it must remain the foundation of bilateral relations and Nepal must think about the consequences of undoing it. Ministry of External Affairs officials, conversation with author, New Delhi, 14 August 2000. See also C. Raja Mohan, "Scrapping the Treaty with Nepal?," *Hindu* (New Delhi), 29 January 2001.

20 See Ministry of External Affairs, "Treaty between India and Bhutan 1949," *India–Bhutan Relations: Bilateral Documents* (New Delhi: Ministry of External Affairs, 1998), 1.

21 Initially India characterized the Norwegian mediation as entirely an effort by Oslo and refused to endorse it. But after a period of consultations and Oslo's effort to keep India informed about the peace process gave India more assurance on the bona fides of the Norwegian initiative. See summary of the press briefing by the spokesman of the Ministry of External Affairs on the visit to Norwegian envoy, Erik Solheim to New Delhi on 11 May 2000,

available at <http://www.meadev.nic.in/news/20000511.htm>; see also C. Raja Mohan, "Norway Hails Jaswant Initiative," *Hindu* (New Delhi), 15 June 2000, and Nirupama Subramanian, "India Fully Backs Peace; Solheim," *Hindu* (New Delhi), 25 March 2001.

22　C. Raja Mohan, "India to Join British Initiative on Nepal," *Hindu* (New Delhi), 14 June 2002.

23　Japan has taken an increasing interest in South Asian regional conflicts. In the name of a 'consolidation of peace' initiative, Japan has sought an active role in the Sri Lankan peace process. See "Towards a Brighter Future: Advancing Our Global Partnership" (speech by the foreign minister of Japan, Yoriko Kawaguchi, at the Federation of Indian Chambers of Commerce and Industry, New Delhi, 8 January 2003, mimeographed), 11.

Chapter Ten: Diplomacy for the Second Republic

1　C. Raja Mohan, "Jaswant Bids Farewell to Foreign Office," *Hindu* (New Delhi), 3 July 2002.

2　Ibid.

3　The Communist leaders in India were trenchant in their criticism of India's foreign policy in the 1990s, particularly under the BJP; see Prakash Karat, "A Hindutva Foreign Policy," *Akhbar Online*, no. 2 (2001), *South Asia Alert 2* available at <http://www.ercwilcom.net/~indowindow/akhbar/2001-02/alert2.htm>.

4　Dileep Padgaonkar, "Resurgent India: Taming the Demon of Inertia," *Times of India* (New Delhi) 1 January 2000.

5　Press Trust of India, "Show Them the Door, Says RSS Chief," *Hindu* (New Delhi), 3 October 2002.

6　N.R. Narayana Murthy, "Western Values and Eastern Challenges," *Financial Express* (New Delhi), 4 October 2002. The article contains excerpts from the Lal Bahadur Shastri Memorial Lecture delivered by Murthy in New Delhi on 1 October 2002.

7　Sanjaya Baru, "An India of Narayana Murthy or Sudarshan?," *Financial Express* (New Delhi), 4 October 2002.

Index